4. Members should not claim nor advertise affiliation with the *International Reading Association* as evidence of their competence in reading.

Ethical Standards in Reading Services

1. Reading specialists must possess suitable qualifications *(See Minimum Standards for Professional Training of Reading Specialists)* for engaging in consulting, clinical, or remedial work. Unqualified persons should not engage in such activities except under the direct supervision of one who is properly qualified. Professional intent and the welfare of the person seeking the services of the reading specialist should govern all consulting or clinical activities such as counseling, administering diagnostic tests, or providing remediation. It is the duty of the reading specialist to keep relationships with clients and interested persons on a professional level.

2. Information derived from consulting and/or clinical services should be regarded as confidential. Expressed consent of persons involved should be secured before releasing information to outside agencies.

3. Reading specialists should recognize the boundaries of their competence and should not offer services which fail to meet professional standards established by other disciplines. They should be free, however, to give assistance in other areas in which they are qualified.

4. Referral should be made to specialists in allied fields as needed. When such referral is made, pertinent information should be made available to consulting specialists.

5. Reading clinics and/or reading specialists offering professional services should refrain from guaranteeing easy solutions or favorable outcomes as a result of their work, and their advertising should be consistent with that of allied professions. They should not accept for remediation any persons who are unlikely to benefit from their instruction, and they should work to accomplish the greatest possible improvement in the shortest time. Fees, if charged, should be agreed on in advance and should be charged in accordance with an established set of rates commensurate with that of other professions.

DIAGNOSTIC AND REMEDIAL READING

for classroom and clinic

Robert M. Wilson
University of Maryland

CHARLES E. MERRILL PUBLISHING COMPANY
COLUMBUS, OHIO

A Bell and Howell Company

Merrill's
International Education Series
Under the Editorship of
Kimball Wiles
Dean of the College of Education
University of Florida

Library of Congress Catalog Card Number: 67-16169

2 3 4 5 6 7 8 9 10 11 12 13 14 15-76 75 74 73 72 71 70 69 68 67

Printed in the United States of America

Foreword

Many classroom teachers, and especially the reading teacher or supervisor, will find this book most helpful. It is well organized and reads easily. Not only does it contain excellent guidelines for organizing the optimal reading environment for the handicapped reader, but it contains practical suggestions for manipulating this environment so the struggling reader will realize success and satisfaction in his attempt to compete with his peers. While some recipes are given which are time-tested, yet I sense a core philosophy — the reading teacher, whether teaching developmental, corrective, or remedial classes should be a creative teacher, judiciously manipulating the reading environment so the child learns to read through discovery.

Certain features of this book are worthy of mention. First, is the types of diagnosis: *Informal-on-the-spot, classroom,* and *clinical.* The alert teacher should consistently and continuously appraise the child's progress towards the previously determined goals of the instructional program, or perhaps it is better to say, "the terminal behaviors elicited." Then, and only then, can she judiciously shift emphasis in the instructional program. If the problem persists after these informal adjustments in the instructional program have been made, the teacher must initiate a more directed and formal analysis of the child's persistent reading patterns. Sufficient content has been provided by the author so the dedicated teacher can glean sufficient understandings and knowledges to conduct the appropriate diagnosis, and subsequently to manipulate the reading environment so the child will acquire the agreed-upon terminal behaviors. While the book is not necessarily designed for the clinician, it contains sufficient substantive content to enable the classroom teacher to properly interpret a formal case study.

Another feature of the book that is worthy of mention is the chapter titled, "Non-educational Diagnosis." Much lip service has been given to the philosophic point of view that before any hypothesis is selected as to factors inhibiting adequate growth in reading skills and the subsequent therapy, an inter-discipline approach should be used. Embracing this point of view, the author calls attention to the contributions such disciplines as psychology, opthalmology, optometry, neurology, bio-chemistry, etc., can render in the diagnosis of reading difficulties.

Another feature which should be highlighted is Chapter IX, "Evaluation in Remedial Reading." All too frequently, the results of therapy in reading have been expressed in grade equivalent gains. While this medium of expressing growth is more or less ubiquitous, it is placing undue emphasis upon one or several skills in reading. The author has, and rightly so, called attention to the affective aspects of reading growth.

Furthermore, it is gratifying to note that a chapter has been devoted to "Parental Roles in Diagnosis, Remediation, and Prevention." A point of view is expressed that should strike a responsive chord in all teachers. In addition to providing adequate physical care and a salutory emotional climate, the author emphasizes that the most significant contribution of the parent to the remedial program is the reinforcement of learned skills. This implies that the parent should, in most cases, refrain from engaging in direct and structured reading therapy.

The professional responsibilities of all concerned for the welfare of the handicapped reader, and also, the reluctant reader, is another viewpoint that is presented by the author. The philosophy presented is sound and deserves the thoughtful perusal of the reader.

While readers may disagree with some of the viewpoints, postulates, and hypotheses drawn from related data by the author, nevertheless, the pages are informative and challenging. After all, shouldn't a book be both informative and challenging? I invite your reflective and critical reading of this scholarly manuscript. You will find the experience most rewarding.

Donald L. Cleland
University of Pittsburgh

March 1, 1967

Preface

Hundreds of problem readers have been diagnosed and provided with the remediation on which this book is based. The fact that a large majority of these children returned to successful classroom experiences resulted,in part, from specific designs of transfer discussed in this book.

Special emphasis has been given to the classroom aspects of diagnostic and remedial reading. The classroom teacher and the reading specialist must work cooperatively to provide the most effective reading program for the problem reader. Through poor communication, misunderstanding, and lack of information, many good remedial programs fail to help effectively the child *in the classroom*. The book has been designed to deal with the various aspects of diagnosis and remediation with special emphasis on communication between clinic and classroom.

Many colleges and universities operate reading clinics to assist classroom teachers in the area of remedial reading. Here, again, there is a difficult transfer for the teacher—from the clinic (ideal) situation to the classroom (real) situation. Therefore, this book is also designed to examine clinic operations and demonstrate how they may best be adapted to the classroom. The clinical aspects of remedial reading are treated thoroughly, but with special direction for the classroom teacher. This book, then, is designed to provide the uninitiated with his first view of diagnosis and remediation.

Chapter ten has been devoted to the role of the parent of the problem reader. Based upon the contention that the parent should maintain a vital role, this chapter presents a specific set of suggestions to assist in making that role as effective as possible.

With a variety of diagnostic and remedial services available, it becomes imperative for the informed teacher to know of their relative merits. A thorough examination of the various types of remedial programs for problem readers is covered in the last chapter.

Before dealing with the problems defined, the author assumes that the reader has a rather complete understanding of the basic reading concepts, including a thorough understanding of the following:

1. *Definition of reading.* Reading involves coordinated physical action, manipulation of a variety of word recognition skills, understanding of simple and complex comprehension patterns, reaction to the printed page in terms of behavior modifications and, ultimately, a wide range of reading experiences. To use the skills of reading, the reader must be willing and able to interrelate the experiences that he has had with those that the author is presenting in print. A requisite to working with children who have reading problems is an understanding of the process of reading, for without a knowledge of this process, it is obvious that a program of diagnosis and/or remediation cannot be formed.

The educator must see reading as basically a two-part process, in which the components are highly interrelated. One part involves the decoding of the printed message, in which the reader generally decodes the print into silent or articulated speech. An essential part of teaching reading, then, is the decoding of the message. The other step is association, in which the reader is required to associate the message which he has decoded with a concept based on something either real or vicarious in his past experience.

The extent to which the reader comprehends the idea of the author depends upon how well his experiences parallel those which the author has assumed that the reader would have. A deficiency in either decoding or associating will result in limited reading. Any factor that can be said to cause a deficiency in either of these processes can contribute to a reading deficiency. It is not uncommon for problem readers to show particular inadequacies in either decoding or association. The child who reads for the first time about the ocean, for example, recalls his only experience with water—the local stream. Without pictures, concept development, or some type of verbal experience prior to reading, this child will be deficient in his association abilities. Obviously then, the two processes, decoding and association, are so closely related that they affect one another.

2. *Implications of the reading act.* The laws of learning are applicable to the teaching of reading. The teacher must also understand

that there are psychological, social, cultural, and personal implications in the act of reading; to overlook any of these areas weakens the possibilities of a successful reading program.

3. *History of reading.* Reading instruction has long been a matter of discussion, for many techniques and procedures have been tried. Furthermore, no one procedure has yet been found to satisfy all needs of this high-level activity. An appreciation of past and present research will likely lead to a more thorough understanding of the reading process, dictating the need for further research.

4. *Basic Methodology.* The basic methods of teaching reading, generally with the assistance of basal readers, are rather effective. The techniques and materials for teaching reading are often appropriate for the average student, but students on both extremes must receive additional consideration beyond the many suggestions in the teachers' manual.

For the reader who does not have these concepts well in mind, the author suggests a study of one or more of the following books on basic reading skills:

Durrell, Donald D., *Improving Reading Instruction.* Yonkers-on-Hudson, New York: World Book Company, 1956

Heilman, Arthur, *Principals and Practices of Teaching Reading.* Second Edition, Columbus, Ohio: Charles E. Merrill Books, 1967

Smith, Nila B., *Reading Instruction for Today's Children.* Englewood Cliffs, N. J.: Prentice Hall, Inc., 1961

Smith, Henry P., Emerald V. Dechant, *Psychology in Teaching Reading.* Englewood Cliffs, N. J.: Prentice Hall, Inc., 1961

Spache, George, *Teaching Reading in The Elementary Schools.* Boston: Allyn-Bacon, Inc., 1964

Tinker, Miles A. and Constance M. McCullough, *Teaching Elementary Reading.* New York: Appleton-Century-Crofts, Inc., 1962

Each section of this book is followed by an annotated list of suggested readings. Some of these suggested readings agree with the views presented in the book; others present contrasting views.

Appendices A and B provide a handy reference for tests and materials for those interested in conducting a diagnostic and remedial program. Although not all-inclusive, these charts present a wide sampling for examination.

Acknowledgements

This writer wishes to acknowledge the many people who have encouraged and guided him to the completion of this book. In particular, two educators deserve a special vote of thanks: Dr. Donald L. Cleland, teacher and friend, and Mr. C. B. Wilson, teacher, psychologist, and father.

For their critical reviews of technical portions of the manuscript, a special note of appreciation is extended to Ward H. Ewalt, optometrist, and William H. Druckmiller, neurologist.

I would imagine that behind almost every book there is one person who has kept it moving and who organized the "disorganized." For this type of assistance and inspiration, I thank Miss Karen E. Kebaugh.

Special acknowledgment should be made of the fine editorial services of Mrs. Barbara McMahan whose diligent work was so helpful in the preparation of this book.

To a family who has sacrificed much to permit the completion of this book—my thanks.

R.M.W.
February, 1967

Contents

1

Working With Problem Readers

Who knows better than the teacher of a child with a reading problem, the importance of reading for school success? And who is in a better position than the classroom teacher to realize that the inability to read, coupled with the lack of desire to read, leads directly to school failure? A teacher knows the type of problems presented by the child who cannot or will not read, for he faces the reality of this situation daily. He must be armed with the diagnostic and remedial techniques necessary to meet these problems as effectively as he can each day, for the exceptional child is not included in the generalizations of most basal series teachers' manuals.

A study of problem readers, then, must keep in mind the reality that the classroom teacher is not only in the best position to help the student, but also is professionally responsible to continue with the education of the child as intelligently and efficiently as he can.

Characteristics of Problem Readers

Although there is no single observable characteristic which isolates the problem reader from his classmates, he will likely demonstrate the characteristics of one or more of the three basic types of problem readers.

1. A child is a problem reader because, for one reason or another, he does not read as well as his ability indicates he should. He should not be

judged by his reading skills in relation to his grade level in school, but rather in relation to his potential. The fact that a dull child reading below his grade level in school may become a problem, does not necessarily imply that he is retarded in his development of reading skills. On the other hand, the bright child, although reading well above his grade level, may be considered a problem reader when his reading level falls short of his intellectual potential. It becomes important to assess accurately the reading level and ability of each child to arrive at a comparison determining whether or not he is operating below his potential.

2. A child may be considered a problem reader when, with the exception of a specific skill deficiency, all measures of reading are up to his potential. He does satisfactorily in most reading situations, but becomes a problem because of a specific type of deficiency. Although more difficult to locate because he appears normal in most reading skills, the deficiency, once located, is more readily corrected due to the precise nature of remediation necessary. The classroom teacher, being constantly alert to this type of deficiency, is less likely to label the child lazy or careless.

3. A child may be considered a problem reader when, with reading skills in good relationship to his potential, he lacks the desire to read. Strang points clearly to this problem when she says:

> "Under test conditions, and for a short period, the individual may score above average, but emotional conflicts, lack of purpose, visual discomfort, dull textbooks and other factors may decrease his reading efficiency in everyday assignments."[1]

These factors, mentioned by Strang, discourage a child from using available skills and tend to dampen the desire to read. It is of utmost importance that a lack of desire to read be considered a reading problem since it often *appears* that this child has no problem. Clinic reports for such children show that they are frequently subject to ridicule and disciplinary action, since it is often assumed that there is no excuse for their poor reading habits. An understanding of the child's real problem, however, will indicate the need for adjustment in the school situation to develop a better attitude toward reading.

As problem readers are studied on the following pages, it must be kept in mind that a child can have these characteristics in any combination with varying degrees of severity.

---

[1] Ruth Strang, *Diagnostic Teaching of Reading* (New York: McGraw Hill Book Co., 1964), p. vi.

Specific Traits

How convenient it would be if a problem reader could be described through easily identifiable traits, but such is not the case. He certainly cannot be identified by sight, for he is not an outcast of society because of his appearance. The problem reader, usually a boy, can be seen in almost any classroom. A study of this type of child generally reveals an individual who recognizes that the majority of his scholastic activities are unsatisfactory experiences. It is likely that he sees little possibility of school being anything but a series of frustrations and failures. Because of this constant frustration and failure, this child is likely to react in one of the following ways: he may withdraw and shyly avoid the reading process whenever possible; he may show resentment and become belligerent towards the reading situation; or he may cover his deficiency by showing a lack of concern, acting as if his problem doesn't make any difference; and finally, he may try to escape the reality of his problem by drifting and spending abnormally large amounts of time with T.V. and comic books, or by diverting the teacher's attention with unacceptable behavior. These and other responses to failure in reading provide us with insights into the difficulties of the problem reader.

A closer look at the problem reader reveals that he is likely to do better in the early grades where required reading skills are fewer and less complicated. His problem becomes more pronounced when he is introduced to the content areas and is expected to learn for himself from a textbook. Here he can no longer rely purely on his memory for word recognition; and, therefore, he reacts poorly to new reading situations. As his scores in all verbal areas fall below the norm, it is likely that arithmetic computation scores will remain relatively high. The teacher finds it difficult to separate the child's reaction to failure from the failure itself. As a result, the child is often misunderstood, coaxed, bribed, threatened, and punished until he, himself, no longer has any confidence that school will ever be a successful situation for him. Thus the problem reader faces many frustrations beyond his failure to read.

Ramifications

The problem reader is not only a problem to himself, but eventually causes problems in school, with his peers, and at home.

In school

In school where pressure is often exerted to have all children achieve a certain grade level of performance, the problem reader is a source of never-ending disappointments. Whether the pressure be subtle or direct, the child and the teacher both sense failure. The teacher may react by giving up on the child feeling that he is indifferent, lazy, or a trouble-maker. This reaction may be followed by punishment that usually fosters a hostile attitude between the teacher and the child who can least accept hostility. Frustrated by the rejection and the labels which he has received, the child either cannot or will not work independently. As more and more frustrating material is heaped upon him, he is likely to busy himself with non-educational activities. He finally decides that an education is just not worth the effort. As he falls behind in his classroom work, he is likely to be forced to repeat a grade, with the threat of further repetition constantly being called to his attention. Excessive absenteeism and complete rejection of the school program are inevitable, as he proceeds through school, being promoted on the basis of age alone. A brief look at the reading level of high school dropouts tells the remainder of the story. Penty says: "More than three times as many poor readers as good readers dropped out of school before graduation."[2]

We realize that not all problem readers end as school dropouts; however, the strained school-pupil relationship increases dropout possibilities with this type of child.

With his peers

Although his peers often treat him kindly, it is not uncommon for the problem reader to be teased and taunted. In either case, he is not with the "in" group and is often found alone at play as well as in the classroom. Other children are not likely to seek his efforts for committee work, since his contributions are limited. Rejections of this type encourage him to seek companionship with others in the "out" group. A further complication of peer group relations is the problem reader's repetition of a grade, which places him one year behind his peers, and he clearly recognizes

[2]Ruth C. Penty, "Reading Ability and High School Drop-Outs,"*Journal of the National Association of Women Deans and Counselors,* National Education Association, October, 1959, p. 14.

that he does not "belong." If he continues to meet peer group disapproval, he is highly susceptible to undesirable influences, the consequences of which are seen in the reports of police authorities who handle juvenile delinquents. Summarizing a study from the Children's Court in New York, Harris reports: "Among those tested . . . 76 per cent were found to be two or more years retarded in reading, and more than half of those were disabled five or more years."[3] Again we do not conclude that all problem readers turn to delinquent behavior, but merely that continued rejection from his peers makes a child more susceptible to undesirable influences.

With his parents

Parents become very anxious when it is obvious that their child is not succeeding at his school tasks. Even the most intelligent of these parents are likely to see the solution to the problem as urging or forcing the child to make a better effort. This is often attempted by piling on more and more of the same type of frustrating work which makes him reject school. When he balks, it is not unusual for him to be compared openly to his brother or sister or to his playmates. Seemingly ashamed of his behavior, parents will often look for someone to blame. The child is not blind to this shame and rejection, and he too will look for someone to blame. Even more important, he is likely to look elsewhere for that acceptance which all children need from their parents.

By observing the problem reader, it can be concluded that the ramifications of his problem are felt not only by himself, but by the school, his peers, and his family. His inability to solve his own problem causes the future to look very dark indeed.

Not all problem readers follow the patterns mentioned above. Indeed, some are quite capable of reasonable adjustment, usually with the help of an understanding, intelligent teacher. The problem facing the teacher, then, is just what can be accomplished in a regular classroom of twenty-five to thirty-five children, when a child with a reading problem is among them. A classroom without at least one such child is rare. The following pages will provide several possible solutions to this problem.

---

[3]Albert J. Harris, *How To Increase Reading Ability* (New York: David McKay Co., 1961), pp. 2-3.

Reactions to Symptoms — Reactions to Causes

When the child with a reading problem is found in the school situation, what diagnostic procedures should be used? Should the *symptoms* of the problem be considered valid enough for a diagnosis, or is it more desirable to conduct a thorough diagnosis designed to establish *causation?* An examination of the following situations will help to place each of these approaches in its proper perspective.

Tony is not alone. He is one of many children across the country who, day after day, sit in an elementary school classroom in which reading situations well above his level are required. Tony, however, may be ranked among the fortunate, for his teacher realized that Tony could not read well enough to do fifth grade work. He found out quickly that Tony could read accurately at the third grade level and that he could read only with frustration at the fourth grade level. He noticed that he would refuse to attack unknown words, and, on rare occasions when he would try, his pronunciation was very inaccurate.

He also noticed that all of his reading was characterized by word pronunciation without fluency, that he was uncomfortable in the reading situation, and that his reading seemed hindered by what the teacher called "word reading." A quick check of the school records indicated that Tony was average in ability but that each year he seemed less responsive to the reading instruction.

Therefore, after careful consideration of the information available to him, combined with his analysis of Tony's reading performance in his classroom, the teacher set into motion a two-pronged program to supplement Tony's regular reading. First, he encouraged fluent reading by providing him with reading material at a lower level of difficulty, in an attempt to stimulate more fluent reading habits; second, he taught essential phonic skills from the sight words that Tony knew. Realizing that Tony's problem might be more deeply rooted, the teacher asked for an evaluation by a reading specialist. This situation demonstrates an interested, informed classroom teacher analyzing a child's problem and attempting to correct it, while waiting for the services of the reading specialist.

When the reading specialist saw Tony, he knew that, to arrive at the cause of Tony's problem, a careful diagnosis would be essential. He realized that, among other things, he needed to have complete information concerning Tony's ability, his knowledge of phonics, his auditory skill, and his emotional stability. Therefore, the specialist set into motion a thorough diagnosis to establish the cause of the problem, without which he doubted that he could properly recommend a program of correction.

This example clearly illustrates two different reactions to Tony's symptoms. The classroom teacher used a pattern of symptoms to set into motion a program of correction. The specialist realized that the problem could best be understood by a more careful study of the child. Both the classroom teacher and the reading specialist reacted properly! The teacher instituted a program of correction as quickly as possible after careful consideration of the symptoms, his basic concern being the continuation of Tony's educational program. The specialist initiated a program of diagnosis attempting to determine the cause of Tony's difficulty as accurately as possible, his concern being the recommendation of the most appropriate program of remediation.

To further clarify the difference between symptoms and causes of reading disability, symptoms are defined as those observable characteristics of a case that lead to an educated guess about the reader's problems. Teachers must look for reliable patterns of symptoms so that an intelligent program of correction can be initiated with minimal delay to the child's educational progress. Harris states: ". . . many of the simpler difficulties in reading can be corrected by direct teaching of the missing skills, without an intensive search for reasons why the skills were not learned before."[4] Consideration must be given to the fact that the average classroom teacher has neither the time, the training, nor the materials necessary to conduct a thorough diagnosis. He must use a reliable pattern of symptoms. His procedure is to: 1. examine observable symptoms, combined with available school data; 2. form a hypothesis; and 3. get to work. With the possible necessity for referral in mind, he must formulate and conduct the most effective corrective program possible within the limitations of the regular classroom situation. It then becomes obvious that the reliability of a pattern of symptoms has a direct influence on the effectiveness of his instruction with problem readers. Reference may be made to the following chapter for patterns of symptoms applicable to the classroom diagnosis of problem readers.

Causation may be defined as that factor or those factors which, as a result of careful diagnosis, can be accurately labeled responsible for the reading problem. This is in agreement with Robinson[5] who elaborates upon a definition for causation. The reading specialist is acutely aware

---

[4]Harris, *How To Increase Reading Ability,* p. 220.

[5]Helen M. Robinson, *Why Pupils Fail in Reading* (Chicago: The University of Chicago Press, 1946), p. 219.

that, since there is rarely one cause for a given problem, a careful examination for causation is necessary. Poor home environment, poor physical health, inadequate instruction, the lack of instructional materials, personality disorders, and many other factors have been established as interfering to some degree with the development of reading skills. More specific references to causative factors are made in future chapters.

The reading specialist realizes first that it is through analysis of cause that programs of prevention are made possible, for as Robinson states: ". . . preventive measures can be planned intelligently only if causes of difficulty are understood."[6] The cause, in Tony's case, may have been a lack of auditory discrimination skills to learn phonics or perhaps an overemphasis on isolated word drill in earlier grades. The reading specialist, after a diagnosis designed to determine causes, sets the groundwork for a program of correction. In Tony's case, this might be a revision of portions of the reading curriculum from grade one on or perhaps the establishment of a more thorough readiness program in the early grades. Thus, a careful diagnosis is the first step toward the implementation of a preventive program.

The reading specialist may also be interested in causation to lead more accurately to the most effective program of correction, especially with the more seriously retarded reader. Strang[7] states that success in working with the seriously retarded reader depends upon accurate diagnosis for the cause of the difficulty. If Tony's classroom teacher's program of correction is not effective, it is obvious that a more thorough diagnosis will be essential. This, then, is the other function of the reading specialist. Based upon his diagnosis, he will be able to assist the classroom teacher with recommendations to implement the most effective corrective program.

The fact that the specialist looks for causation and the classroom teacher for patterns of symptoms in no way excuses the classroom teacher from being aware of possible implications and complications concerning the causes of reading problems. Nor does it excuse him from gathering as much diagnostic information as possible. Certainly, the more informed he becomes concerning causation, the more effective he will become in analyzing a pattern of symptoms intelligently. And, as Harris states, he should be ". . . able to carry out the simpler parts of a diagnostic study."[8] At the

---

[6]*Ibid*, p.219.

[7]Strang, *Diagnostic Teaching of Reading*, p. 7.

[8]Harris, *How To Increase Reading Ability*, p. 220.

same time, the teacher's major job is to better instruct all the children in his care, and, as stated above, this generally precludes thorough diagnosis in any one case. It is also possible that, after a most careful diagnosis, the reading specialist will not yet be able to accurately identify all of the causes of the child's reading problem. Causative factors may be elusive, but this condition does not free the reading specialist from attempting to identify those causes as accurately as possible.

To better understand these concepts, the following examples illustrate the effectiveness of both procedures when applied to the four major areas of reading problems, that is, physical, intellectual, emotional, and educational. For a more complete pattern of symptoms and a more thorough discussion of causation, reference is made to Chapters 3 and 4.

Physical Problems

"Bill, how many times have I told you not to hold your book so close to your face?"

Despite repeated efforts to have Bill hold his book at the proper distance, he insisted on this type of visual adjustment. Knowing this to be a symptom of a visual disorder, the teacher began to observe Bill more closely. He noticed unusual watering of the eyes and an unusual amount of blinking, especially after longer sessions involving seat work. His response was to adjust the classroom situation to allow Bill the maximum amount of visual comfort, i.e., regulating visual activities to shorter time periods and assuring Bill of the most favorable lighting conditions. Realizing that he might have a serious vision problem he referred him to a vision specialist.

The teacher's job then was one of recognizing the symptoms and reacting: first, to continue to teach Bill by adjusting the physical setting to enable him to perform as comfortably as possible; and second, to refer him to a specialist for whatever visual correction was necessary.

The reading specialist's reaction to Bill was a little different. He saw the symptoms of the difficulty, and he also realized that referral was a possibility. However, in this case, a visual screening test involving near point vision was first administered in an attempt to determine whether Bill's problem was one of visual disability or one of bad habit.

In all physical problems referral to the proper specialist is the appropriate action for personnel in education. Therefore, both the reading specialist and the classroom teacher considered the referral of Bill for vision analysis. The difference in their approach is important. The classroom teacher observed a pattern of symptoms which told him that there was a good possibility that vision was interfering with his educational progress. Since Bill's education is his first responsibility, the teacher's proper reaction was to adjust the educational climate so that he could operate as effectively as possible. He also was obligated to make a referral for the proper visual analysis. The reading specialist, however, was not immediately confronted with Bill's day-to-day instruction; rather, he was obligated to determine as accurately as possible whether vision was the factor interfering with Bill's education. He was justified in his attempt to screen thoroughly before making recommendations for visual referral or for adjustment to educational climate.

Intellectual Problems

Jim scored poorly on the group intelligence test given at the beginning of fifth grade. His teacher noticed that his mental age and reading achievement age were about the same; however, the teacher realized that his oral vocabulary seemed much better than average and that he seemed to be much better in arithmetic than in other content areas. He concluded that Jim may have more ability than his mental age indicated and that perhaps his intelligence test score was a result of the reading performance necessary in this type of test. His assumption then was that he had more ability than his records indicated. Therefore, he urged him to perform at a higher academic level. To assure himself of the most accurate information, he referred Jim for an individual intelligence test. While waiting for the results of this test, he saw it as his job to motivate him to achievement beyond his present levels. He was obligated to rely upon a pattern of symptoms for his analysis of Jim.

The reading specialist's reaction was to administer an individual intelligence test to determine, as closely as possible, Jim's actual potential. Without accurate knowledge in this area, it would be difficult to make precise recommendations for his educational program. Again, notice that the reactions of the classroom teacher and of the reading specialist were proper, for both realized the limitations of group tests with children who do not read well, and the necessity for the administration of an individual intelligence test. The teacher, however, while waiting for the results of this examination, relied upon a pattern of symptoms which told him that Jim may well have more potential than the school records indicated. He, therefore, increased the tempo of instruction and encouraged Jim toward a higher level of academic performance. The specialist again used diagnostic procedures. His first task was to determine as accurately as possible the degree of the student's actual potential. In the area of intellectual problems, we notice that the classroom teacher is seriously limited by training, time, and the availability of testing materials. He has no recourse but to rely upon a pattern of symptoms of scholastic aptitude, such as group intelligence tests, oral vocabulary, and arithmetic skills. It should also be noticed that the reading specialist *with* the training, the time, and the appropriate materials, is in an excellent position to conduct an examination for a more precise measure of scholastic aptitude. It is also important to notice that in both cases the personnel involved were aware that they should not rely upon *one* measure of ability and that each searched for the most effective technique available.

Emotional Problems

"Sally, haven't you finished your library book yet?" Sally continually resisted her teacher's efforts to encourage her reading. She lagged behind in all personal reading assignments. Concerned about Sally's attitude, her teacher also noticed that she seemed extremely anxious for praise and, at the same time, frequently drifted off into a private world of day dreams.

A check of the development of Sally's reading skills through the school records assured the teacher that his primary task was not going to be one of instruction in the basic reading skills. Correspondingly, it became obvious that her reading situation was in need of adjustment to insure more successful, pleasant experiences which would merit her teacher's praise. In an effort to alleviate Sally's rejection of her personal reading, her teacher lowered the level of difficulty in reading assignments. At the same time, he continued to observe any reaction for possible emotional complications. If such occurred, he would make a referral for a thorough psychological evaluation.

When the reading specialist saw Sally, his first reaction was to administer certain personality evaluations and to study her life at home, with her peers, and in the classroom, to determine the degree of deviations as they may apply to her reading problem. If such deviations appeared to be significant, the specialist would refer Sally's case to a psychologist, a psychiatrist, or a social worker.

While recognizing the potential of Sally's emotional problems, the classroom teacher realized that though he could not give up on the child, he did not have training, time, nor the materials to make a thorough diagnosis.

Again we see both the classroom teacher and the reading specialist willing to refer — the teacher upon the basis of recognition of a pattern of symptoms. Since his primary concern is for immediate educational progress, he attempted to make adjustments in the learning climate to facilitate Sally's progress.

The specialist, being alert to the possible complications in this case, again used diagnostic procedures. Although he realized that he wasn't a psychiatrist, a thorough evaluation through tests and case analysis, would put him in a better position to: first, refer to the proper person; and second, make recommendations for the adjustment of the educational situation. So we see again that both reactions were proper, yet different. The specialist does not feel inclined to start corrective programs with children, who in his opinion, have basic emotional problems. The classroom teacher does not have that choice, so, with an intelligent reaction to a pattern of symptoms, he proceeds with the education of the child, ever alert to problems which may arise!

Educational Problems

As you may recall, Tony was weak in his ability to use word attack skills and was considered by his teacher to be a word-by-word reader. The teacher clearly saw that his reading problem was educational in nature, i.e., he had either missed some instruction, instruction had been skipped, or he had received poor instruction. Although he was concerned about the cause of Tony's problem, he could not stop and trace the problem to its source; rather, he attempted to improve his learning situation through individualization of the classroom procedure. Bond and Tinker[9] hold the view that remedial reading instruction is the same as good classroom instruction which is individualized. Quite properly, the teacher arranged for this individualized instruction and proceeded with Tony's education. The reading specialist began a thorough diagnosis. He was aware of Betts' warning, "Poor teaching in a large sense is the chief cause

---

[9]Guy L. Bond and Miles A. Tinker, *Reading Difficulties, Their Diagnosis and Correction* (New York: Appleton-Century-Crofts, Inc., 1957), p. 13.

of retardation in reading."[10] He realized further that, at best, the teacher had closed the gap for Tony, but that unless a preventive program was instituted, Tony's problem would appear again and again in other children. The specialist finds support again in Betts who says: ". . . each community will find the need for a careful analysis of its peculiar problems."[11] It is obvious that the reading specialist is more capable of making this "careful analysis," and that it cannot be the responsibility of the classroom teacher. By analysis of groups of students, often in different grades, the reading specialist may well find the flaw in the educational program and prevent future problems from occurring. Herein lies a major responsibility for the reading specialist to alleviate the problem through preventive educational programs. Because of his insights into the problem, the specialist has the additional opportunity of advising the classroom teacher concerning individual students with the more serious reading problems.

Summary

It should be remembered that the teacher's first responsibility is to educate all of the children in his classroom as effectively as possible, reading problems notwithstanding. He most effectively fulfills this responsibility by: 1. examining observable symptoms; 2. evaluating the child's difficulty through this pattern of symptoms; 3. adjusting the educational climate; and 4. considering the possibility of referral. In contrast, the reading specialist's first responsibility is to upgrade the effectiveness of reading instruction of all of the children through diagnosis of reading problems within and among the various classrooms. He is, furthermore, responsible for the accurate diagnosis of seriously retarded readers. Herein lies the basic difference between diagnosis using a pattern of symptoms and more thorough diagnosis for causation, both of which are acceptable and proper when dealing with problem readers in the schools.

---

[10]Emmett A. Betts, *Foundations of Reading Instruction* (New York: American Book Co., 1946), p. 52.

[11]*Ibid*, p. 54.

Suggested Readings

1. Bond, Guy L., and Miles A. Tinker, *Reading Difficulties, Their Diagnosis and Correction.* New York: Appleton-Century-Crofts, Inc., 1957, 17. The reader will find Chapter IV in this book to be of particular benefit under this topic; entitled "General Nature of Reading Disability," it is quite thorough.
2. Brueckner, Leo J., and Guy L. Bond, *The Diagnosis and Treatment of Learning Difficulties.* New York: Appleton-Century-Crofts, Inc., 1955, 45. This entire book is directed toward the classroom teaching situation. Chapters III and V have particular relevance to this topic.
3. Harris, Albert J., *How To Increase Reading Ability.* New York: David McKay Co., 1961, 33. Chapters V (III) and VI provide a broad outlook to supplement students' reading under this topic. The more inexperienced reader will want to examine this reference closely.
4. Strang, Ruth, *Diagnostic Teaching of Reading.* New York: McGraw Hill Book Co., 1964, 14. Chapter II, "The Role of the Teacher in Diagnosis," is an excellent discussion of diagnosis in the classroom. The student will find this to be a very handy reference for this and the following chapter.

2

Introduction To Diagnosis

Regardless of the educator's professional position, diagnosis is essential in formulating a remedial program which will be both effective and efficient. Implied by the term diagnosis are the kinds of activities which will assist the educator in evaluating the present state of the child's skill development and the developmental history of the child's attitudes and habits toward reading and learning. Diagnosis can be accomplished quickly or it may be quite time consuming. However, believing that instruction should take the child ahead as rapidly and efficiently as possible, there is no alternative to effective diagnosis prior to instruction. It is necessary for the classroom teacher to enter diagnosis with as much accuracy and confidence as possible. The day is past when diagnosis of reading problems could afford the aura of mystery which once surrounded it. In facing the problem realistically, the reading specialist will not be able to handle the number referred unless the classroom teacher starts to assume major responsibilities in diagnosis. The type of diagnosis used will be dependent, however, upon the educator's ability to use the diagnostic tools at his disposal and his specific educational situation. Thus, the teacher or the reading specialist must evaluate the need for extended diagnosis in terms of the difficulty that the child is having, the availability of specialized services, and the needs of the other children in the room. The three types of diagnoses to be discussed in this chapter are: informal-on-the-spot, classroom, and clinical.

Informal-on-the-Spot Diagnosis

This type of diagnosis is constantly taking place in the modern classroom where the teacher recognizes symptoms of educational lag through informal procedures. As a result of such diagnosis, the alert teacher makes immediate adjustments in his teaching techniques to allow for maximum efficiency in his classroom. Involved in this type of diagnosis are evaluations of the child's reaction to classroom situations such as: questions asked by the teacher; informal teacher made tests; reading class exercises; and the use of library facilities. Ever alert to the first signs of pupil frustration, the teacher will prevent serious reading problems from developing by using informal diagnosis, followed by immediate instructional adjustment. The good teacher will always make certain beforehand, through evaluation of child performance, that the child is ready for the next step in learning. He will continuously assess the child's learning performances, repeating or adapting instruction as necessary. Some of these diagnoses may be conducted with groups of children and some may be individualized, but the process is an on-going, vital part of the total learning situation in the classroom. How well a teacher can conduct informal-on-the-spot diagnosis will relate directly to his understanding of the children whom he is teaching and the skills which they need. However, since this type of diagnosis will not suit the needs of every child, the teacher will need to evaluate some children more carefully.

Classroom Diagnosis

If the problem persists even after informal adjustments have been made, the teacher initiates a classroom diagnosis which involves a more formal and directed effort without removing the child from his classroom environment. In this type of diagnosis, the teacher utilizes the diagnostic material available to him to formulate a pattern of symptoms which will assist him to more clearly understand a particular child's reading skills. This understanding necessitates the direct observation of the child in the reading act; use of school records; direct testing of noted skill deficiencies; assessment of intellectual potential; and a compilation of relevant data. In this type of diagnosis, the teacher gathers information, evaluates its appropriateness, and relates his findings to his instructional situation. This, in contrast to on-the-spot diagnosis, involves more analysis and time in a directed study of an individual child. Based on the resulting understanding, the teacher then carefully plans the child's reading program.

Clinical Diagnosis

As the term implies, this type of diagnosis is reserved for the more complex type of reading difficulty. Conducted by the reading specialist, (often with the assistance of noneducational specialists), it requires the removal of the child from the classroom so that individual examinations may be administered by a qualified person in surroundings that are conducive to full performance. Characteristic of this type of diagnosis are more precise measures of intellectual potential, word attack skills, visual screening, etc. These measures, presented in the form of a case study, will be evaluated to diagnose as accurately as possible the precise nature of the child's reading problem. Clinical diagnosis involves more detailed planning, more careful analysis, and more precise instruments for testing than does classroom diagnosis.

Sequence of Diagnosis

The following sequence will provide a better understanding of the relationships between the types of diagnosis:

The classroom teacher makes an informal on-the-spot diagnosis and adjusts instruction accordingly. If this fails, the teacher conducts a classroom diagnosis and again instruction is individualized. Should this step be unsuccessful, the teacher refers to a reading specialist for a more thorough analysis via clinical diagnosis. Once more instruction is adjusted according to the recommendations of the specialist. When the entire sequence cannot produce the desired results, referral outside the school is likely. It is unlikely that a single failure will result in the teacher's moving immediately to the next type of diagnosis; rather, he will utilize each diagnostic step thoroughly and repeatedly, if necessary, before moving to the next. It should be noticed at each step in this sequence, that the possibility of referral is present. (For a clearer understanding refer to Chart I.)

Since all effective learning relies upon informal on-the-spot diagnosis and its subsequent follow-up, it is assumed that this type of diagnosis is normal to good teaching situations. Further discussion of diagnosis in this book, then, will more directly relate to classroom and clinical diagnosis which involves more careful diagnostic techniques.

CHART I — SEQUENCE OF DIAGNOSIS

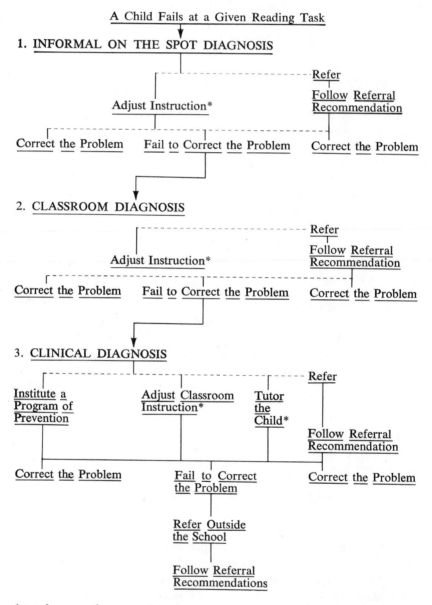

A Child Fails at a Given Reading Task

1. INFORMAL ON THE SPOT DIAGNOSIS

Refer

Follow Referral
Recommendation

Adjust Instruction*

Correct the Problem   Fail to Correct the Problem   Correct the Problem

2. CLASSROOM DIAGNOSIS

Refer

Follow Referral
Recommendation

Adjust Instruction*

Correct the Problem   Fail to Correct the Problem   Correct the Problem

3. CLINICAL DIAGNOSIS

Refer

Institute a
Program of
Prevention

Adjust Classroom
Instruction*

Tutor
the
Child*

Follow Referral
Recommendation

Correct the Problem   Fail to Correct
the Problem   Correct the Problem

Refer Outside
the School

Follow Referral
Recommendations

*may be more than one attempt

Diagnostic Procedures

Diagnostic procedures vary with the purpose and scope of the diagnosis. While similarities exist, there are noticeable differences in classroom and clinical diagnostic procedures.

Classroom diagnostic procedures

Classroom procedures must be designed with the idea in mind that the teacher has obligations and responsibilities to other children as well as the problem reader. The following procedures may be studied in chart form on Chart II.

CHART II

PROCEDURES FOR CLASSROOM DIAGNOSIS

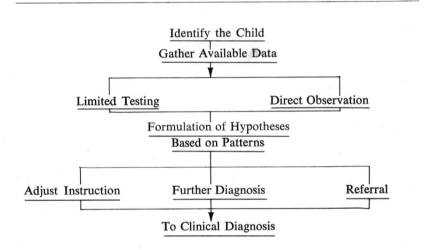

1. *Identifying the child:* The classroom teacher, unlike the reading specialist, is in the best position to first notice potential problem areas. In this way the classroom diagnosis is actually underway by the time the child has been identified, for informal-on-the-spot diagnosis has previously

established certain diagnostic information which the teacher will use in classroom diagnosis.

Hopefully, the tendency for educators to wait until the problem is well developed can be avoided by increased attention to classroom diagnosis at all age levels, including first grade. It is through immediate attention to the reading problems of children that the number of seriously handicapped readers can be reduced.

2. *Gathering available data:* The classroom teacher then makes an intensive search for available information on the child and organizes it for further consideration during the diagnosis. Using school records, interviews with past teachers, health reports, and the like, considerable data may be available concerning past development, successes, and failures of this child.

3. *Limited testing:* When necessary, the classroom teacher may be prepared to administer and interpret appropriate tests designed to provide information in the area of the difficulty. Testing, of course, is limited in terms of the time that a teacher has for individual testing as well as his skill in using these instruments.

4. *Direct observations:* Based upon the information available at this stage of classroom diagnosis, the classroom teacher will find it advantageous to observe the child in various reading situations with particular emphasis on the verification of this information. When observations and other data complement previous findings, the next step can be taken. When they do not support each other, there is a need for a re-evaluation, more observation, possible testing, and new conclusions.

5. *Formulation of hypotheses:* Based on the patterns observed, the teacher will then form hypotheses about adjustment of instruction within the group or individually, and about the possibility of referral.

By following the suggestions in this book and by adapting this material to information which the classroom teacher already has available to him, classroom diagnosis should be conducted effectively in about one hour. The classroom teacher will need to find periods of time, not necessarily in one hour blocks, for this type of individual study. As the teacher grows proficient in classroom diagnostic techniques, he will find them more rewarding and less time consuming.

The classroom teacher's job has obviously just begun, as he will now teach in accordance with his hypotheses, make referrals, evaluate his effectiveness, and adjust his instruction; in addition, he must be ever alert to the possibility that a more thorough diagnosis may be necessary. His situation permits continued diagnosis through the remediation periods. In fact, classroom diagnosis has the strong advantage of often achieving better understandings by working with the child, than were possible by pre-remedial diagnosis itself. In the remedial program the finer points of technique and the real interests of the child can be determined.

Clinical diagnostic procedures

Clinical procedures may be designed without attention to the needs of other children in the classroom. Clinical procedures are charted on Chart III.

CHART III

PROCEDURES FOR CLINICAL DIAGNOSIS

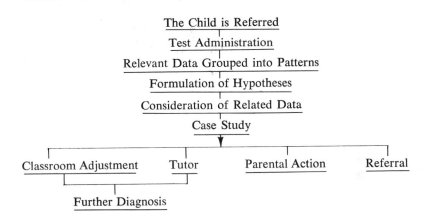

1. *The child is referred:* The specialist has the advantage of starting to work with a child previously identified as a possible reading problem. The classroom teacher has either attempted classroom diagnosis or identified the child as one in need of clinical diagnosis. He should be expected to have accumulated all available information about the child and, upon referral to the reading specialist, should submit such information for the specialist's use. It is not uncommon for parents to identify the child as needing clinical diagnosis; however, it is the specialist's job, in these cases, to consult with the classroom teacher to make certain that clinical diagno-

sis has not previously been conducted. He encourages the teacher's support and obtains his opinions and records.

2. *Administration of a battery of tests:* Based upon a tentative evaluation of the child and his needs, the reading specialist proceeds with the administration and analysis of a battery of tests necessary to gather objective data concerning the child's reading skills.

3. *Observation of patterns:* The reading specialist then makes careful observations of behavior patterns during the testing, which, when combined with test scores and an inner analysis of the child's errors on tests administered, will permit him to group relevant data into more meaningful patterns.

4. *Formulation of hypotheses:* From the observable patterns, the reading specialist then forms tentative hypotheses concerning the causes of the child's problem. The hypotheses are formulated upon his findings alone. It is important that his original hypothesis be untainted by parental opinion, for often this fresh, unbiased examination of the child leads us to the discovery of previously unavailable information.

5. *Consideration of related data:* Once the hypothesis has been formed, the specialist weighs related data in the form of parent and teacher conferences, school records, previous diagnostic results, etc. In many instances the specialist, finding that his hypothesis is true, becomes more confident about his findings. At other times conflicting information forces him to reconsider his original hypothesis and, in many cases, to test the child further or re-examine the results of previous tests to gain clearer insights into the child's problem.

6. *Formulation of recommendations and referrals:* After consideration of all relevant data, the reading specialist develops a case study which includes recommendations for adjustments of school programs, remedial treatment, possible parental action, further testing, and/or necessary referral.

The amount of time needed for effective clinical diagnosis will vary with (1) the age of the child, (2) the effectiveness of classroom diagnosis, and (3) practical matters such as clinician load. Normally, a clinical diagnosis would not be handled in less than three hours nor more than ten hours.

It is to be remembered that the reading specialist's job does not end here, for he is often involved directly in remediation or in the institution of preventative programs, both of which may call for further diagnosis. Morris includes the following thoughts in his discussion of diagnosis:

". . . the challenge is to get to grips more directly with the problem and by working with the individual pupil try to understand what is leading him astray."[1] It is sufficient to say that diagnosis may often reach its ultimate conclusion during instruction.

In fact, we have found it profitable for the clinician to conduct a few lessons upon the drawing of diagnostic conclusions. In such a manner, the final case study can include positive statements concerning the type and level of instruction to which the child can best respond. For example, if diagnostic conclusions call for working in the area of initial consonant substitution and if Speech to Print Phonics is recommended, then the clinician teaches a few lessons in this area. Case reports can become more practical and recommendations more specific through the use of this technique.

Sources of Data

The reading specialist and the classroom teacher have many sources of diagnostic data available to them. Much, but by no means all, of the data available in a reading diagnosis is in the form of tests. Harris views the diagnostic use of tests as follows:

> . . . the heart of diagnosis is not testing, it is, rather, the intelligent interpretation of the facts by a person who has the theoretical knowledge and the practical experience to know what questions to ask; to select procedures, including tests, which can supply the needed facts; to interpret the meaning of the findings correctly; and to comprehend the interrelationships of these facts and meaning.[2]

The reader should therefore remember that it is the person conducting the diagnosis and his ability to interpret the data, not the data itself, which leads to effective diagnosis.

Data for classroom diagnosis is more informal. School records, observation of the child in his classroom reading, evaluation reports from past teachers, interviews with students and parents, home visits, and available test scores form the major sources of data for a classroom diagnosis.

Data for clinical diagnosis normally take the form of tests of intellectual performance, tests and evaluations of personal adjustment, physical screening tests, tests of reading performance, interviews and

---

[1]Ronald Morris, *Success and Failure in Learning to Read* (London: Oldbourne, 1963), p. 159.

[2]Harris, *How To Increase Reading Ability,* p. 221.

questionnaires, and professional reports. Data is supplemented by observation of the child during testing and is normally compiled in the form of a case study which illustrates the importance and inter-relationships of the data collected.

Anyone conducting a diagnosis will want to use all of the available diagnostic data which he is competent to interpret. The classroom teacher who has had course work and/or experience in clinical diagnosis will find considerable use for portions of the data listed for the reading specialist. Normally, however, the factors of time, educational background, experience, and access to materials will limit the classroom teacher to less formal types of data.

Principles of Diagnosis

The examiner conducts a diagnosis to understand and then correct a child's difficulty. Implied in principles of diagnosis is the examiner's thorough knowledge of the learning process and of the procedures of teaching reading. Without this knowledge, the educator will find it difficult to apply properly the information gained in a diagnosis, for he will tend to rely solely on the data he has collected, instead of interpreting that data in terms of reading skills and learning environment for the child.

Although the classroom teacher is not always able to comply with the following principles of diagnosis, it is important for him to be as aware of these principles as is the clinician, for to violate them would threaten the reliability of his diagnostic findings. Classroom diagnostic procedures and data are designed with the inherent limitations of the classroom in mind.

1. *To establish rapport:* For a child to perform at his best, a situation must be established where tensions are relaxed and the child is encouraged into a cooperative attitude. The reading specialist confronted with conducting his diagnosis outside normal classroom situations must be more alert to the necessity for establishing rapport than must the classroom teacher who, through daily contact with the child, is more likely to have rapport established.

2. *To provide for individual study:* Since group testing procedures tend to produce unreliable results for the child with a reading problem, individual study becomes requisite. This principle demands that the individual be studied apart from, as well as within, the group to insure an as accurate as possible analysis of his reactions to learning. Through individual study

it is possible to analyze accurately the child's skill development, alleviating the aspects of competition which often cause this type of child to perform below his capacity.

3. *To test, not to teach:* During testing procedures, special effort must be made to resist the temptation to prompt the child to give the proper answer through "teacher-type" comments such as, "Sound out the first letter" or "That's almost right, try again." The teacher's comments can make the child become justifiably encouraged or discouraged. In either case, this action invalidates the diagnostic findings. This principle applies only to the diagnostic period in which the child is expected to perform in a variety of ways without the encouragement or discouragement of success and/or failure. As has been previously stated, both the classroom teacher and the reading specialist will find numerous diagnostic opportunities while instruction is taking place.

4. *To assure thoroughness:* Normally continuing in remedial sessions, diagnosis seldom terminates with the initial diagnostic period. In most cases, informal diagnosis and shorter periods of formal diagnosis will be interspersed during remedial sessions where precise diagnostic findings are formulated and put to use.

5. *To maintain efficiency:* In terms of efficiency, a diagnosis includes only those tests which are likely to help the examiner arrive at pertinent results. There is a tendency to rely upon a systematic diagnostic procedure regardless of the needs of the child, creating pointless testing situations which at best, are often frustrating experiences. An efficient diagnosis, then, is one which includes those measures needed by the educator to properly arrive at a solution to the problem; it eliminates those which have questionable value in relation to the final objective of the diagnosis.

6. *To evaluate diagnostic data in terms of patterns:* The examiner must look for patterns in data and hesitate to rely upon a single measure as being meaningful or significant. This principle, then, requires a diagnosis to, in effect, include several interrelated measures of the child's reading abilities. For example, it would be best to compare one's results on a word recognition test with the results on both oral reading and word meaning. When similar errors occur on all three tests, a pattern of errors is established, when they occur on only one or two, a different pattern appears. Both of these patterns are important, and it is essential that data be evaluated in this manner.

Diagnosis for Causation

As diagnosis has been presented thus far, the role of the reading specialist in clinical diagnosis has been contrasted to the role of the classroom teacher in classroom diagnosis. Each has been encouraged to use the best diagnostic procedures and data available. The classroom teacher will utilize his time and efforts most effectively in diagnosing patterns of symptoms to adjust his classroom approach to the child with a reading problem. The reading specialist, in clinical diagnosis, will be more thorough in attempting to arrive at a cause. Although diagnosis directed toward the detection of causation is primarily the responsibility of the reading specialist, and although it is through clinical diagnosis that causes are most accurately evaluated, the classroom teacher's awareness of the causes of reading difficulties will aid him in obtaining a better diagnostic understanding of the child.

We have previously established that reading disabilities are caused by a variety of factors. The areas indicated by Bond and Tinker[3] (intellectual, physical, emotional, and educational) are inclusive enough to provide consideration for this variety of causes. Non-educational causes (intellectual, physical and emotional) will be discussed in Chapter 3. Chapter 4 will contain a discussion of educational causes. It is important for the reader to be reminded that it is the specific responsibility of educators to diagnose and correct reading problems in this fourth area, educational.

Summary

Through an understanding of the similarities and differences in the diagnostic procedures, data, and principles as they apply to the classroom and clinical situations, the educator is most likely to be effective and satisfied with his efforts The nature of classroom and clinical settings establish clear limitations. There are advantages and limitations to both types of diagnosis, and therefore each can be viewed objectively and used most effectively.

---

[3]Bond and Tinker, *Reading Difficulties,* p. 104.

Suggested Readings

1. Bond, Guy L., and Miles A. Tinker, *Reading Difficulties, Their Diagnosis and Correction,* p. 104. New York: Appleton-Century-Crofts, Inc., 1957. Chapter VII contains a careful introduction to the broad principles of diagnosis. The reader who desires more specific information on this general topic will find this chapter rewarding.
2. Strang, Ruth, *Diagnostic Teaching of Reading.* New York: McGraw Hill Book Co., 1964. As an introduction to this book on diagnosis, Chapter I provides a very up-to-date, carefully organized discussion of the principles, approaches, and other concepts related to the diagnosing of reading disabilities.

3

Non-Educational Diagnosis

Diagnosis which is non-educational in nature refers to situations in which the final analysis rests with a specialist outside of the field of education. The responsibility of educators in non-educational diagnosis is to screen the child either with the tools which he has available or through observations of symptoms of difficulty. Once a problem is identified, the child is referred to the appropriate specialist, who will conduct a thorough examination and either correct the deficiency or make recommendations to the educator for remedial approaches. This chapter will assist the educator to identify potential problems, refer effectively, and recognize the difficulties involved with diagnosis in each of the areas.

Intellectual Diagnosis

The classroom teacher and the reading specialist are obligated to estimate as accurately as possible the child's reading potential. To recognize both the limitations and the advantages of such an estimate is a necessity. The child's estimated potential should serve as a goal for instructional achievement for the teacher. This goal will of necessity be flexible, for even the best estimates of intelligence are subject to error. As a cause of reading disabilities, intelligence is suspect. In fact, intelligence is related to *causes* of reading problems only in relation to the ability of the school to adjust the educational program to the abilities of various types of children. It is essential to realize that not because of his intelligence, or lack of it, does a child not read up to his potential; rather, it is that school programs, usually geared to the majority of children who are average, give little consideration to children found at the extremes (the bright and dull children). The inability or the impossibility of a given situation to provide these necessary adjustments often *causes* these bright or dull children to become reading problems.

Complications of intellectual testing

Complicating the position of intelligence is the educator's tendency to misuse intelligence test scores by grasping at high or low scores as the most easily observable division between the problem and the normal reader. Although accurate measures of intellectual performance are essential to the diagnosis of children's reading, the intelligence of a given child per se is not the cause of his problem.

This controversial relationship of intelligence to reading has been researched extensively, resulting in reports of both high and low correlations between reading success and mental ability. The variation in these findings, however, can often be credited to non-comparable research designs, poor means of measuring intelligence, and/or improper interpretation of test results. A brief look at a few of the problems in measuring intelligence will lead to a clearer understånding of the obstacles encountered in using measures of intellectual performance in a diagnosis.

1. Even the best measures of intelligence evaluate only a few of the many aspects of this complex concept. Presumably, the most prominent aspects have been selected by the more carefully designed tests; however, the educator must place the results of these tests in proper perspective to their obvious limitations. A test of intellectual performance which measures auditory comprehension, for example, concerns a critical aspect of intelligence; however, the resulting score is limited by the narrow nature of the performance required by an auditory comprehension as an estimate of intellectual potential.

2. Many measures of intelligence have been criticized because they favor certain socio-economic classes, rendering less valid the scores for large groups of certain types of children. It is acknowledged, for example, that children with weak language experience backgrounds reflect this deficiency in verbal test scores. Poor scores for these children do not necessarily mean they are dull. Therefore, when interpreting results of

intelligence tests, the examiner must acknowledge that scores may be influenced by the lack of similarity between the child being tested and the population upon which the particular test was standardized.

3. The examiner often has scores available from intelligence tests which he personally did not administer. He must be aware that testing situations about which he is unfamiliar may lack rapport, causing scores taken at face value to be highly misleading. He must also evaluate, if possible, the competency of the other examiner in administering and interpreting the test, for it falls upon the test administrator to interpret properly children's responses on many of these tests in order to obtain reliable results. When the test administrator cannot be identified, the resulting score may properly be held suspect until supporting evidence can be accumulated and evaluated.

4. The age of the child when the test is given may affect the test results. While some tests are designed for preschool or elementary school children, others are better measures of older children. Familiarity with this type of information leads the examiner to a more valid interpretation of a given score. For those unfamiliar with the various tests, *The Mental Measurements Yearbooks* by Buros[1] provides descriptive analyses.

5. Since many group intelligence tests are strongly influenced by the ability of the child to read the questions, they are, in fact, reading tests also. The poor reader often scores poorly on this type of test simply because he cannot read. MacDonald comments on this conflict:

> Because both group type intelligence tests and reading achievement tests involve reading, the common element present in both kinds of tests represents two measures of the same categories of skill. Poor readers are doubly penalized with significant underestimation of probable mental ability.[2]

Awareness of the limitations inherent in measures of intellectual performance will lessen the possibility of intelligence test scores being used or interpreted improperly. To assure correct assessment of intellectual performance, at least one of the measures of intelligence must be individual and non-reading in nature. Major discrepancies between test scores are justifiable reasons for referral for psychological examination. An accurate I.Q. is *not* found by averaging conflicting scores.

---

[1]O. K. Buros, ed., *The Fifth Mental Measurements Yearbook* (Highland Park, N.J.: The Gryphon Press, 1959).

[2]Arthur S. McDonald, "Research for the Classroom," *The Journal of Reading,* VIII:2, (November, 1964), pp. 115-18.

Acknowledging these limitations, it remains desirable to establish as accurately as possible the level of intellectual performance (an index of potential reading ability) to measure the degree to which the child is retarded in reading. A fifth grade child with the estimated intelligence of the average fourth grader, reading one year below his grade level, is not normally considered retarded in reading; he reads as well as he is able. He is, however, a problem to his teacher for he is less likely to be capable of profiting from instruction with the materials he has available for his fifth grade class. This child is a problem, not as a retarded reader, but as a product of the failure of our schools to provide materials at varying levels of difficulty (or of the teacher to effectively use the materials and techniques available to him). This child does not need a reading diagnosis; rather, he needs the normal development program available in fourth grade. Harris claims ". . . children of limited mental ability cannot be brought up to age and grade norms . . . Failure to realize this has clogged up many remedial programs with the wrong children."[3] On the other hand, a fifth grade child, reading at a sixth grade level with the estimated intellectual performance of the average eighth grader, may not cause his teacher instructional problems in the classroom, but he *is* retarded in reading. So quite often the retarded reader is of normal or above average intelligence, reading below his potential.

It remains important, therefore, for the person conducting a diagnosis of reading problems to evaluate carefully the intellectual performance of each child or to obtain that evaluation from a reliable source.

Measures of potential reading ability suitable for clinical diagnosis

1. *Revised Stanford Binet Intelligence Scale**. Generally considered the most accurate single test for measuring intelligence, the Binet may be administered and scored only by personnel with formal course work and/or clinic experience. The test ranges from preschool to adulthood, yielding a mental age and an intelligence quotient. The test measures several aspects of intelligence, takes about 45 minutes to administer, is individual in nature, and requires precise administration and interpretation for reliable results.

2. *Wechsler Intelligence Scale for Children (WISC)**. Another popular,

---

[3]Harris, *How To Increase Reading Ability*, p. 227.

*See Appendix A.

very accurate test of intellectual performance, the WISC requires individual administration and formal course work and/or clinical experience for valid results. Measuring several aspects of intelligence, the WISC yields a performance and a verbal score, with the verbal score normally considered the most valid predictor of performance in reading. With problem readers, however, it is the performance score that is most likely to provide the best measure of reading potential. The child's verbal score is likely to be limited by the same factors that limit his performance in reading. When WISC scores show a higher performance than verbal rating, there is just cause to encourage the child with his development in reading. Deal[4] summarized fourteen studies of WISC sub scores and found that the researchers were far from unanimous in their findings. It would appear, then, that the educator will be treading on dangerous ground to venture into the interpretation of WISC sub scores. The *Wechsler Adult Intelligence Scale* (WAIS), also available, may be used with older children and adults. It takes approximately 30-60 minutes to administer.

3. *The Peabody Picture Vocabulary Test (PPVT)**. Designed to test the child's ability to associate one of four pictures with the word pronounced by the examiner, the *PPVT* is a test of oral vocabulary taking approximately 15 minutes for individual administration and requiring little special preparation by the teacher. Although limited to one aspect of intelligence, i.e., auding, Neville[5] found no significant difference between the performance scores of 54 children on the *PPVT* and on the *WISC.* Strang contends, "Ability to comprehend by listening, sometimes called auding, is one of the best single indications of potential reading ability."[6] We have found it valuable to refer to the M.A. score on the *PPVT* as the child's "auding age" . . . and the IQ as the "auding quotient." By changing these names, we find that college students who work with these tests are more likely to use the resulting scores properly. For a quick indication of intellectual performance, the *PPVT* is considered to be practical and useful when *Binet* and *WISC* scores are not available.

4Margaret Deal, "A Summary of Research Concerning Patterns of WISC Subtest Scores of Retarded Readers," *The Journal of the Reading Specialist,* IV:4, May, 1965, pp 101-111.

5Donald Neville, "The Relationship Between Reading Skills and Intelligence Test Scores," *The Reading Teacher,* XVIII:4, January, 1965, pp. 257-61.

6Strang, *Diagnostic Teaching of Reading,* p. 13.

*See Appendix A.

4. Durrell-Sullivan Reading Capacity Test*. As another measure of auding ability, this test requires a child to associate words and paragraphs which are read by the examiner with pictures designed to represent the words and paragraphs. Yielding a word meaning and paragraph meaning capacity score, it is a group measuring device which takes 30-40 minutes and requires little formal preparation for proper administration. This test may be compared to the *Durrell-Sullivan Reading Achievement Test**, for the achievement test measures the same factors in reading achievement as the Capacity Test does in auding (reading potential). Designed in 1939, the Capacity Test has been a long time favorite in clinic study.

5. Botel Listening Test*. This is a test in which the examiner reads one word and asks the child to listen to three or four other words, one of which contains the opposite meaning. The test provides a measure of grade level performance in word auding and should be considered a screening test. It has the advantage of group administration, and takes approximately 10-20 minutes. The Botel test series also includes a *Word Recognition Test** and a *Reading Word Opposites Test** which may be compared to the listening test, as are the Durrell-Sullivan tests.

6. Arithmetic computation. For children who have attended school for two or more years, a test of arithmetic computation, not involving verbal problem reading, is useful in estimating reading potential. Included as a factor on several intelligence scales, arithmetic computation scores show how well the child succeeds in school in non-verbal tasks, indicating the level of potential. Arithmetic computation scores verify suspicions of potential that have gone undetected when they vary noticeably from reading achievement. In some types of more seriously handicapped children, arithmetic computation scores do not indicate potential. This is especially true when the child reacts against the learning environment with emotional rejection. Arithmetic computation, however, remains a valuable tool as one of the first indicators of intellectual potential.

7. The Knox Cube Test*. A sub test from the *Grace Arthur Point Scale**, it is useful in reading diagnosis since it provides a measure of the child's performance in memorization of non verbal sequences. It can be expected that most children with reading problems will score two to three years below their chronological age. Scores which exceed this margin may be considered as one symptom of more complicated organizational disabilities.

The tests mentioned above, which are most likely to be available, provide fairly accurate measures of reading potential. Other measures of

---

*See Appendix A.

intellectual performance are also available for clinical diagnosis; however, most of them require special preparation and/or clinic experience, as do the Binet and the WISC.

Measures of potential reading ability suitable to classroom diagnosis

1. Although the Binet* and the WISC* are not normally administered by the classroom teacher, their scores are often found in the school records of the problem reader. The other tests mentioned under clinical diagnosis can be administered by a classroom teacher as a part of normal school procedures or as a part of classroom diagnosis.

2. Group intelligence tests: Although most group intelligence tests are strongly controlled by the child's reading performance, there are several of them which separate reading and non-reading factors. The *California Test of Mental Maturity**, for example, provides a mental age and I.Q. for both language and non-language performance. The teacher who uses this type of test and finds a major discrepancy between the two scores (non-language I.Q.—140; language I.Q.—100), should assume that the pattern is unusual and that reading may be limiting the language score. Other measures of reading potential such as those mentioned under clinical diagnosis should then be checked, or the child should be referred for an individual intelligence examination. One must note that unless group intelligence tests have non-language features, they are not particularly useful in estimating the reading potential of children with reading problems.

3. Teacher observation: The experienced teacher is often able to note characteristics of reading potential through direct observation of the child's response to various school activities. Roswell states that a teacher ". . . can form some idea of the child's intellectual ability from his general responsiveness in class."[7] Specifically, noticeable characteristics are:

1. Ability to achieve higher in arithmetic than in subjects requiring reading.
2. Ability to participate effectively in class discussions, both listening and speaking.
3. Ability to participate effectively in peer group activities.
4. Ability to demonstrate alert attitudes to the world around him.
5. Ability to perform satisfactorily on spelling tests.

---

[7]Florence Roswell and Gladys Natchez, *Reading Disability* (New York: Basic Books, Inc., 1964), p. 27.

*See Appendix A.

Admittedly, such observations are neither highly valid nor reliable indications of reading potential; however, limited ability in these areas is often the first symptom to be noticed. By such observations, children who have been intellectually misjudged may be referred for a more accurate evaluation.

Reading potential and degree of retardation

Measures of intellectual performance greatly aid in determining the degree of reading retardation. A comparison of the best estimates of reading potential with the best estimates of reading achievement will result in an arithmetical difference. Finding that potential exceeds achievement, concern is legitimate that the child is not working up to his capacity. The larger the difference, the more serious the degree of retardation.

Perhaps the most common technique for estimating the seriousness of retardation is a simple comparison of the child's mental age (I.Q. divided by 100, multiplied by chronological age (C.A.)) to his reading achievement.[8] This technique is particularly limiting with very young children of high ability, as it assumes a considerable development of reading skills prior to school attendance. A six year old child with an I.Q. of 140 entering first grade may be considered to have a mental age of 8.4, ($\frac{140}{100}$ x 6.0 = 1.4 x 6.0 = 8.4) but should not normally be expected to be reading at the third grade level because he lacks social, emotional, and educational experiences for that degree of achievement. Even with older children, this technique tends to place reading potential scores unrealistically high. Acknowledging these limitations, seriousness of retardation can be determined by this technique, and many wrongly placed children can be screened out of remedial programs.

Bond and Tinker circumvent the limitations mentioned above by using the formula ($\frac{I.Q.}{100}$ multiplied by years in school + 1.0)[9] as compared to reading achievement. The child discussed above would have a reading potential of 1.0 upon entrance to first grade.

---

[8]Harris, *How To Increase Reading Ability,* p. 299.

[9]Bond and Tinker, *Reading Difficulties,* pp. 78-9.

$$(\frac{140}{100} x \ 0) \ + \ 1.0 \ = \ 1.0$$

As the child advances through school, this approach expects him to make accelerated progress, so that upon entrance to third grade, this same child is expected to be reading at the 3.8 grade level:

$$(\frac{140}{100} x \ 2.0) \ + \ 1.0 \ = \ 3.8$$

Their research shows that this formula is much more realistic than formulas using mental age such as that mentioned above.[10] In using this formula, consideration must be given three factors. First, it must be understood that the term "years in school" does not mean the child's grade placement, rather, the actual number of years that he has attended school. Therefore, for a child who has a grade placement of 4.8 and who has not accelerated or repeated a grade, the appropriate entry would be 3.8 for "years in school." (For this formula, kindergarten does not count as a year in school.) Second, the teacher must have accurate data concerning the grades repeated or accelerated. Third, the examiner should understand that the addition of 1.0 years in the formula is to compensate for the manner in which grade norms are assigned to tests, 1.0 being the zero month of first grade. Despite its obvious advantages, many teachers, lacking complete understanding of it, refrain from using this formula.

Cleland [11] prefers to average four factors, giving equal weight to each, in arriving at a reading potential score which is compared to reading achievement. In his formula he computes the grade equivalents of chronological age, mental age, arithmetic computation, and the Durrell-Sullivan Reading Capacity Test:

$$C.A.-5 = 6-5 \ \ = 1.0$$
$$M.A.-5 = 8.4-5 = 3.4$$
$$Arith. \ C. \ \ \ \ \ = 1.5$$
$$D/S \ Cap. \ \ \ \ = 2.5$$
$$8.4 \div 4 = 2.1$$

This formula has several advantages: first, although mental age is used without the compensation that Bond and Tinker give, it is equalized somewhat by the use of chronological age; secondly, the use of reading capacity adds auding as a factor; and thirdly, the use of arithmetic computation provides measures of the child's ability to do non-verbal

---

10Bond and Tinker, *Reading Difficulties,* pp. 78-9.

11Donald L. Cleland, "Clinical Materials for Appraising Disabilities In Reading," *The Reading Teacher,* XVII:6, March, 1964, p. 428.

school work. It is important to note that grade equivalents of M.A. and C.A. are obtained by subtracting 5, for the 5 years the child did not attend school. This formula, or variations of it, is commonly used in clinical diagnosis. We find that it compares much more favorably to the Bond and Tinker formula than to the mental age formula, and is preferable to either of these for a precise clinical diagnosis.

A convenient and fairly accurate technique for determining the degree of retardation is to compare the scores on the *Durrell-Sullivan Reading Capacity Test* with those of the *Durrell-Sullivan Reading Achievement Test*. The difference between the two scores measures the degree of retardation. When the reading capacity score is higher than the reading achievement score, the examiner has reason to assume that the child is not working up to his potential.

To compare the child's score on a test of auding with his achievement test performance is another relatively easy way of determining the degree of retardation. In this case, the auding score is an estimate of reading potential and may be obtained from tests such as the *Peabody Picture Vocabulary Test* and the *Botel Listening Test*. On the Peabody the auding age equivalent may be converted to grade equivalent by subtracting 5 years.

The classroom teacher in his diagnosis will first use symptoms observed in the classroom to determine which children appear to have the potential to read better. In comparing the child's reading achievement with observable estimates of the child's potential, he will have made the initial identification of the child in need of diagnosis.

How large the difference between reading potential and achievement must be, to be considered serious, will vary with the grade placement of the child. There may be many children who fall slightly short of full reading potential, yet would not be considered problem readers. In fact it is rare for children to reach their full potential. Older children can manage a larger variance between potential and achievement without the severe ramifications that occur with younger children.

The scale in Table 1 may be useful in selecting a cut-off point between a tolerable difference and one that is sufficient to interfere with the child's progress in reading and other subjects.

Tolerable differences are presented in this table in column I, by individual grade level and in column II by groupings for primary, intermediate, and junior and senior high school levels. A child in the primary

TABLE 1
Degree of Tolerable Difference Between
Potential and Achievement

End of:	I	II
1st grade	- .3)	
2nd grade	- .5)	.5 of a year
3rd grade	- .7)	
4th grade	- .8)	
5th grade	-1.0)	1 year
6th grade	-1.2)	
7th grade	-1.3)	
8th grade	-1.5)	1.5 years
9th grade	-1.7)	
10th grade	-1.8)	
11th grade	-2.0)	2 years
12th grade	-2.2)	

grades retarded .9 of a year has exceeded the minimum tolerable difference, while a child in an intermediate grade with this same difference has not exceeded his tolerable difference. Although this scale should not be adhered to rigidly, it does provide reasonable limits useful in categorizing most children. However, since diagnosis includes considerably more analysis than the estimation of potential and achievement, it would be folly indeed for the educator to evaluate a child's progress in reading by this technique alone.

When selecting the method for computing the degree of reading retardation, the following should be considered: 1. The number and type of children selected as retarded in reading will vary with the method employed. 2. Each method is only as good as the instruments used to obtain the scores for its computation. 3. A child with a specific skill deficiency may not be discovered by these types of formulas. 4. The ultimate selection of a method may have more to do with availability of the data required than the inherent values of the system. 5. The confidence that a given examiner has found in the method and materials used has much to do with his ultimate selection. The examiner after weighing the above factors employs that method best suited to his situation.

In summary, the educator is encouraged to view scores from intelligence scales as indicators of potential for reading. Although intelligence per se is not to be considered the cause of a child's reading problem, assessment of intelligence remains basic to the diagnosis of reading problems to identify properly those who will profit most from a program of correction. The classroom teacher is encouraged to use techniques available to him to make estimates of reading potential, allowing the reading specialist or appropriate psychological personnel to make more precise identifications. An understanding of the limitations and advantages of the measures of intelligence will greatly enhance the educator's use of the resulting scores.

Physical Diagnosis

A physical limitation is considered a cause of a reading problem when it is identified as a factor interfering between a child's potential and his performance. If it can be determined that a child cannot adequately see a printed page, he cannot be expected to read that printed page as well as his potential indicates he should. The question then arises as to whose job it is to assess the severity of physical disability. Although it is often in a classroom or clinical diagnosis that physical limitations are first recognized, the responsibility falls to medical personnel or other specialists for specific identification, corrective measures, and recommendations. Both the reading specialist and the classroom teacher are in a position to refer children either on the basis of reliable patterns of symptoms or as a result of certain screening devices available to educators. Conceivably, the educator, in daily contact with the child in a variety of situations, often sees symptoms of possible physical limitations which non-specialized medical personnel, in a given, brief medical examination, cannot detect. This is not to say that the classroom teacher's observation is a substitute for a specialist's evaluation; rather, it is to strongly indicate the place of the teacher in the initial identification of a physical problem, through the observation of symptoms in his daily contact with the child.

Specifically, the areas of physical diagnosis of reading problems are: general physical, visual, auditory, and neurological. Limitations which are serious enough in these areas to interfere with the child's performance in reading are also likely to interfere with the child's general educational performance. Bond and Tinker[12] also note this in reference to emotional and personality problems. Therefore, a general educational deficiency

---

[12]Bond and Tinker, *Reading Difficulties*, p. 37.

does not necessarily indicate only physical disabilities. So, although it may be through the diagnosis of a reading problem that a physical limitation is first identified, it is likely that the ramifications of that limitation will show in other areas of school performance.

General Health

Large numbers of children are not healthy enough to profit efficiently from the instruction provided under even the best of conditions. Although difficult to estimate, the exact size of a given school population affected by this area of physical limitations varies greatly from one community to the next. It behooves the educator to know those aspects of general health which interfere with school progress and which should be evaluated in the diagnosis of reading problems.

Persistent malnutrition causes the child to lose weight or to lag behind in physical and mental vitality.

Glanduar defects have also been diagnosed as causing educational problems. When the glands which maintain important balances in the body fail, more than physical discomfort may result.

Fatigue, mental or physical, caused either by lack of sleep, poor sleeping habits, or over-exertion, can cause children to be inattentive and easily distracted in a learning situation.

Poor general physical condition, often characterized by frequent illness, causes a lack of stamina with resulting gaps in the educational instruction.

Each of these areas may first be discovered in a reading diagnosis; however, one must have the cooperation of the family, medical personnel, and the school to place the child in the most desirable learning situation.

The classroom teacher combines information from school records, reports from the school nurse and family doctor, information obtained from the parents, and observable symptoms which are characteristic of children with general physical deficiencies. Sluggishness, inattentiveness, failure to complete assignments, apparent lack of interest, sleeping in school, and general lack of vitality are often the same symptoms which cause a child to be labeled lazy or indifferent. A classroom teacher, finding a pattern of these symptoms, properly contacts the home to report his evaluation of the problem and makes a medical referral when it is appropriate. At the same time, he adjusts the instruction for the child to prevent these symptoms from becoming complicated medical problems. This adjustment may take the form of relaxing the tension caused by the child's apparent indifference, allowing the fatigued child a program of varied activities and necessary rest periods, and following the recommendations of medical personnel, if possible. It does not take a medical report to make us aware that all children, not just those with reading problems, need good health for optimum school performance. Necessities such as adequate rest, three meals a day (particularly a good breakfast), annual physical checkups, and large doses of play activity after school are vital requirements for good school performance.

Referral, then, is the responsibility of the teacher any time that a child in academic difficulty shows symptoms of general physical limitations. It is the responsibility of school personnel to consult the home and make medical referrals when there is evidence that a child needs medical attention.

The reading specialist's job in diagnosing is to evaluate reports received from medical personnel in terms of the total case picture of the child involved and to recommend the appropriate classroom adjustment and/or remedial program. Prior to referral, the reading specialist is likely to obtain much of his diagnostic information from the same symptoms mentioned under the classroom teacher's diagnosis or from the classroom teacher himself. His duty, then, is to apply this information to his overall diagnosis. The reading specialist must note particularly the onset of the physical deficiency. Was this limitation prevalent at birth, or did it arise later in the child's life? Thus by considering this time element, the reading specialist most accurately assesses the degree to which a limitation has actually interfered with the child's learning processes.

Visual Diagnosis

The classroom teacher is aware that deficiencies in visual ability and ocular comfort may well impede a child's growth in reading. Reports relate that from fifteen to forty percent of our school children need professional visual attention. The relationship of vision to reading problems is complicated, since many children with visual problems are not problem readers. The more careful research reports show a strong relationship between certain types of visual deficiencies and failure in reading and have found that certain visual disabilities and ocular discomfort greatly interfere with a child's reaching his reading potential. In general, functional problems such as awkward eye movements and poor fusion more often cause reading difficulty than do organic difficulties such as nearsightedness, farsightedness, or astigmatism. A review of some of the aspects of vision and ocular comfort pinpoints the relationship.

Acuity. Acuity, the clearness of vision, is normally measured at far point targets (a Snellen Chart[13] 20 feet away from the child). Such screening tests of acuity provide us with information as to the child's acuity at the far point, i.e., his ability to see the chalk board. The results of this type of visual screening are expressed in terms of what the average person can see at twenty feet. The term 20/20 means that a child can see at 20 feet the same target that a person with normal vision can see at 20 feet. This test, when used alone, however, cannot detect all visual deficiencies. In the first place, we do not normally read from targets which are 20 feet from the eyes: Neither do we read with one eye at a time. The eyes must efficiently move from one target to another rather than merely fixing on and identifying a target. Kelley claims: "The misconception that the Snellen Chart will do an efficient job of screening out children who need visual care is a major block in the road of those trying to establish good school visual screening programs."[14]

Screening devices to measure near point acuity are essential in the diagnosis of a problem reader, although they generally take more time and training to administer properly. Today, a child who passes the *Snellen Chart* may still have a visual deficiency which is causing problems in his reading performance. The farsighted child, seeing far point targets better than near point targets, may pass the *Snellen Chart* yet not see well enough or efficiently enough to read with comfort at the near point. The nearsighted child, who sees near point targets better than far point targets, is likely to fail the *Snellen Chart* and, while obviously limited by a visual defect, may read effectively in most cases. Therefore, proper visual screening must measure both far and near point acuity. This limitation has been partially met by the development of a type chart for use at a distance of 14 inches. Additional techniques, described below, are generally more desirable for accurate near point screening.

13"The Snellen Chart" (Southbridge, Mass.: American Optical Co.).

14Charles A. Kelley, *Visual Screening and Child Development* (Raleigh, North Carolina: North Carolina State College, 1957), Chapter II, p. 11.

Fusion. Fusion involves the ability of the brain to blend or fuse the image from each eye into an adequate image. A child who looks with one eye and psychologically blinds the other gets a clear image but does not have good fusion. A child with sluggish fusion seldom sees a clear target adequately, experiencing ocular discomfort and inefficiency that should be identified in a near and far point visual screening. It is not the educator's job to determine the degree of fusion; rather, he must identify the problem area for referral purposes.

Color recognition. It is important for the young child to recognize colors accurately. Simple far point color blindness tests are generally adequate for screening, with the precise measurement of color limitation left to the vision specialist. The reading teacher, with a knowledge of the child's color confusion problems, does not expect the child to perform in tasks requiring color discrimination.

Ocular motility. The efficient operation of the eye in motion is a requisite for effective reading. In particular, we are referring to good left to right motion (pursuit), saccadic movement, fixations and focusing power. Screening devices are available for evaluation in these three areas and should be considered in a diagnosis of reading problems.

1. *Left to right motion.* In the reading act the eyes must fix on a target, move to the right, fix on another target, move to the right, fix on another target, then sweep back and take hold of the next line in a manner which is not natural at birth, but learned. A child who is grossly inefficient at this task of left to right eye movements or accurate fixations will likely experience difficulty in the reading act.

2. *Pursuit eye movement.* Eyes should be able to follow a moving target smoothly, not stopping and starting, but following with an effortless fluid movement. The ability to do so allows a child efficient eye motion between fixations without which he is likely to have trouble following a line of print.

3. *Saccadic eye movement.* Accurate change of fixations from one word to another or from the end of a line of print to the beginning of the next line is an important ocular-motor skill related to reading. When deficient in this skill, the child loses his place, skips words, and reads more slowly than is necessary.

4. *Focusing power.* Prolonged reading further demands the power to maintain focus on a target for a long time. The child with deficient focusing power is likely to become fatigued much sooner than others.

5. *Binocular vision.* During the reading act some children tend to suppress the vision of one eye and do all the reading with the other. The

continuation of this type of reading can lead to serious visual complications which can only be evaluated by the visual specialist.

The areas of ocular motiety are seldom investigated in usual school screening; however, when diagnosing a reading problem, every effort should be made to evaluate them.

The reading specialist should visually screen any child referred to him as a problem reader in all the areas mentioned above. We feel that the following screening process satisfies this requirement. First, a *Telebinocular** test provides near and far point screening on acuity, stereopcis, and fusion as well as a test of color vision. The proper administration and analysis of this test requires supervised experience to assure reliable results. It should be noted that the telebinocular screens the visual skills related to the ability of the eyes to fix only on a given target.

The reading specialist must also be concerned about the eyes as they operate in reading situations. The *Binocular Reading Test** by Spache provides an analysis of binocular vision during the reading act. In this test, the child looks at a card that has been placed in the telebinocular and reads a story containing some words that only the right eye can see and some that only the left eye can see. By marking the child's responses, the examiner can determine the degree to which each eye operates in the reading act. Referral is based on certain characteristics which are identified in the accompanying manual.

Another test of the operation of eyes in the reading act is the *Reading Eye Camera.** Similar to an eye motion camera formally called the opthalmograph, the film produced in this examination supplies information concerning the number of fixations, regressions, span of fixation, and duration of fixation of a child's reading. As Spache has explained, "The use of the camera reveals that many pupils of primary and intermediate levels manifest reading errors that reflect faulty or inadequate training in the visual components of the reading act."[15] When carefully interpreted, an analysis of eye motion in the reading act can supply important information. Although the equipment for this test is costly and the administration is time consuming, it enables a reading specialist to obtain an accurate picture of the eye in motion.

For screening pursuit, saccadic eye movements, and focusing power,

---

[15]George D. Spache, *Reading in the Elementary Schools* (Boston: Allyn and Bacon, Inc., 1964), p. 11.

*See Appendix A.

a pocket flashlight is used in the following way: holding the light upright, approximately 18 inches from the eyes, the examiner asks the child to look at the light. The examiner then moves the light in a plane 18 inches from the eye in straight, vertical, horizontal, and diagonal lines 12-18 inches in length, and then in a circle with a radius of about 12 inches clockwise and counterclockwise. The child should be considered for referral if: 1. he cannot follow the light without moving his head, even after being told to hold still; 2. the reflection of the light cannot be seen in both pupils at all times; and 3. the eye movements are saccadic, that is, they follow the light jerkily instead of smoothly. To test converging power, the light is again held 18 inches from the eye, moved slowly to a position one inch directly between the eyes, and held for one second. Since some children do not understand this test the first time, there is justification for referral only if the child cannot hold this fixation after three attempts.

The reading specialist is not likely to have all the equipment necessary to test in these four areas; however, efforts should be made to provide for as thorough as possible a visual screening.

Not having any of this screening equipment available to him, the classroom teacher must rely upon a pattern of symptoms observable in the reading act or in other school situations. The check list prepared by the American Optometric Association[16] (Chart IV) includes a list of these symptoms. Copies of this check list may be secured from the American Optometric Association, 4030 Chouteau Avenue, St. Louis, Missouri. Note that this check list recommends that *all* students who are not performing well in terms of their capacity should be referred for visual examinations.

CHART IV

TEACHER'S GUIDE TO VISION PROBLEMS

WITH CHECK LIST

To aid teachers in detecting the children who should be referred for complete visual analysis, the American Optometric Association Committee on Visual Problems in Schools has compiled a list of symptoms—a guide to vision problems. The committee recommends:

---

[16]"Teacher's Guide To Vision Problems," (St. Louis: American Optometric Association, 1953).

1. That all children in the lower third of the class, particularly those with ability to achieve above their percentile rating, be referred for complete visual analysis.

2. That every child in the class who, even though achieving, is not working up to within reasonable limits of his own capacity be referred for a complete visual analysis.

Following are other symptoms which may indicate a visual problem, regardless of results in any screening test:

Observed in Reading:

Dislike for reading and
    reading subjects. —
Skipping or re-reading lines. —
*Losing place while reading. —
Slow reading or word calling. —
Desire to use finger or marker
    as pointer while reading. —
*Avoiding close work. —
*Poor sitting posture and posi-
    tion while reading. —
Vocalizing during silent read-
    ing, noticed by watching
    lips or throat. —
Reversals persisting in grade
    2 or beyond. —
Inability to remember what
    has been read. —
Complaint of letters and lines
    "running together" or of
    words "jumping." —
*Holding reading closer than
    normal. —
*Frowning, excessive blinking,
    scowling, squinting, or other
    facial distortions while
    reading. —
*Excessive head movements
    while reading. —

Poor perceptual ability such
as confusing o and a; n
and m; etc. —

Other Manifestations:

Restlessness, nervousness,
    irritability or other unac-
    counted for behavior. —
Writing with face too close to
    work. —
Fatigue or listlessness after
    close work. —
Inattentiveness, temper tant-
    rums or frequent crying. —
Complaint of blur when look-
    ing up from close work. —
Seeing objects double. —
Headaches, dizziness or nau-
    sea associated with the use
    of eyes. —
*Body rigidity while looking
    at distant objects. —
Undue sensitivity to light. —
Crossed eyes—turning in or
    out. —
Red-rimmed, crusted or
    swollen lids. —
Frequent sties. —
Watering or bloodshot eyes. —

*Found to be particularly significant in a recent study.

Burning or itching of eyes or eyelids. ___	Poor hand and eye co-ordination as manifested in poor baseball playing, catching and batting or similar activities. ___
*Tilting head to one side. ___	
*Tending to rub eyes. ___	
Closing or covering one eye. ___	
Frequent tripping or stumbling. ___	*Thrusting head forward. ___
	*Tension during close work. ___

Only a complete case study will determine whether inadequate vision is a significant factor in non-achievement.

Referral of children with these symptoms will normally be to the school nurse; however, if her screening equipment is limited to the *Snellen Chart,* the classroom teacher has the obligation to present his information to the parents, with the suggestion of a complete visual case study by a specialist. Until the child receives treatment, the teacher should make every effort to provide the child with the most comfortable and efficient visual environment. This may be accomplished by placing the child in a position of maximum lighting, by eliminating glare, by adjusting seating to ease board work, or by reducing the reading load.

Visual referral problems. Referral in vision is complicated by the reluctance of educators to over-refer; that is, referring a child who may not be in need of help. Kelley[17] views the problem as follows:

> The cardinal purpose of school visual screening procedures is to refer children who may need visual care. It is generally considered more serious for a screening program to *fail to refer* a child in real need of care than for it to *refer* a child not actually in need of care.

Shaw says:

> "My opinion is that a child's first ophthalmological examination should be given at about age three . . . The persistence of abnormal symptoms would suggest the need for eye examination regardless of the results of a screening test."[18]

---

*Found to be particularly significant in a recent study.

[17]Charles A. Kelley, *Visual Screening,* Chap. ii, p. 11.

[18]Jules H. Shaw, "Vision and Seeing Skills of Preschool Children," *The Reading Teacher,* XVIII:1, October 1964, p. 36.

Under-referral is the only alternative since it is unlikely that a visual screening test will result in completely accurate referral. Ewalt sees the problem of over-referral as follows:

"You have heard screening programs seriously criticized because they refer too many youngsters for visual examination. Nonsense! Most of the agencies of this country, dealing with vision, whether they represent the ophthalmologists as the National Association for the Prevention of Blindness, or the optometrists as the American Optometric Association agree that every school child should have an annual examination. If all school children need an annual examination, we need not be too concerned with an occasional over referral.[19]

The schools have been notorious for their reluctance to refer, thus causing many children to operate daily with eye strain which leads to more complicated, permanent problems. We are of the opinion that all children should have periodic visual examinations by a specialist. Until the schools assume this responsibility, it remains a parental obligation. The teacher, then, should not hesitate to refer any child who demonstrates the symptoms indicated in Chart IV. This in no way implies that an indiscriminate attitude toward referral should be adopted; however, it is the best way in which many children can receive visual attention.

The necessity for referral in vision is further complicated by changes in the eyes following visual adjustment. The nature of school, requiring hours of close work, may make it necessary for lenses to be changed periodically. Therefore, the teacher should not hesitate to refer a child who has symptoms of visual discomfort even if the child is wearing glasses.

A third complication of referral is the strongly motivated student who, regardless of visual strain and discomfort, persists in his school work, and shows no signs of academic deficiency. Again this child, showing symptoms listed in Chart IV, should be referred without hesitation before the possibility of consequential harm.

Finally, one must choose to whom the referral should be made. We have used the term vision specialist to avoid complication. By vision specialist we mean either an optometrist, an ophthalmologist, or an oculist. A competent specialist in any of these fields should be considered satisfactory for referral. Ophthalmologists and oculists are medical doctors who have specialized in vision. The optometrist has a doctor's degree in optometry. Each is qualified to prescribe lenses and visual training. In the

---

[19]Ward H. Ewalt, Jr., "Visual Problems of Children and Their Relationship to Reading Achievement," *The Optometric Weekly,* October 22, 1959.

case of eye disease, an optometrist will refer the patient to the ophthalmologist or oculist. Regardless of the degree held by the vision specialist,
educators should make an effort to seek out those who have a special interest in the visual development of children and in the problems of functional vision that relate to reading achievement.

To aid in the referral, a form such as the following will aid the vision
specialist to understand the reasons for referral and will provide him with
basic educational information.

VISUAL REFERRAL FORM

_____(name)_____ was screened visually and did not
perform satisfactorily in the following area(s):

_____

_____

His present reading level is_____, but his reading
potential is about _____

Will you please inform us if, after your examination, a visual deficiency
may have been causing this student some problems in reading.

_____
                    Signed

In summary, both the reading specialist and the classroom teacher
should consider every child with a reading problem a potential visual
problem. They should therefore use screening devices and observe symptoms to refer possible problem cases. Under no circumstances should the
teacher or the reading specialist consider a battery of screening devices,
no matter how highly refined, a substitution for a thorough eye examination and visual analysis. Screening tests, at best, are limited to their
designed function: the identification of children in need of visual attention.

Auditory Problems

Obviously, a child who cannot hear adequately faces problems in school. Many children with auditory limitations are placed in special schools or special classes for the deaf and hard of hearing so that they can receive specialized educational opportunities. Many children with hearing losses, however, remain in the normal school situations. For the most part, school nurses have been able to identify these children early and refer them to specialists. Nevertheless, for one reason or another, auditory problems continue to plague children.

It has been our experience that very few children need auditory referral; those who do show marked difficulties in reading. In the first place, a child with a significant hearing loss is quite likely to find phonic instruction beyond his grasp because of a distortion of sounds or the inability to hear the sounds at all. Most auditory deficiencies concern high frequency sounds; therefore, due to the high frequency of many of the consonant sounds, the most common limitation that a hearing deficiency places upon a child is in the area of consonant recognition and usage. A child with a hearing difficulty is also hindered by his inability to follow directions, since he might not hear them clearly. He is therefore, likely to lose his place in oral reading class when listening to others, fail to complete home assignments, and appear inattentive and careless.

It is important to recognize the difference between the child who is unable to hear a word and the child who is unable to discriminate the differences between sounds. In the first case, the child has a hearing loss which is a physical problem, and in the latter, he has an auditory discrimination problem which has educational implications. Auditory discrimination will be discussed under educational diagnosis in Chapter IV.

Ideally, auditory screening should include a test of pitch (frequency) ranging from low to high, and one to measure varying loudness (decibels). This screening can be adequately conducted using an *audiometer**, an instrument adaptable for either group of individual auditory testing. Although opinions vary as to the satisfactory audiometer score, it is safe to conclude that a loss of 30 decibels or more within the speech range (1000-4000 frequency) is a possible interference with reading instruction and that such a child should be referred.

The classroom teacher. Again, it is unlikely that the classroom teacher

---

*See Appendix A.

has the time, experience, or equipment to conduct the type of screening mentioned above. Classroom teachers have been advised that a watch-tick test or a whisper test is possible in the classroom. However, we feel that classroom teachers do not use these tests because they have not had enough supervised experience with them, and the possibilities of over-referral are too great. Therefore, the classroom teacher should be encouraged to rely upon a pattern of symptoms which, when occurring in a child who has failed in reading, is justified cause for referral. These symptoms are:

(1) speech difficulties (particularly with consonant sounds)
(2) inability to profit from phonic instruction
(3) tilting of the head when being spoken to
(4) cupping of the ear with the hand in order to follow instructions
(5) inability to follow directions
(6) general inattentiveness
(7) strained posture
(8) persistent earaches
(9) inflammation or drainage of the ear
(10) reports of persistent buzzing or ringing in the head
(11) excessive volume needed for comfortable radio and phonograph listening.

Normally the pupil is referred to the school nurse for audiometric screening. In an effort to encourage as much success as possible in the classroom for a child with a suspected hearing loss, the classroom teacher should not hesitate to move the child's seat so that it is: 1. in the center of a discussion area; 2. close to the teacher; and 3. away from outside distractions such as radiators, fans, cars, traffic noises. A teacher must also be willing to repeat assignments for this child to insure that they have been properly understood. Referral outside the school would normally be made to a general practitioner or to an otologist, a medical doctor with a specialization on problems of hearing. Again the medical referral is to be made in terms of the observed symptoms of auditory difficulty, with a request for results of the audiometric examination.

The reading specialist. Required information may be obtained from a recent report of a medical examination or from a screening conducted through the use of an audiometer. Although the reading specialist may not plan to conduct an audiometric examination with every child, such an examination is certainly called for when the child shows signs of problems in speech and/or phonics instruction. The reading specialist must also attempt to establish the period of time during which the hearing loss first noticeably interfered with school work and then relate this information to the entire case study. For example, the child affected by a hearing loss after the primary years, in which oral instruction and basic phonic sounds are presented, *had* the opportunity to learn his basic skills while he had normal hearing. Although this child may be handicapped, remedial techniques will vary in terms of the type of instruction the child received prior to the hearing loss.

Neurological Disorders

Neurological disorders include direct damage to the brain and defective neurological systems resulting from either malfunction or disorganization. There is little evidence that neurological disorders are a major cause of reading problems. Bond and Tinker state, "Evidence indicates that brain damage is seldom or never the cause of ordinary reading disability."[20] Nevertheless, there continues to be a large number of investigations annually based upon the observation that many problem readers show symptoms of abnormal neurological patterns. Robinson[21] named neurological disorders as one of the causal factors in eighteen percent of the cases in her classic study. It is our experience that approximately eight percent of the children tested in the university clinic have enough symptoms of neurological disorders to be referred for neurological examination. Initially, the problem for the educator in this complex area is to identify the child who may be neurologically handicapped; however, precise identification is ultimately the job of medical specialists, who themselves have some concerns about the accuracy of diagnosis in this area. Let us say simply that most problem readers are adequate enough neurologically to preclude this area as a cause of reading disability; at the same time, let us admit that there remains a small percentage of problem readers who do, in fact, have these symptoms and need medical referral.

The classroom teacher and the reading specialist are likely to find themselves relying heavily upon a pattern of symptoms for initial identification. Due to the fact that individual symptoms used for neurological referral are, when viewed in isolation, not peculiar to the neurologically

---

[20]Bond and Tinker, *Reading Difficulties,* p. 99.

[21]Helen M. Robinson, *Why Pupils Fail in Reading* (Chicago: University of Chicago Press, 1946), p. 218.

disturbed child, it becomes necessary to seek a highly reliable pattern. Without this pattern, the educator is subject to the error of interpreting educational indifference to neurological causes. If the identification is made in the initial diagnosis, it is necessary to have a pattern of several symptoms (three to four) to properly refer a child for neurological examination. However, if a child fails to respond after the best diagnosis and remedial instruction, then one or more of these symptoms or any history of the following causes of neurological disorders should be considered when deliberating a neurological referral. These causes include:

1. difficulties at birth—birth complicated by prematurity, use of instruments, or by anoxia or hypoxia.
2. head injuries—blows or accidents in which the head is severely bruised.
3. diseases—those resulting in inflammation and/or pressure in the area of the brain, i.e., rheumatic fever, encephalitis, continuously high temperature and the like.

Symptoms for neurological problems fall into two categories, physical and educational. Physical symptoms include:

1. physical incoordination—grossly awkward walking, running, writing, etc., in relation to overall physical development.
2. over-activity—inability to concentrate, causing the child to seldom complete his assignments, to annoy others, and to appear disinterested.
3. headaches—history of persistent headaches.
4. speech impediments—persistent blockage of speech or articulation difficulties which are peculiar for his age level.
5. visual incoordination—saccadic eye movements, inability of the eyes to focus or to visually hold a line of print.
6. mixed dominance—confused preference for the dominant hand, eye, or foot.

(Although the various types of dominance may be observed informally, dominance tests such as the *Harris Test of Lateral Dominance** in which hand, eye, and foot tasks are required have been found to be of assistance.)

Educational symptoms of neurological problems include:

*See Appendix A.

1. average or better than average intelligence—general educational development deficient in terms of valid measures of intelligence.

2. phonic blending deficiency—knowledge of sounds but inability to blend them into words.

3. poor contextual reader—knowledge of the sight vocabulary but inability to use known words in sentences.

4. slow reading speed—poor reading rate, even with easy, familiar material.

5. poor auditory discrimination—inability to discriminate between sounds of letters, without evidence of a hearing acuity deficiency.

6. distractability—inattentive to designated tasks.

7. abnormal behavior—over-reaction to stimuli, i.e., he laughs long after others have ceased.

8. poor ability to remember sequences—although apparently normally intelligent, difficulty in remembering sequences, verbal and non-verbal. The *Knox Cube Test* (see p. 34) is good for this evaluation. Scores here must fall well below the chronological age (4-8 years) to be significant. Smith and Carrigan[22] cite the Knox Cube as one of the first tests to give in cases for screening of neurological disorders. References for further study of children with these symptoms are often found under the terms dyslexia and specific language disability.

Obviously, these symptoms in isolation do not necessarily indicate neurological disorder. It is imperative that a pattern of symptoms which includes four or more of the above be gathered. Children with this number of symptoms, whether identified in classroom or in clinical diagnosis, should be considered legitimate referrals for neurological examinations.

There is a reluctance among educators to make neurological referrals, however, for it seems that we are overly concerned about either the psychological effects of such a referral or the great possibility of over-referral. An understanding of the procedure generally followed in a neurological examination may reduce the educator's hesitancy to refer. Neurological referral will normally include an office appointment, during which the child will receive a detailed neurological examination, and the medical specialist will obtain case history information. If, at that time, the medical

---

[22]Donald E. P. Smith and Patricia M. Carrigan, *The Nature of Reading Disability* (New York: Harcourt Brace and World 1959), p. 47.

specialist finds symptoms of abnormal tendencies, another appointment will be made for a more involved neurological examination, often requiring hospitalization.

Professionally justified in these instances, the educators should not be reluctant to refer. If, in fact, we should happen to over-refer, we are relieved to find that the child's problem is *not* neurological in nature and that we can proceed with an educational diagnosis.

The reading specialist, upon receipt of the neurological report, relates the findings to other information which he has gathered for the case study. Again the relationship of neurological problems to the entire case history must be considered in the recommendations for educational adjustment.

The classroom teacher, while waiting for the neurological report, should relieve the child from unnecessary frustration by relaxing tension and allowing for reading experiences in the area of the child's strengths. If the report indicates that the child does not have a neurological problem, the teacher will continue with a classroom diagnosis in an effort to find the area where correction should start. However, if the report does reveal a neurological problem, the classroom teacher should refer the child to a reading specialist who will conduct a careful case evaluation of the child, noting all educational aspects and precise recommendations concerning remedial techniques.

The final analysis of all physical difficulties is the responsibility of medical personnel; however, since physical problems frequently interfere with reading efficiency, the educator often finds himself in the position of first identifying a physical problem. Based upon reliable patterns of symptoms, the educator is obligated to refer to the medical specialist and, while awaiting his diagnosis, to make practical classroom adjustments. The educator considers medical recommendations carefully in terms of the child's total diagnosis.

Emotional Diagnosis

Emotional difficulties, when considered as causes of reading problems, create cause and effect confusion. Sometimes emotional disturbances cause reading problems; however, many emotional problems are not the cause, but the result of a failure in reading. Unfortunately, there is often no clear line of distinction. When emotional disturbances cause reading problems, performance in all learning areas suffer. It is often in the diagnosis of a problem reader that this area of difficulty is first uncovered; however, assessing the severity of that difficulty is properly the task of psychological personnel. Conversely, although emotional reactions may complicate a reading problem, they are often not the cause, but rather an effect of the reading failure itself. It is our experience that most children referred as problem readers exhibit some symptoms of emotional conflict and that these symptoms often diminish or disappear with proper instruction after the diagnosis. In summarizing the research, Bond and Tinker conclude, "Examination of all the evidence, however, does make it pretty clear that the emotional maladjustment is much more frequently the effect than the cause of reading disability."[23] An effective diagnosis may result in relieving the child of some home and school pressures, by exposing the fact that the child's difficulty is not due to a poor attitude or a low level of intellectual potential, but rather to a skill deficiency which, when corrected, will permit the child to perform as expected. When these diagnostic conclusions are satisfactorily explained to cooperative parents, a more favorable learning atmosphere can be established.

The classroom teacher and the reading specialist must be aware that most children with reading problems react emotionally to their failure through such behavior patterns as refusing to read, not enjoying school, disliking their teacher, or causing problems at home. Emotional reactions to specific situations, however, may be opposite within a given child at a given moment, and they may be opposite between two disturbed children. For example, when frustrated, an emotionally disturbed child may (1) withdraw and be quiet or (2) slash out in defiance. In comparing emotional diagnosis to intellectual diagnosis, Carroll states: "Personality traits are more complex and less consistent than intelligence and so more difficult to measure objectively."[24] The more thorough an understanding the teacher has of the child's inner-family, peer, and school relationships, the more likelihood of an effective diagnosis. The examiner must anticipate certain types of emotional reactions, note them, include them in his diagnosis, and consider them in his recommendations; however, it is with caution that these reactions be labeled as causative, for their presence does not necessarily make the child a candidate for referral.

Realistically recognizing their limitations as detectors of emotional difficulties, and at the same time recognizing the emotional entanglement

---

[23]Bond and Tinker, *Reading Difficulties,* p. 107.

[24]Herbert A. Carroll, *Mental Hygiene* (New York: Prentice Hall, Inc., 1947), p. 246.

of these types of children, the reading specialist and the classroom teacher follow similar diagnostic procedures. Through the cooperation of all the educators in contact with the child, information may be gleaned concerning the child, his home, his school situation, and his reactions in peer group situations.

Information concerning the child

Due to his daily contact with the child, the classroom teacher is in the unique position to obtain valuable information about the child's reactions to many situations. The reading specialist is obligated to rely upon the information supplied by the teacher and parents or obtain if from a personal interview with the child. Desirable information should include:

1. the child's attitude toward his family, school, teacher, and friends;
2. the child's awareness of his problem and his suggestions for its solution;
3. the child's attitude and reaction to reading;
4. the child's development of worthwhile personal goals.

Gathered informally by the classroom teacher or formally by the reading specialist, all information in questionable areas must be checked for reliability. One can do this easily by comparing sources of available data; if they concur, one can view their source as both reliable and respectable. A child may have said that he makes B's and C's in school. One will rely more readily on his other statements about school if, when checking the school records, one finds that he does indeed make B's and C's.

Personality testing of a formal nature is available. The *California Test of Personality,** one of the more popular instruments for classroom usage, provides standardized evaluations of the child's reactions to questions concerning personal and social adjustment. This test may be administered individually or in classroom-sized groups. Since adequate performance requires the child to possess reading skills close to the grade level of the test, the seriously retarded reader is placed in the position of being unable to read the questions. In evaluating the *California Test of Personality,* caution is urged in the tendency to place undue emphasis on any low

*See Appendix A.

set of scores; however, they may be considered as areas of potential personality problems. Scores indicating the necessity for referral are described in the test manual. Final verification will not come from this type of testing, but rather from referral to psychological personnel.

Personality testing through the use of incomplete sentences is an informal way of obtaining valuable information. The child is expected to respond to 20-30 incomplete sentences, some examples of which might be: "I like books, but . . .", "My home is . . .", "I like my brother and . . .". Strang[25] provides an example of responses in informal inventory including some advice on the techniques of interpretation. The most reliable use of this type of device is to note patterns of responses and to verify them by direct observation of the child in situations where these responses may be reflected in the child's behavior. Again the examiner is cautioned against excessive analysis of any slightly deviate responses, leaving for psychological personnel final assessment of the child's emotional stability.

Personality tests of the paper and pencil variety are considered inherently weak, since the child often anticipates what he considers to be the acceptable response. When this occurs, it is obvious that the scores obtained, not validly indicating personality traits, have severely limited use in diagnosing emotional problems in children.

A technique for noting personality characteristics in a more natural situation is to observe the child at play. An investigation of play behavior may be based on the following type of questions: Does he play with others his own age? Does he prefer to play with children of his own sex? Does it appear that he is accepted by his peers? Does he play fairly? Does he play enthusiastically? Answers to such questions provide further analysis of the child's total behavior pattern, without the limitations of paper and pencil tests. Shafer and Shoben feel that this approach has definite advantages in emotional diagnosis: "Many diagnostic suggestions may be drawn from watching a child in free play . . . The communications of very young children tend to be symbolized only in the activities of play . . ."[26] Forest also feels that such observation of play is desirable. "Emotional release through play activities due to a sense of competency and mastery may be observed in normal groups of children."[27] Note that both

---

[25]Strang, *Diagnostic Teaching of Reading,* pp. 256-8.

[26]Laurance F. Shafer and Edward J. Shoben, Jr., *The Psychology of Adjustment,* 2nd ed. (Boston: Houghton Mifflin Co., 1956), p. 508.

[27]Isle Forest, *Child Development* (New York: McGraw Hill Book Co., 1954), p. 64.

of these authorities suggest that this technique has particular value with younger children.

A study of the home

Although the home is not usually visited as a result of a reading diagnosis, under certain circumstances such a visit is profitable. When it appears that situations at home are impeding the child's language and/or emotional development, the educator who hopes to improve these conditions is proper in using this approach. In cases when a home visit would be useless, it is common to gather information concerning home conditions through parental interviews or questionnaires. These are constructed to obtain the following types of information: socio-economic status of the home; availability of books; inner-family relations; parental efforts to assist the child; general family activities; and overall acceptance of the child in the home.

Abnormal home conditions should be brought to the attention of appropriate personnel (school officials, home-school visitors, social workers, psychologists). Neither the classroom teacher nor the reading specialist is justified in offering unsolicited advice to parents about home conditions unrelated to the child's educational progress. There are times when parents will turn to an educator and ask for consultation in non-educational areas. Although it depends upon the individual situation, it is our opinion that an educator is normally acting out of his proper professional role to offer advice in such cases.

The educator will want to contact the social worker when home problems appear to be a basic source of difficulty for the child. These professional persons are skilled in working with parents and investigating home situations. Many schools have found it worthwhile to have social workers on their professional staff.

A study of the school

The classroom teacher normally gathers relevant data for a classroom diagnosis and submits it to the reading specialist for his case analysis. From the school it is necessary to obtain information relating to the child's attendance, his behavior, his ability to work and play with others, and his reactions to various types of success and failure. School records do not always contain this type of information, although teachers are often encouraged to write comments concerning outstanding characteristics of the child. When such notations are available, they should be included in the diagnosis; when not accessible, the information should be gathered through interviews or questionnaire response from the teacher.

Teachers, for example, should accustom themselves to notice peculiar reactions of children in the reading act which reflect anxiety, frustration and emotional disturbance. Roebuck[28] found that emotionally disturbed children tend to read orally with tense voices, to react more definitely to the material being read, and to read compulsively. In compulsive reading, the child never stops or hesitates; rather, he reads on whether he knows the words or not, skipping and/or mispronouncing unknown words. Other noticeable symptoms are: refusal to read aloud; profuse sweating of the hands during oral reading; and peculiar book selections for free reading.

If the educator is to be effective in obtaining such information, students and parents must be assured that it will be handled confidentially and will not find its way into the hands of irresponsible people. A cooperative attitude on the part of both parents and educators will bring about the most effective diagnosis in this area.

One of the most justifiable reasons for an educator to give consideration to emotional difficulties, other than for possible referral, is that it will discourage him from improperly labeling children. It is extremely easy to decide that a problem reader is lazy, a trouble-maker, or a delinquent, before considering his emotional difficulties. These symptoms are quite often displayed by children with emotional problems; the unwarranted label complicates the difficulty.

After psychological referral has been made, the classroom teacher adjusts his instruction so as not to further complicate potential emotional difficulties while awaiting referral recommendations. This adjustment includes: avoiding the placement of the child in failing situations which cause unnecessary embarrassment; avoiding implications to the child that he is lazy or stupid; and providing a sensible program of discipline in which the child can gain a degree of composure and self-reliance. Carroll points out some of the difficulties involved with discipline for children with these symptoms:

> The causes of misconduct insofar as classroom conditions are concerned, are not hard to identify. Every child needs to succeed. If the

---

[28]Mildred Roebuck, "The Oral Reading Characteristics of Emotionally Disturbed Children," *International Reading Association Proceedings,* VII, (1962), pp. 133-8.

academic tasks set for him are too difficult, he feels frustrated. Frustration is uncomfortable, and he feels driven to do something about it . . . Denied the opportunity to satisfy his need for scholastic achievement, he strikes out against environment.[29]

He goes on to say that this child must have his success recognized by the group and by the teacher, whether the success is large or small. Furthermore, he states, "She (the teacher) will be more lavish with praise than criticism. She will help every child to maintain his self respect."[30] Concerning the control of the group when this child is acting in such a manner as to disrupt the group, Carroll points out that disciplinary measures will have to be taken in such instances but adds, "She should never use fear as a technique of control."[31]

For this advice, the classroom teacher must consider this child as one who needs and deserves special considerations; he is always aware that negative reactions from him can only drive the child further into his rejection of the learning processes and environment. At the same time the teacher has an obligation to the other children in the room and is obliged to provide an environment for them which is conducive to learning.

When the child with symptoms of emotional problems disrupts this environment to the detriment of the entire group, the teacher must act to meet the needs of the group.

Prevention of complex emotional disorders is also in the hands of the classroom teacher. His reaction, for example, to the initial signs of frustration and failure within a given child may cause the child's acceptance of his temporary situation or his reaction against it. Although children must be challenged in school, not all children will meet these challenges with the same degree of success. The teacher may relax tensions and feelings of failure by his attitude toward the efforts of the less successful. Conversely, all children must succeed in school. The successes of all children, but particularly the less successful, should be highlighted. Beware, however, of false praise—children resent it. In its place, situations must be structured in which, with a little effort, this child can legitimately succeed and be praised. More of these types of techniques are discussed under remediation and in Chapter 10 when parents are discussed.

All information and notations concerning the child's emotional be-

---

[29]Carroll, *Mental Hygiene,* p. 210.

[30]*Ibid.,* p. 210.

[31]*Ibid.,* p. 211.

havior should be included and evaluated in the case analysis. The reading specialist applies the recommendations for the necessary educational adjustment. If the classroom teacher, after the institution of these recommendations, finds further complications, referral to the reading specialist is recommended.

Summary

Educators are involved in non-educational diagnosis. They are likely to be the first to identify a child's potentially non-educational problem. Knowing that he cannot finally judge the severity of non-educational problems, the educator collects his data carefully, refers the child to an appropriate specialist, follows the advice of the specialist, and makes classroom adjustments. The reading specialist will be expected to give more careful consideration than would the classroom teacher to these non-educational areas in his diagnosis. Both educators, however, have important roles and it is imperative that the roles be understood by each. By refraining from involved non-educational diagnosis, the educator frees himself for the task of educational diagnosis—his primary diagnostic obligation.

Suggested Readings

1. Cleland, Donald L., "Clinical Materials for Appraising Disabilities In Reading," *The Reading Teacher,* XVII:6, March, 1964, p. 428. This interesting, easy-to-read article presents summaries of the various appraisal materials available for clinical diagnosis. Of particular interest is the discussion of reading capacity and appropriate techniques for determining it.
2. Delacato, Carl H., *The Diagnosis and Treatment of Speech and Reading Problems.* Springfield, Illinois: Charles C. Thomas, 1963. The reader who is interested in a more thorough discussion of diagnostic as well as remedial techniques to be used with children with neurological disorders, should consult this book. This is the second book in which Dr. Delacato presents his theories; this one includes summaries of his previous investigations.

3. Stuart, Marion, *Neurophysiological Insights Into Teaching.* New York: Pacific Books, 1963. For relatively elementary explanations of diagnosis and treatment of readers with neurological limitations, this book treats the issues involved in a specific manner.

4. Robinson, Helen M., *Why Pupils Fail in Reading.* p. 218. Chicago: University of Chicago Press, 1946. Robinson presents a discussion of the multiple causation theory in terms of the most prominent authorities and also in terms of her research in this area. Of particular importance are the conclusions which Robinson reaches through her technique to determine causation.

5. Strauss, Alfred A., and Laura E. Lehtinen, *Psychopathology and Education of the Brain-Injured Child.* New York: Grune & Stratton, 1947. This book provides the rationale for the syndrome of distractability and perseveration. A basic book for those who are interested in more thoroughly understanding the aspects of minimal brain injury. The reader will find explanations in terms designed for educators.

6. Kelly, Charles R., *Visual Screening and Child Development,* The North Carolina Study, North Carolina State College, Raleigh, North Carolina, 1957. A little-known, but carefully organized study is reported in this book concerning the scope and sequence of vision and scholastic effectiveness. The reader who is interested in more detailed study will find it worthwhile.

7. Woolf, Maurice D. and Jeanne A. Woolf, *Remedial Reading.* New York: McGraw Hill Book Co., Inc., 1957. For detailed discussion of the emotional involvement of problem readers, this selection is recommended. Theory backed by case study illustrations makes meaningful reading in this difficult area.

4

Educational Diagnosis

An analysis of the child's reading skills and attitudes is the major function of educational diagnosis. Unlike non-educational diagnosis, in which final evaluation is the consideration of a specialist outside the field of reading, educational diagnosis rests solely with the classroom teacher and the reading specialist. It is here that their professional competencies best suit them to complete the task which has been delegated to them by the public, i.e., the education of children.

The classroom teacher, having a relatively long acquaintance with the child, relies heavily upon observation and informal testing procedures for educational diagnosis. The reading specialist, permitted only short term pupil acquaintance, finds a more formal testing and evaluation program to be most effective. Before careful examination of the two approaches to educational diagnosis, it is essential to consider briefly the causes of problems in this area. Educational difficulties can be said to cause a reading problem when, through the adjustment of the learning climate, the problem can be corrected or when the adjustment of the learning climate can prevent this problem from recurring.

Educational Causes

Educational causes can be grouped in the following five categories:

65

Instruction; Absence; Classroom size; Materials for instruction; and Reading systems.

Instruction

In the primary grades the child normally has one teacher each year. If that teacher is incompetent, indifferent, poorly educated, or insensitive towards children, this year of exposure to him can seriously harm some children. While most children survive a year of poor teaching without permanently harmful results, others fall far enough behind in their reading skills to be considered problem readers. The solution to the reading problem caused by this type of teacher is twofold: first, the children so handicapped must receive the appropriate instruction at a later date; and secondly, this teacher must either be assisted to correct his limitations or be replaced. Poor instruction is considered by many to be the major cause of reading problems in children. To this we must agree, but we hasten to add that it is most common to find other interferences complicating the problem.

Absence

When returning to school after long periods of continuous absence, a child is likely to suffer in the sequential development of his skills, yet be pushed along to more advanced skills without that basic background upon which future success depends. It is often difficult for the teacher to provide the amount of good instruction necessary to counter-balance excessive absence. Reading disability can occur when no provisions have been made to assist the child to learn the skills that have been missed. Permitted to continue without program modifications, the child may progress to more complicated problems.

Classroom size

In overcrowded classrooms it is difficult for the teacher to follow the sequential development of reading skills with each child. Here a child may falter undetected until he falls too far behind to catch up without special instruction. Although particularly damaging in the primary grades where the development of reading skills follows a closer sequence than in the later elementary years, the failure to provide basic skill development may cause difficulty during the remainder of the child's schooling, To alleviate overcrowded classrooms, some schools have found it practical to hire teacher assistants. By assuming many of the less important routine tasks, the assistant frees the teacher to provide the needed instruction.

Materials for instruction

Economy-minded school administrators frequently fail to provide adequate materials to enable the classroom teacher to adjust instruction for children with reading skill deficiencies. Unless a teacher can devise materials and techniques to instruct children with minor skill deficiencies, the possibility of these children becoming problem readers increases. With adequate materials and knowledge of their use, most teachers can prevent serious skill deficiencies. Considering the wealth of materials available to educators today, one must seek out the most helpful. Many larger school districts have established curriculum libraries in which a wide variety of materials is available to individual teachers and teacher committees to examine and consider. In this manner, it is possible to maintain reasonable economy and, at the same time, permit careful analysis and wise selection of materials.

Reading systems

School systems selecting methods for teaching reading to keep up with the latest fads quite frequently adopt a system which limits their children in the development of some part of their reading skills. This unfortunate choice leads the child to a mistaken conception of reading, and creates reading problems in those who become confused. Such methods, if adopted, must be modified to correct their inherent weaknesses, or children may suffer from lack of proper skill development.

As the classroom teacher and the reading specialist proceed with educational diagnosis, they must have a well-established understanding of the skill sequences necessary for good reading, for it is assumed that effective instruction in the proper area and at the right level will correct the problem. Seeking to improve reading skills, educators must establish effective prevention and remedial programs.

Classroom Diagnosis

Educational diagnosis in the classroom has been hampered by test administration, a time consuming, costly, and sometimes questionable operation. The classroom teacher is encouraged to use that diagnostic tool already available to him in the classroom, direct observation of the child in the reading act. Through this observation, the teacher may place all reading errors within one of four *basic skill areas*:

Orientation involves the ability to approach the printed page with effective mechanical skills.

Sight vocabulary involves the recognition and meaning of the word instantly and constantly.

Word attack involves an efficient ability to decode words not recognized by sight.

Comprehension involves the ability to bring meaning and understanding to words and groups of words and their inter-relationships.

The reader is asked to note that each of these skill areas affects the total reading process—that is, each influences the manner in which a child decodes the printed message and associates his decoded message to past experiences. These terms, then, appropriately include the skills necessary for effective decoding and association, i.e., reading. In each of these skill areas, the classroom teacher must obtain the answers to the following three questions:

1. What is the instructional level of the child in this area? It must be determined at which level this child can most effectively respond to instruction; normally, it is a point where the child makes errors but does not fail completely.
2. Specifically, what type of errors appear to be causing the skill area deficiency? The diagnostic responsibility is to note a pattern of symptoms, relate it to the appropriate skill area, determine the pattern's significance, and formulate a program to correct it.
3. What diagnostic conclusions can be reached by adjusting classroom instruction to correct the deficiency? Using direct observation of the child in the reading act, the teacher will note patterns of symptoms to arrive at the factors most probably limiting a child's reading ability.

To answer each of the above questions, the teacher makes a direct observation of the child in three reading situations: word recognition exercises, oral reading, and silent reading. Reading situations differ from skill areas in that each situation requires the use of one or more of the skills for acceptable performance. Improvement in the skill areas results in improvement in the reading situations when the diagnosis has been effective in establishing the instructional needs of the child.

In word recognition

While observing the child in word recognition exercises, the teacher can notice the following errors:

1. Failure to pronounce the word. The child simply stops, unable to go on until assisted in the word pronunciation. Five seconds is generally recognized as ample time to pronounce a given word.
2. Hesitation. Although waiting a second or two, the child finally pronounces the word properly.
3. Mispronunciation. Distorting vowel or consonant sounds or accent. The child makes an inaccurate, non-contextual guess at the pronunciation of the word, e.g., *cutch* for *catch*.
4. Substitution. The child replaces the correct word with another word, e.g., *sit* for *sat*.
5. Word and letter reversal. The child completely distorts the word by reversing the order of letters, e.g., *was* for *saw,* or he reverses the letter itself, e.g., *big* for *dig*.
6. Letter order confusion. The child does not necessarily reverse the word but he confuses the order of the letters in the word, e.g., *pincicknig* for *picnicking*.

In oral reading

While observing oral reading, the teacher can notice the following errors:

1. Failure to pronounce words, substitutions, mispronunciations, reversals, and hesitations in oral reading. These occur also in word recognition.
2. Word-by-word reading—The child tends to emphasize words rather than phrases even in easy, familiar material. This causes nonfluency.
3. Failure to keep place—The child frequently loses his place either by skipping lines of print or by failing to follow left to right through a line.

4. Omission—The child skips one or more words in a line of print.
5. Failure to observe punctuation—The place and purpose of various punctuation marks are not observed clearly.
6. Inability to comprehend—After pronouncing words correctly, the child cannot demonstrate an understanding of what he has read.
7. Repetition—The child repeats words already properly pronounced. A repetition to correct a mispronounced word should not be considered an error, rather, an effective use of context.

In silent reading

While observing silent reading, the teacher can notice the following errors:

1. Lip movement—Particularly with easy material, the child is readily observed moving his lips while reading the words. (Many children exhibit lip movement on difficult material.)
2. Failure to keep place—The child needs physical crutches such as finger pointing or markers to hold his place.
3. One-word errors in recall—Upon questioning, the child is able to answer accurately except for one word in the answer which distorts the author's meaning.
4. Inability to recall—Although apparently having read the story, the child fails to recall the ideas of the author during questioning.
5. Inability to follow directions—The child fails to follow written directions, although he obviously knows the words involved.

The above mentioned, readily noticeable reading errors may be interpreted in a classroom diagnosis by using the checklist in Table 2. To use it, the teacher tallies each observable symptom in the appropriate column representing the four skill areas. For example, in a word recognition situation, a child who makes many hesitations should receive a tally under sight vocabulary (column 2). If he moves his lips in a silent reading situation on easy material, a tally is placed under comprehension (column 4). In order for a reading error to be considered a symptom, it should be a relatively constant interference with the successful reading act, i.e., an error committed once or twice in a given reading test is seldom considered significant. Each type of error observed often enough to be considered a symptom should be tallied.

The use of this chart and the diagnostic technique involved is not

TABLE 2
CLASSROOM DIAGNOSIS CHECK LIST

READING SITUATIONS	1 ORIENTATION	2 SIGHT VOCABULARY	3 WORD ATTACK	4 COMPREHENSION
In Word Recognition	___reversals* ___letter order confusion*	___failure to pronounce word ___hesitations	___mispronunciations ___substitutions* ___failure to pronounce word	
In Oral Reading	___omissions ___repetitions ___loss of place	___failure to pronounce word ___hesitations ___omissions	___substitutions* ___mispronunciations ___failure to pronounce word	___disregard of punctuation ___inability to comprehend ___word by word reading
In Silent Reading	___loss of place	___one word error in recall		___inability to recall ___inability to follow directions ___excessive lip movement
TOTAL	Orientation	Sight vocabulary	Word attack	Comprehension

*Also readily identified in spelling exercises.

71

without limitations. An awareness of these limitations will assist in placing in proper perspective the results obtained by this technique. First, most classroom teachers experience some difficulty in their initial efforts to observe accurately errors in word recognition, oral reading, and silent reading. Spache[1] cautions the inexperienced teacher to practice such identification. We have found that with directed practice, teachers can accurately record the errors made by children. Exercises with children's reading efforts recorded on tapes and played for students to practice with has been especially effective. Despite the degree of difficulty encountered in his initial attempts to make such direct observations, the teacher will find that his skills will improve with practice to give him accurate results. Secondly, the technique used in this type of diagnosis lacks the precision and scope found in clinical diagnostic techniques. As has been stated, the classroom teacher is not normally in the situation to obtain all of the types of information available to a reading specialist. The use of the proposed technique will, however, assist the classroom teacher to detect many reading deficiencies. With full realization of what the classroom diagnosis is attempting to do, the teacher will find the technique is extremely practical and useful.

For the teacher who is unfamiliar with the skill sequence program to which his children have been exposed, Barbe[2] presents charts and explanations of reading skill development from readiness through grade six. One may find this reference to be of value in initial work in classroom diagnosis.

Error patterns

Once a skill area is established (that area in which tallies appear most frequently) the teacher is obligated to determine the significance of each *type* of error pattern in terms of appropriate classroom adjustment.

___

If *Orientation skills* appear to be deficient, answers to the following questions will assist the classroom teacher in pinpointing the difficulty:

1. Was the orientation symptom accompanied by signs of visual discomfort? There is a possibility of physical interference when gross

___

[1]Spache, *Reading in the Elementary Schools*, p. 249.

[2]Walter B. Barbe, *Educator's Guide to Personalized Reading Instruction* (Englewood Cliffs, New Jersey, Prentice Hall, Inc., 1961), Chap. vii and viii.

orientation errors are observed.

2. Was the orientation symptom accompanied by symptoms of nervous reading?

If the answers to numbers one and/or two is YES, there is valid reason to reconsider visual and emotional referral. The remaining questions are educational in nature. Answers to these questions identify skill deficiencies that are highly related at times, for the task of each involves an awareness of the organization of the print on the page, on a given line, and within words.

3. Does the child exhibit visual difficulty in following the line of print left to right?

4. Were the orientation errors basically ones of habitual letter, word and/or phrase reversals?

> *big-dig* = letter reversal
> *was-saw* = word reversal
> *stop-spot* = partial reversal
> *many were-were many* = phrase reversals

5. Were words habitually omitted without destroying context?

6. Was the symptom one in which the child habitually lost his place? Through observation it should be determined further whether the child lost his place while going from line to line or within a line of print.

If the answer to questions three, four, five, or six is YES, the teacher is led to educational adjustment, in an effort to correct the skill deficiency. (See Chapter 6, pp. 111)

If *Sight vocabulary skills* appear to be deficient, the answer to the following questions will assist in pinpointing the difficulty. To obtain accurate answers, each error must be examined.

1. Does the child miss small, similar words—*sat, cat, mat*—or does he falter on words which are obviously different—*city, water, phone*? It is important to establish that the child has actually looked at the word. It is not uncommon to list a child's errors only to find that, upon instruction, the child knows the word and the word patterns, but had not looked carefully at them during testing.

2. Does the word missed represent a concrete or abstract concept— *boy* and *dog* or *with* and *where*?

3. Does he know the word in isolation but not in context?

4. Does he pronounce the word properly but fail to associate it with the correct meaning?
5. Is the error one in which the child eventually pronounces the word, but not without undue hesitation? In this instance, the child is apparently using a word attack skill but does not know the word as a sight word.

A YES answer to any of the above five questions calls for educational adjustment. See Chapter 7, pp. 125)

If *Word attack skills* appear to be deficient, the answer to the following questions will pinpoint the phonic, structual, or contextual nature of the error. To arrive at these answers, each mispronounced word must be examined.

In examining phonic errors:

1. Is the problem basically the child's inability to hear likenesses and differences in the sounds (auditory discrimination)?
2. When the child mispronounces or substitutes words, is there a pattern of consonant or vowel errors? If so, in what part of the word are these errors made—initial, medial, or final?

> *dig* for *dog* = vowel, medial position
> *sat* for *mat* = consonant, initial position

3. Does the child need instruction in the usage of known sounds—(blending and syllabication)?

In examining structural errors:

4. Do the words which are substituted or mispronounced contain prefixes or suffixes, or are they compound words? Problem readers commonly have trouble with suffixed words. It must further be determined if the child knows the base word without the suffix, e.g., a child can pronounce "want" but not "wanting."

In examining contextual errors:

5. When the child made his contextual errors, were there contextual clues available which, if observed, could have prevented the error?
6. Did the error result from failure to observe punctuation clues?

A YES answer to any of the above six questions calls for educational (See Chapter 7, pp. 137)

7. Do the child's errors seriously distort the author's intended meaning? If the child reads the following sentence: "Tom has a big cat," as "Tom has a large cat," the child has not made an error which seriously distorts the author's meaning. However, if he were to read: "Tom has a big dog," this would be a serious contextual error and is basically one of sight vocabulary.

If *Comprehension skills* appear to be deficient, an analysis of the errors will assist the teacher in pin-pointing the difficulty:

1. Do the child's comprehension difficulties appear to increase as he encounters larger units of material? (Words, to phrases, to sentences, to paragraphs, to combinations of paragraphs.)
2. Were the basic errors due to the type of comprehension expected, i.e., were they in the area of factual recall, or were they involved with the more subtle areas of comprehension such as obtaining main ideas, inferences, sequences, or evaluations?
3. Was the child able to paraphrase the author's ideas or was he able to relate them only in the words of the author? Quite often we find children able to parrot the words of the author but unable to obtain deeper meaning.
4. Can the child recall the author's ideas but remain unable to perform in content area reading situations? Does he have difficulty in following directions and organizing the author's ideas?
5. Is there a total failure to respond to comprehension situations?

A YES answer to any of the above five questions calls for educational adjustment. (See Chapter 8, pp. 157)

Habits and attitudes

An evaluation of a child's habits in reading must also be considered in a classroom diagnosis. The classroom teacher is in the most effective position to accurately evaluate the child's reading habits, for he sees him in reading situations such as book selection and independent reading. An effort should be made to note effective and ineffective habits which seem to vary considerably from those of the average children; he does this most effectively in terms of undesirable but correctable situations. The classroom teacher is likely to be asked by the reading specialist for information of this type; therefore, observations should be carefully noted. Specifically, the classroom teacher should obtain answers to the following questions:

1. What use does the child make of free reading opportunity? Does he appear eager to use free time for reading, or is reading only the result of constant prodding?
2. Does the child appear anxious or reluctant to read orally . . . silently? Does there appear to be a difference in his attitude between oral and silent situations. His area of least reluctance should be noted specifically, for this gives us direction when remediation starts.
3. Are signs of reluctance noticeable in reading situations only or in all learning situations? A child who hesitates in all learning situations must be motivated, whereas one reluctant in reading alone needs success and reward in reading.
4. In what reading situations is the child most or least effective? Can he summarize or answer direct questions better? Does he do better when he tells you answers or when he writes them? Again, this will direct us to desirable remedial situations.
5. Does the child have to be prodded to finish his reading assignments? If the child cannot work without supervision even when specific assignments have been made, unsupervised reading situations should be avoided in initial remedial instruction.
6. What type of book selections does the child make in the library? Considerable information can be obtained about a child's interests by noticing the type of book he chooses from the library. Remedial efforts should start with the type of material in which he has indicated an interest.

Answers to the above questions will become important guides to the initial remedial sessions. The teacher will find it useful to record his findings so that (1) he will have a record of accurate data, and (2) he will be able to inform the reading specialist. Although these questions will be answered for the most part by informal observation, we have found it most satisfactory if the teacher gives them special attention and becomes an active agent in collecting information.

At times it is not possible to obtain precise "yes" or "no" answers to the questions needed for classroom diagnosis. In these cases the classroom teacher may place the child under continued observation until he can substantiate a more accurate pattern of errors. Specifically, the teacher may provide the child with individualized exercises to do at his seat, go over his responses, and even have a short conference with him about why he marked the exercises as he did. A part of informal on-the-spot diagnosis, this technique can be useful in verifying classroom diagnosis. Suppose, for example, that one has diagnosed irregular patterns of difficulty with final consonant sounds. Several carefully prepared exercises with final consonant sounds can be developed, administered, and analyzed for the purpose of verification. Further verification can come from information available in school records, from parental interviews, and from past observations (both his and other teachers'). All of this information should be used to effect an accurate classroom diagnosis.

Four Final Questions

The teacher must reflect upon the answers to the following four questions to complete an effective classroom diagnosis and assist him in more clearly establishing the validity of his findings.

1. Did the child make the same error in both easy and difficult material, or did the observed errors indicate frustration with the material? We are most interested in the errors made at the instruction level— the level at which we hope to make improvement. All children make errors when reading at their frustration level; these errors, however, do not normally lead us to diagnostic conclusions, for these are not the errors upon which remediation is based.

2. Were the errors first interpreted as slowness actually an effort on the part of the child to be especially careful and precise? Beware of diagnostic conclusions drawn from the child's responses to questions on material which he did not read, due to slowness. We find this to be particularly true when timed standardized tests are used or when testing situations make the child aware of being evaluated.

3. Can the child be helped as a result of this classroom diagnosis, or must he be tested further, either in the classroom or in a clinical diagnosis? If the teacher has reached a point at which he can effectively adjust classroom learning situations, he should do so; otherwise, he must evaluate the need of further diagnosis. Further testing with any of the instruments mentioned under clinical diagnosis may be in order and is entirely proper when the teacher has the time and knowledge of their proper usage and interpretation. It is at this point, however, that the services of a reading specialist are required.

4. Did the child appear to concentrate while being directly observed, or did he seem easily distracted? The child who appears to be distracted during observation may have produced unreliable symptoms.

Summary Sheet

With a technique for summarizing his diagnostic findings, the classroom teacher may find much of this valuable information more readily applicable to the adjustment of classroom instruction. It is our feeling that much diagnostic information is lost through the lack of recording techniques. Of course, the classroom teacher may, as does the reading specialist, form a case study on the problem reader. We have found, however, carrying essential information on one page, as in Chart V, to be more valuable and less burdensome for the classroom teacher. By consolidating the information on one page, the classroom teacher will find the information more accessible for reference and that various findings can be related to one another quite accurately.

The summary sheet provides basic information at a glance. In short, it illustrates how far the child is reading below grade level and how far he is reading below his potential. The teacher then indicates the remedial skill areas in which he has identified specifically needed classroom adjustment. And, finally, he notes symptoms requiring referral along with the date that the referral was made. The teacher maintains accompanying information on the child in a folder with this form stapled on the inside cover.

His diagnostic task has been to observe the individual child through analysis of symptoms, to associate the symptoms to appropriate skill areas, to determine the significance of the error, and to organize his information in terms of practical classroom adjustments. On only few occasions will diagnosis be concluded at this point. An on-going process, diagnosis will normally continue during the remedial sessions, always attempting to obtain more precise information concerning the child's deficiency. Morris feels that this is the important advantage for the classroom teacher. He states: "To the teacher . . . the challenge is to get to grips more directly with the problem and by working with the individual pupil try to understand what is leading him astray."[3] To this we add, "and to determine more precisely his skill deficiencies."

---

[3]Morris, *Success and Failure in Learning to Read*, p. 159.

CHART V

SUMMARY SHEET — READING DIAGNOSIS

Diagnostician *J. E. M.*

John Jones   *5*   *April 6, 1966*

Name of child   Grade in School   Date

Grade in School	Reading Potential	Word Recognition	Oral Reading	Silent Reading
	X			
				X
			X	
		X		

Deficient Skills Area(s) Identified:

1. Orientation

   Instruct. Level_____

   Type of Error_____

   _____

2. Sight Vocabulary

   Instruct. Level *3 - 1*

   Type of Error *words of minimal difference*

3. Word Attack

   Instruct. Level *3/4 - 1*

   Type of Error *syllabication blending*

4. Comprehension

   Instruct. Level *5 - 1*

   Type of Error *getting main idea*

Referral

Type	Symptoms	Date of Referral
1. Emotional	*none*	
2. Physical	*visual discomfort - holds book too close*	*April 6, 1966*
3. Intellectual	*none*	
4. Clinical Diagnosis	*no*	

Miscellaneous Information *The child has basic interests in animal stories. Home conditions - good.*

Clinical Diagnosis

Through a testing program, the reading specialist evaluates the same four skill areas as in classroom diagnosis. He obtains, as did the classroom teacher, the instructional level of each skill area, establishes the skill area that appears to be most basic to the child's deficiency and through answers to specific diagnostic questions, pinpoints more precisely the nature of the difficulty.

The reading specialist, however, does not consider his diagnosis in terms of classroom adjustment alone, for he must also consider:

1. Possible remediation in a clinic situation.
2. Possible adjustment in school to prevent development of similar problems.
3. Potential parental corrective action and adjustment of home situations.
4. More precise evaluation for possible referral.

Therefore, clinical diagnosis must be extended: first, by obtaining more precise measures of skill development in questionable areas; and secondly, by analyzing all potential causes, relating information from the non-educational areas. It is important to note that through the relating of all available data one is directed towards an analysis of possible causes of the problem, the case study being the tool for recording these relationships.

While discussing techniques for clinical diagnosis, no attempt is made to reproduce carefully prepared teacher's manuals and test instruction; rather, many of the major types of tests are presented with an indication of their usefulness in clinical diagnosis. (Appendix A contains a summary of basic test information.)

Limited to a shorter time period to obtain diagnostic information, the reading specialist will conduct his diagnosis through testing rather than through direct observation as used by the classroom teacher. Testing will be conducted in the same three reading situations which were observed in classroom diagnosis, i.e., word recognition, oral reading, and silent reading.

In word recognition

The first reading test to be administered in a clinical diagnosis is one of word recognition. This test must be designed to screen the ability of the child to accurately pronounce words normally found at the various grade levels. From a screening of word recognition, the reading specialist is able to make the same analysis made from direct observation in classroom diagnosis (p. 69). It also assists him to make the following two basic judgments concerning the next steps in clinical diagnosis:

1. From the instructional level of word recognition (the level at which a child can recognize at least seventy percent of the words), the reading specialist is able to select tests of the appropriate level for use in the remainder of his diagnosis. Without this information, it is quite possible to find oneself administering tests upon which the child cannot score at all or upon which he can obtain a nearly perfect score because it is too easy. In neither case will this type of testing produce usable diagnostic information, for tests must be administered upon which students can start with success and upon which they ultimately fail.

2. From the word recognition test, the reading specialist initially determines the *type* of testing which should follow. He may find, for example, that further testing of sight vocabulary, as such, is unnecessary, but that a complete phonic analysis is in order. Or, he may find that the child has adequate sight vocabulary and word attack skills, but needs a test with words in context to determine the child's understanding of the meaning of words in relation to each other, as well as their pronunciation.

Two of the widely used tests of word recognition are the *Botel Reading Inventory** and the *Dolch Basic Sight Vocabulary Cards.** The Word Recognition section of the Botel Inventory samples groups of twenty words found in the various basal readers, grades one through four. A child pronounces the word while the examiner records his pronunciation errors.

A sample of one half of the first page of the Botel Word Recognition Test is shown. Notice that the child's responses must be accurately recorded. This child made most of his errors in final consonant sounds and then in vowel sounds. Accurate inner test analysis requires an examination and marking of each type of error as shown. (v stands for vowel, fc for final consonant, ic for initial consonant, and mc for medial consonant, √ for correct response.)

---

*See Appendix A.

BOTEL READING INVENTORY A*

WORD RECOGNITION SCORING SHEET

Pupil_____

Date_____

Instructional Levels_____

Teacher _____

A (Pre-Primer)		B (Primer)		C (First)	
Word	Response	Word	Response	Word	Response
1. a	√	all	√	about	√
2. ball	√	at	√	as	√
3. blue v	blow	boat fc	boak	be	√
4. come	√	but fc	bud	by	√
5. farther mc	fatter	do	√	could v	cold
6. get	√	duck	√	fast v	first
7. have fc	half	find fc	fine	friend fc	friet
8. house v	horse	girl	√	guess fc	guest
9. in	√	he	√	hen	√
10. it	√	kitten v	kitton	how fc	hot

The *Dolch Basic Sight Vocabulary Cards* represent a sample of 220 common words found in most first and second grade basal readers.

Many clinicians prefer to construct lists from words found in the basal series. When this is done, it is suggested that the lists contain a minimum of twenty words (preferably more) per reader used, with an adequate sampling of the following types of words:

1. Words that have a variety of vowel and consonant sounds and positions.
2. Words that are prefixed and suffixed (for children above grade 2).
3. Compound words.

---

*Morton Botel, *Botel Reading Inventory* (Chicago: Follett Publishing Co., 1961).

4. Words that are similar in configuration.
5. Words which have concrete meanings as well as words that have abstract meanings.

The specialist who is inexperienced with informal test construction will find this task quite difficult and may find it more profitable to use the ready-made tests. Informal word lists are available[4, 5] and may be used when desired.

In oral reading

The reading specialist will next find a test of oral reading skills to be valuable. From the oral reading tests, the reading specialist can again gather diagnostic information in the same manner as did the classroom teacher when he observed oral reading in the classroom (see p. 69). It also enables him to do the following:

1. He will be able to verify the findings obtained on the word recognition test. Does the child consistently make errors on the same kinds of words or in the same parts of words as were noted in tests of word recognition?
2. Further diagnostic information is obtained while determining if those words unknown in word recognition are known when they are seen in their relationship with other words. The ability of the child to use contextual word attack skills is obtained by comparing the instructional level of word recognition with the instructional level of oral reading. A large difference in favor of oral reading indicates effective use of context. A score difference in favor of word recognition may be an indication of contextual confusion.
3. Oral reading tests also provide the examiner with an understanding of the child's reading characteristics in oral school situations. Although this particular diagnostic information may not have a direct relationship to specific remedial procedures, it will provide the reading specialist with an understanding of the child's reaction to oral reading and of the problems which he may be causing in his classroom.

There are several tests already available with prepared oral reading

---

[4]Mary C. Austin, Clifford L. Busch and Mildred H. Huebner, *Reading Evaluation* (New York: The Ronald Press, 1961), p. 13.

[5]Emmett A. Betts, *Handbook on Corrective Reading for the American Adventure Series* (Chicago: Wheeler Publishing Co., 1956), pp. 37-9.

selections and norms for grade equivalents. Some of these are: *Gilmore Oral Reading Test,* * *Gray Oral Reading Test,* * *Diagnostic Reading Scales,* * *Durrell Analysis of Reading Difficulties,* * and the *Gates-McKillop Reading Test.* * Although the direction for administration of these tests vary, they have the following basic ingredients in common: the child reads aloud from graded reading selections, ranging from simple to difficult; the examiner records the reading errors in a manner outlined by the manual; he then asks several comprehension questions which normally provide a measure of the child's ability to recall specifically stated facts from the story (the Gates-McKillip test does not have this feature). The reading specialist will want to examine each of these tests and make his selection in accordance with his philosophy of oral reading and the characteristics of the specific tests.

Oral reading tests as diagnostic tools are plagued by several limitations. In the first place, there is considerable disagreement about what an oral reading error is. Certainly, we would recognize mispronounced words, hesitancy on unknown words, or disregard of punctuation marks as obvious limitations to effective oral reading, at least as far as the audience is concerned; but is it an error when a child repeats words to correct oral reading mistakes? Is it an error when a child stops to use word attack skills on words not known at sight? And are all these errors of equal importance, or do some more seriously cripple reading efficiency? Fully aware of these limitations, test constructors, in an effort to standardize oral reading tests, have had to establish some easily recognizable arbitrary standards of accurate and inaccurate oral reading. Although these arbitrary systems vary, most of them include markings similar to those listed in the Gilmore Oral Reading Test Manual.[6] Substitutions and mispronunciations are written above the word for which the substitution was made; omissions are circled; repetitions are underlined; words inserted are put in the appropriate place; punctuation which is disregarded is marked by an x; hesitations of two seconds or more are marked by a check mark above the word; at five seconds these words are pronounced for the reader and two check marks are indicated. Diagnosis, of course, depends upon the accurate marking of errors and a valid interpretation of them.

---

*See Appendix A.

[6]*Manual of Directions,* Gilmore Oral Reading Test, (New York: Harcourt, Brace and World, 1952), pp 8-9.

Another limitation of oral reading tests concerns the ability of the examiner to hear and record accurately the errors that the child is making. It has been our finding that supervised practice is necessary to obtain proficiency in oral reading test administration. It is obvious that if the examiner is not able to hear or record the child's errors accurately, the results of his testing will be of questionable value. Through practice, competency can be developed to assure satisfactory administration and interpretation of oral reading.

With these limitations in mind, the reading specialist will continue to find tests of oral reading extremely valuable in the reading diagnosis due to the information obtained from the answers to the analysis suggested above.

In silent reading

The third step in a clinical diagnosis is the evaluation of the child's silent reading skills through specially-constructed tests. Through an evaluation of these tests, the reading specialist gathers information as did the classroom teacher when he observed silent reading (see p. 70).

In clinical diagnosis, silent reading tests have several additional advantages. First, an instructional level is established at which a child can get meaning from words and paragraphs silently. The instructional level in silent reading is considered to be that level at which a child reads without undue frustration, but at which he is obviously in need of instruction for improved performance. The grade score earned on a silent reading test, however, does not necessarily represent the instructional level, as this score usually includes measures of the child's performance at the frustration level. To accurately obtain the instructional level, the reading specialist must carefully examine silent reading comprehension errors to determine where the child falls short of errorless reading. Secondly, it is through the inner analysis of test errors that the reading specialist is able to determine the type of comprehension that is limiting the child's reading proficiency. An inner analysis of the child's responses will assist the examiner in determining the type of errors with which the child is having the most difficulty. Most well constructed test manuals guide the examiner to this type of analysis. Thirdly, through a comparison of the child's scores in word meaning and paragraph meaning, the examiner obtains insights into the broad area of most severe deficiency. Prepared with such information, he is enabled to proceed with the precise selection of future tests. It is important that the reading specialist understand what these various tests have to offer in terms of the skills measured and the interpretation of resulting scores.

Several of the better known tests of silent reading ability are: *The California Reading Tests,* *The Diagnostic Reading Tests,* *Durrell Sullivan Reading Achievement Test,* *The Gates Reading Survey,* *The Gates Reading Tests,* *The Iowa Test of Basic Skills,* *The Metropolitan Achievement Tests,* and *The Stanford Achievement Test.** Being silent tests, they may be administered in group situations in which the child is normally expected to complete the process in a generously alloted time period. It is important that the reading specialist remembers to consult his word recognition test scores to determine the proper level for the selection of silent reading tests. Although each of the mentioned tests provide a measure of a child's performance in word and paragraph meaning, the difference in the items involved to obtain these scores is great. For example, some tests stress the recall of directly stated facts while others sample the ability to handle main ideas, inferences, map reading, etc. Both tests are likely to call the resulting scores an indication of the child's ability to comprehend. The reading specialist will necessarily need to examine the nature of each test prior to its interpretation.

Silent reading tests are also plagued with limitations. First, if the child's instructional level is not measured by this test, the score which he obtains will not be meaningful. For example, if a child is to take a test designed for intermediate grade children but cannot read beyond the first grade level, his test score is likely to be invalid since the test did not measure his instructional level. He will not likely score on any item except by pure guessing. All we will know from this type of test is that he is a poor reader, and we knew that before we gave the test to him.

Secondly, the author's definition of what comprehension actually is may make quite a difference in the resulting score. For example, the *California Reading Test* measures comprehension at the elementary level by combining the ability to follow directions, the ability to read maps, charts, and graphs, and the ability to get meaning from paragraphs. Obviously, this score is not comparable to the score on an achievement test measuring only paragraph meaning. The reading specialist, then, will want to administer that test which agrees most directly with his definition of comprehension.

---

*See Appendix A.

Another limitation is that standardized populations vary considerably, resulting in grade equivalent scores which are not always accurate for the child upon whom the diagnosis is being conducted. Efforts must be made to determine the nature of the standardization population; otherwise, the resulting score cannot be evaluated accurately for a given child.

Finally, the reading specialist shoud be cautioned about the limitations in using certain silent reading tests to make reliable inner test analysis and diagnosis. On the *California Reading Test,* for example, the child taking the elementary form of the test answers three questions to indicate whether he can obtain the main idea. Conclusions based upon a child's response to only three questions must, it seems to us, be held suspect. If the reading specialist is to interpret this score as an area in which further investigation seems warranted, the test has a useful function. More reliable diagnosis is possible, however, on this same test when comparing the major sections such as Following Directions, Reference Skills, and Interpretation of Materials. The *Diagnostic Reading Tests* and the *Gates Reading Tests* have entire sections which are devoted to an analysis of a child's competency in specific types of silent reading comprehension. Gates, for example, has a separate test for (1) Reading for General Significance, (2) Reading to Note Details, and (3) Level of Comprehension, as well as Reading to Follow Directions and Reading Vocabulary.

Informal inventories

Occasionally, scores in the diagnosis conflict to the point that they are confusing. If the reading specialist finds such to be the case, he may conduct an informal reading inventory constructed from the type of materials the child will be expected to use in the classroom. One of the major advantages of using informal testing devices is that they can be designed to sample much larger units of material at one level, permitting a more reliable pattern of errors to develop. Wherever the score conflict has appeared, be it word recognition, oral reading, silent reading, or a combination, the reading specialist has the child read from basal series type materials, at the various grade levels, in an attempt to determine how well he can function at these various levels and in these various reading situations. Informal inventories produce results which are only as good as the efforts of the reading specialist in the tasks of selecting the appropriate materials, asking the proper questions, and listening accurately to the types of errors made. It is not assumed that the reading specialist will, in an informal manner, measure skills better than professional test constructors; however, he will find this a valuable technique to obtain specific diagnostic information and to verify conflicting test scores on larger samples of the same materials that will be used for instruction.

Austin and others[7] have prepared an inventory for use with the Allyn Bacon Series Readers. Betts[8] has prepared one for use with the American Adventure Series. Smith and others[9] have developed one for the primary grades. Reading specialists who are unfamiliar with the construction of these inventories will want to refer to these sources or to the book on informal inventories by Johnson and Kress.[10] Spache has carefully prepared standardized paragraphs in the *Diagnostic Reading Scales* which provide teachers with a rather large sampling of oral and silent reading test materials. However, he has standardized this test, making interpretation easier.

Hypothesis

At this point in the diagnosis, tentative hypotheses are made, based upon the evaluation of word recognition, oral reading, and silent reading tests. From these hypotheses the reading specialist determines the skill area(s) in which a child appears to be having his basic difficulty and plans further diagnosis in terms of his findings. His procedure here is identical to those used by the classroom teacher in classroom diagnosis (see pp. 72). Although the questions asked in relation to each skill area are the same questions asked in classroom diagnosis, the resulting conclusions are likely to be more accurate, since the reading specialist has used more precise diagnostic tools and is more qualified to interpret the results. Based upon these tentative hypotheses, the reading specialist will now extend the diagnosis to those skill areas which have been identified as deficient. These two aspects of clinical diagnosis, preciseness of the tools and the extension based upon the hypotheses, plus the evaluation of in-

---

[7]Austin, Busch and Huebner, *Reading Evaluation,* Appendix.

[8]Betts, *Handbook on Corrective Reading for the American Adventure Series,* Chapter III.

[9]Nila B. Smith and others, *Graded Selections for Informal Reading Diagnosis* (New York: New York Universal Press, 1959).

[10]Marjorie S. Johnson and Roy A. Kress, *Informal Reading Inventories,* Reading Aid Series (Newark, Delaware: International Reading Assoc., 1965).

formation from non-educational diagnosis, often make the detection of causation possible.

Extension of Diagnosis

If the tentative hypothesis identifies the area of *Orientation* as a problem in reading, diagnosis should be extended through an evaluation of eye motion during the reading act, normally done through careful observation of the child during oral and silent reading. Do the eyes appear to move with a reasonable number of fixations across the line of print? Or, do the child's eyes move backwards, making many regressions? Everyone makes regressions in reading, and without experience in observing children in the reading act, it would be difficult to make an accurate diagnosis in this area. It is suggested that the reading specialist observe groups of good, fair, and poor readers so that he may obtain an idea of what might be expected in the observation of eye movements. The Reading Eye Camera* is designed to photograph the precise movements of each eye while a child is reading. This will afford the reading specialist an opportunity to carefully evaluate several aspects of the mechanics of reading and to compare a child's performance with established norms. It should be noted that the evaluation of eye motion films also requires considerable practice because the patterns of poor readers do not follow the normal analysis patterns set forth in the manual.

Another extension of diagnosis to be made in the area of orientation skills is in terms of dominance preference. It has been our experience that children who lack normal lateral dominance patterns are generally more poorly oriented to the printed page than are children who are unilateral. In this area of diagnosis, we would consider lateral dominance of importance to only the reading specialist since remedial techniques are limited and there is a great deal of confusion in the interpretation of dominance test results. Our conclusion is that confusion in lateral dominance does not cause reading problems, in and by itself, but that children with confused dominance do have more difficulty orienting themselves to the printed page, and therefore, when other complications occur in the child's reading processes, the child's lack of strong dominance complicates the teaching of reading. We have found that children without clearly established dominance patterns are less accurate in oral reading and have

---

*See Appendix A.

more directional confusion than others. Clinical diagnosis of a child with orientation problems should attempt to establish the place of confused dominance in the overall diagnosis. If, after extended diagnosis in these two areas, the reading specialist finds a child's patterns to be abnormal, clinical remediation should be considered (see p. 111).

If the tentative hypothesis identifies the area of *Sight Vocabulary* as the problem in reading, diagnosis should be extended through a more careful analysis of tests previously administered to determine consistent patterns of sight vocabulary errors (see p. 74).

It is of particular importance to obtain a measure of the child's ability to obtain meaning from words which he can pronounce. A test of word meaning can provide this information. The *Botel Word Opposites Test**, a test upon which a child performs silently to indicate his ability in arriving at word meaning through an understanding of word opposites, may be compared with word pronunciation on the *Botel Word Recognition Test**. Such comparisons lead directly to diagnostic conclusions.

Tests may also indicate the speed at which the child responds to recognized words. A word cannot properly be called a sight word unless a child recognizes it instantly at sight, without hesitation. Standardized word meaning tests which are timed will provide this information, especially if the child answers his word correctly but scores poorly on tests which are designed to test his working speed in reading (*Gates Reading Survey**, Speed and Accuracy Section); this may also indicate a hesitancy in word recognition. Durrell[11] suggests that the word not known at sight should be used again to see if the child can analyze the word and then use word attack when time is not a factor. Obviously, if the child does not know the word at sight but does know it when permitted to examine it, we may conclude that the child has skills to properly attack the word but has not overlearned it to the extent that it can be called a sight word.

If the tentative hypothesis finds the area of *Word Attack* as the basic weakness, it is necessary to re-examine the errors made in word recognition and oral reading through analysis similar to that made in the classroom diagnosis (see p. 74). There are tests available for clinical diagnosis which measure precise word attack skill performance. *The Botel Phonics Test*, The Silent Reading Diagnostic Tests** by Bond, Clymer,

---

11Donald D. Durrell, *Manual of Directions,* Durrell Analysis of Reading Difficulty (New York: Harcourt World and Brace, 1955), p. 14.

*See Appendix A.

and Hoyt, and the *Doren Diagnostic Reading Tests of Word Recognition Skills**, are three well-known, quite different evaluations of a child's word attack skills. Each of these tests may be administered to groups of students who respond to oral presentations by the teacher. The Botel test is quite short, the Silent Reading test takes about 45 minutes, and the Doren test takes three hours. The needs of a given child determine which is most appropriate in his diagnosis. The various diagnostic test batteries also contain an analysis of word attack skills; however, they are usually limited to phonics.

Reading specialists will generally want to see how well a child with specific word attack problems handles himself in a spelling test. A test of this nature should be given on the child's instructional level. Through an analysis of spelling errors, the reading specialist is able to extend his diagnosis and verify previous findings. A child who substitutes one consonant for another or one vowel for another is indicating disabilities in handling phonics, e.g., *perty* for *party*. If he confuses the order of the letters, e.g., *picinc* for *picnic* he is indicating directional confusion. And, of course, spelling errors can confirm suspicions of reversal tendencies, e.g., *was* for *saw*. An analysis of the child's performance on these tests, combined with the diagnostic data previously available, should lead the reading specialist to a thorough evaluation of the type of word attack skills with which the child is having his basic problem.

It bears repeating that if a child does not know his letter sounds, one must evaluate whether he has the *auditory discrimination skills* necessary for learning them. Test exercises in auditory discrimination are available in teacher's manuals of most basal series and can readily be adapted for clinical diagnosis. *The Wepman Auditory Discrimination Test** gives a quick, accurate analysis of the ability of the child in this area. If the child does not hear the differences in the sounds of letters, further word attack diagnosis becomes unnecessary, for this is the place where remediation must start.

The reading specialist is cautioned that many children have learned to do an adequate job in attacking words in isolated drill type exercises but are not capable of performing the same task when they see these words in contextual situations. It would be erroneous, therefore, for the reading specialist to conclude that a child does not have a word attack deficiency simply because he performs successfully on all diagnostic tests of word attack skills. Evaluation must be made in an oral reading situa-

*See Appendix A.

tion where the child is faced, not with a single unknown word, but with the unknown word found in a group of familiar words here too, clues to meaning have as much importance as clues to proper pronunciation.

If the tentative hypothesis identifies the area of *comprehension* as the problem, attention must again be directed to those questions asked in classroom diagnosis (see p. 75). Clinical diagnosis will be extended to review the history of the child's reading instruction in terms of basic types of approaches used. From this type of analysis, it is often possible for the reading specialist to understand the gap in areas of instruction and suggest remedial programs to fill these gaps. In the area of *comprehension,* we want to establish the answers to four additional questions before proceeding to remediation:

1. Is the child's poor performance on a comprehension test due basically to weak comprehension skills, or is it more closely related to inadequate vocabulary? One technique for determining the answer to this question is to make a careful comparison between word meaning and paragraph meaning scores. Poorer performance in word meaning usually indicates that a child's vocabulary skills are prohibiting maximum performance in comprehension.

2. Is there a need for further comprehension testing to verify scores upon which there is conflicting evidence? It may be necessary to administer a test which has more items, one which has a better variety of items, or one which measures a certain type of comprehension skill not measured in the previously administered silent reading test. When children have basic comprehension difficulties, the reading specialist will seldom find one silent reading test capable of satisfying all of the child's diagnostic needs. If another test is administered, the results of that test will undergo the same diagnostic scrutiny as did the previous test.

3. Is the child's poor performance on a comprehension test due basically to reading speed? In classroom diagnosis, the ability to complete the reading assignments in a given time period was given basic consideration; in clinical diagnosis equal consideration must be given to the child who fails to complete reading tests in the allotted time. There is no possibility of obtaining this information from the grade scores on silent reading tests; rather, a careful inner analysis is needed to obtain information relative to the amount of material covered by a child in a given test. A test is now available to determine the flexibility with which a child attacks print designed for

different purposes. The *EDL Reading Versatility Test** is designed to provide this type of information when speed of reading is being considered as a limitation to the child.

4. Is the child's poor comprehension on specific text exercises due to his insufficient experiences to draw upon in relating to the printed words of the author? It is easy to understand that a city child, unfamiliar with farm life might score poorly on a story test about farming yet be quite capable of comprehending a similar story about city life. Diagnosis, however, is not so easy. Broad areas of experience may be identified, yet a child's background of experiences is quite personal and involved. A child who can pronounce the words yet fail in comprehension is likely to have a basic weakness in experential background so that he cannot form the concepts that the author's words would indicate to us.

If the tentative hypothesis identifies the area of *Reading Habits and Attitudes* as the problem, the reading specialist has found that the child has the basic skills to read adequately, but does not care to read. Again this involves a careful consideration of information from the areas of emotional and physical diagnosis in which the child may indicate either that he has a poor attitude towards school-type tasks and books or that he is physically uncomfortable to a point that he does not eagerly pursue the reading act. Further evaluation is needed in terms of past efforts made by the school to encourage the child to read; availability of books in school and at home; and the general atmosphere which may either encourage or discourage reading in these situations. A child who can read, but doesn't, is not normally considered a reading problem in need of a specialist's attention; rather, he is a classroom teacher's responsibility as long as the difficulty is educational in nature. The reading specialist's obligation, therefore, is one of making specific recommendations to the classroom teacher to assist him in encouraging the child to read. It will be helpful, therefore, for the reading specialist to use a measure of the child's interests in his diagnosis. Fully aware that interests are of-the-moment and ever-changing, the reading specialist will nevertheless attempt to assess the child's interests either formally through an established interest inventory or informally through informal interest inventories and/or a personal interview with the child, his parents, and his teacher. We have found, for example, that many children, although reading as well as can

---

*See Appendix A.

be expected, are placed in frustrating reading situations daily in school. It does not take a specialist to realize that reading is not much fun for this child and that he might have easily developed a negative attitude toward reading. Information gleaned in such a manner will be important to include in the diagnostic consideration for a problem reader.

Diagnostic batteries

There are available for clinical diagnosis a group of tests which, in a single unit, contain a diagnostic battery. These tests are designed for use by the reading specialist for a rather complete educational analysis on a given child. The more prominent of these batteries are the: *Durrell Analysis of Reading Difficulties**, *Gates-McKillop Reading Diagnostic Test**, *Diagnostic-Reading Scale**, and *Monroe-Sherman Group Diagnostic Reading Aptitude and Achievement Tests**. The first three are individual in nature, and the last is a group test. A careful examination of these diagnostic batteries is essential for the appropriate selection for clinical diagnosis. The only items that all these tests have in common are measures of silent or oral reading and word attack skills. Some tests also include: word recognition, oral reading, arithmetic, spelling, auditory and visual discrimination, and auditing.* The main advantage of using a diagnostic battery is that the results of the subtests are truly comparable since they are standardized on the same population. Another advantage is that there is one manual and one test to learn to administer and interpret. One does not have the overwhelming job that occurs in some other types of testing combinations. The resulting information will provide an individual analysis of how a student is reading and how his skill development is related to his total reading scores. These diagnostic batteries are not without limitations; some are too brief and some are standardized on very small population. Most important, quite possibly the reading specialist will find that all aspects of the test do not measure the types or quantities of skills that he wishes to measure. Therefore, in clinical diagnosis, it is unlikely that any of these diagnostic batteries will be, in themselves, adequate for a complete diagnosis. Note that subtests of these batteries have been

---

*See Appendix A.

recommended for use in certain areas of clinical diagnosis, for they measure specific skills rather precisely.

The so-called non-reader

Unfortunately, not all diagnosis falls into neat packages of specific skill deficiencies. A small portion of children appear unable to profit from even the best instruction in any of the skill areas. They cannot learn to read from conventional methods. The diagnosis of this type of child is the responsibility of the reading specialist.

Commonly referred to as dyslexia, neurological deficiency, minimum brain damage, or specific reading disability, the non-reader has disabilities complicated by multiple factors. The child is almost always emotionally involved in his gross failure. He is likely to be physically deficient and may appear to be dull. Trying to please the teacher is often no longer of interest to him. Diagnosis has failed to identify a consistent pattern of error. Educators have attempted to teach him by all known methods; each of these methods have failed to teach him to read.

Effective diagnosis calls for an interdisciplinary approach to this child. All diagnostic facilities, educational and non-educational, must be called into action. With this child every effort should be made to seek out the sources of his deficiency. It is often necessary that this child be diagnosed in clinics which have been established to work efficiently with him. Diagnosis and initial remediation will most effectively be accomplished in these clinic-type situations.

In some cases, despite all our efforts, these children continue to fail. Multi-disciplinary efforts are continuously explored in hopes of establishing new areas of diagnosis and remediation for them. Gilbert Schiffman, Maryland State Supervisor of Reading, has initiated major efforts to establish communication lines between the disciplines.[12] As a result, better understandings of the role of each discipline have been established, and communication lines have been identified. When such cooperative efforts are not available, we can at least be sure of the following. Early identification is essential. Any educator who finds such a child must refer him without delay to the specialist who is equipped to handle these types of children. When extended into the secondary schools, remediation is extremely difficult, time consuming, and expensive.

---

[12]John Money, *The Disabled Reader* (Gilbert Schiffman, Advisory Editor in Education), (Baltimore, Maryland: John Hopkins Press, 1966).

The Culturally Disadvantaged

Another group of children who do not fall into neat diagnostic patterns are those with cultural backgrounds different from those in the materials which they meet in school. Culturally disadvantaged children are limited by degree of deprivation, not by whether they suffer. Almost impossible to measure, the degree of cultural disadvantage is seldom truly known, even after careful diagnosis. The outstanding characteristics of children with some degree of cultural disadvantage are:

1. They may be from poor families.
2. They may have inadequate speech patterns.
3. They may have foreign backgrounds.
4. They may not have traveled much beyond their neighborhood.
5. They may not accept school eagerly.

Due to different experiences, their difficulty lies in their inability to associate with the printed message. Once these children have failed, they are likely to become discouraged with reading, thereby failing with decoding as well as association. Appearing careless, lazy, and disrespectful, they are likely to be punished, pushed, and badgered, while needing the exact opposite type of treatment.

Identification of these children as early as possible, preferably in kindergarten or first grade, is also a necessity. Specifically, the teacher can observe children with: limited language functions, inability to express themselves, and weak experiential backgrounds. A reliable test of auding can be used to identify children who are not up to norm in their ability to get meaning from speech. Enrichment programs for them must be started in conjunction with or prior to reading skills instruction. Concern about these children has initiated federal interest and federally sponsored programs.

The Case Study

As in classroom diagnosis, the information accumulated in a clinical diagnosis is useless unless it can be organized in a manner which is readily understood. This organization must differ for the various recipients of the report—the reading specialist, the classroom teacher, or the parents.

A case study is the normal approach to preparing diagnostic information for clinical use. Although the precise form may vary, it is suggested that the following format be used so that persons unfamiliar with this child can make optimum use of case information:

1. The first page should contain a concise summary of the essential data included in the report, i.e., name, age, address, and school of the child, degree of reading retardation, and a summary statement of the diagnostic findings, including intellectual, physical, emotional, and educational diagnosis.
2. This page should be followed by as many pages of examination as necessary. The explanation should include all test scores, dates upon which they were administered, and the name of the test administrator as well as diagnostic interpretations of the test performance and evaluations of the child's responses. It should also include non-educational data from screening tests and referral reports. It is here that the relative importance of each piece of data is evaluated and interrelated and that causative factors may be identified.
3. The last page of the case study should be reserved for specific recommendations and referrals. Recommendations should include those to the clinic, the classroom teacher, and the parents specifying preventive as well as remedial procedures.

Reports to the classroom teacher are generally not effective when in case study form; however, they should contain the more important test scores and a concise, readable, usable set of recommendations for corrective action. This report does not preclude the classroom teacher's examination of the case study if he so desires. The main purpose of the report to the classroom teacher is to enable him to understand the child's reading in order to facilitate proper classroom adjustment.

In reporting diagnostic findings to parents, we do not recommend the use of the case study, nor the reporting of precise scores. The reports to parents can contain a general statement in each of the four areas of diagnosis and, most importantly, recommendations for parental action and referral. Test scores without careful explanation tend to be taken as absolutes, causing many problems between the parents, the child, the schools. It is highly desirable to discuss diagnostic results with parents so that questions can be answered and emphasis placed on certain conclusions as desired. Chapter 10 covers the area of the parental roles and the problem reader more thoroughly.

Initial Screening

The reading specialist is going to find that an accurate diagnosis of reading disabilities as mentioned above is a process which will take large amounts of time and effort. It is unfortunate that time is wasted in the complete clinical diagnosis of large numbers of children who do not have reading problems, but are referred to reading specialists who have no means of knowing the child until the entire diagnosis or a major part of it is complete. It seems advisable, then, that the reading specialist have a technique which will permit him to screen children prior to the administration of the entire diagnosis. A second reason for a screening technique is that most reading specialists have long waiting lists of children in need of diagnosis, and it is therefore difficult to justify the diagnosing of children not in need of it.

It is for the above mentioned reasons that the concept of "initial screening" is introduced. Initial screening should be a brief, concise evaluation of the child's reading skills, taking no longer than one hour. We recommend the following:

> *Peabody Picture Vocabulary Test*
> *Botel Word Recognition Test*
> *Botel Word Opposites Test*
> *Botel Phonics Test* (if necessary)
> *Gilmore Oral Reading Test*
> *Telebinocular*—including *Spache Binocular Vision Test*
> Flashlight Test
> A measure of silent reading
> Basic information from the parents
> Basic evaluation of the child's reaction to reading

This material may be presented on the following form which enables the reading specialist to talk with the parents or the classroom teacher with regard to the child's problems and permit him to decide whether further diagnosis is necessary.

It has been our finding that approximately one-fourth of the children referred for clinical diagnosis can be eliminated from complete diagnosis on the basis of an initial screening, because their problem is not basically one of poor reading. We have found that many children are referred by parents who have not accepted their child as an average student and are anxious to see a child of limited abilities earning A's and B's in school. And we find children referred for poor grades in school for

CHART VI
INITIAL SCREENING FORM

Case No. _265_

Name _John Jones_ Date _April 6, 1966_

TEST RESULTS:

Gilmore Oral Rdg. Test.   Botel Informal Inv.   Dominance Screening:

Accur. _____   Word Recog. _2.2_   Hand preference:

Comp. _____   Word Oppos. _3.1_   L.H. _4_ R.H. _2_

Rate _____   Phonics _satisfactory_   Eye Preference:

Silent Rdg. Test   Peabody Picture Vocab. _____   L.E. _0_ R.E. _6_

Name _California Rdg._ C.A. _9-6_

Accur. _2.0_   A.A. _10-4_

Comp. _1.7_   A.Q. _108_

GRADE EQUIVALENTS OF:

School Grade	C.A.	M.A.	School Grade	Gilmore Accur.	Gilmore Comp.	Word Recg.	Word Opp.	Silent Reading
10			10					
9			9					
8			8					
7			7					
6			6					
5			5					
4			4					
3			3					
2			2					
1			1					

VISUAL SCREENING:

Telebinocular   Spache   Eye Motion

Near point acuity _sat._   R.E. _sat._   Focus _poor_

Far point acuity _sat._   L.E. _sat._   Eye Motility _sat._

EDUCATIONAL INFORMATION:

School _Baker Elementary_   Behavior _good_

Principal _Mr. Brown_   Attendance _good_

Grades Repeated _1st_   Grades: Arith. _B_

Reading _D_ Spelling _C_

PERSONAL INFORMATION:

Birth _normal_   Medical Data _____

Siblings _sister_ Grade _1_   Emotional Data _____

sister Grade _6_

RECOMMENDATIONS: **REFERRAL:**

poor in oral training   _visual_ Date _April 6, 1966_

TUTORING: Yes No

CLINICAL DIAGNOSIS: Yes No   (signed)

99

which there appears, as a result of initial screening, to be no blame on reading skills. The amount of examination time and effort saved by the early identification of these children can be used for more thorough diagnosis for those children in real need.

Classroom teachers who have had the opportunity to use initial screening techniques in college courses have found it to be usable in classroom diagnosis. Initial screening is recommended as a classroom diagnostic technique only if the teacher has had supervised experience with the administration and interpretation of the specific instruments suggested.

Pitfalls of Diagnosis

In concluding our comments on diagnosis, it seems necessary to warn the inexperienced examiner of certain pitfalls which may prevail in diagnostic situations. They are:

1. *Over-generalizations*
   The tendency to use total test scores without examination of the pattern of test scores, the tendency to draw conclusions before all facts are in, the tendency to rely upon the first significant symptom, and the tendency to hazard guesses outside of the professional field are all examples of over-generalizing in diagnosis.
2. *Over-extension of diagnosis*
   Extending diagnosis beyond that which will help to arrive at an accurate picture of the child may cause the child to become overconcerned about his problem and is a waste of time. In commenting on the disadvantages of extended diagnostic periods, Strang concludes, "He may feel more strongly than ever that something may be wrong with him."[13] Over-extension of diagnosis occurs more commonly in the clinic than in the classroom, for it is in the clinic that the most careful study of the child is conducted and a wide variety of tests are available. Some clinics suggest that each child should receive a complete diagnostic analysis regardless of his needs. This can only be justified in the interests of gathering research data, but the expense to the child must always be kept in mind, for not all children can accept these large quantities of diagnosis. Nevertheless, every effort must be made to arrive at a true picture of the child's problem.

---

[13]Strang, *Diagnostic Teaching of Reading*, p. 8.

3. *Abbreviated diagnosis*

In the other direction, we often find that abbreviated diagnosis does not investigate to the proper degree in a given child's reading problem. This type of diagnosis is most common in the classroom where time and materials place constant pressure upon the teacher's efforts. Regardless of the limitations of the classroom situation, the teacher must use all available data to insure that the information obtained is reliable and valid. Through abbreviated diagnosis it is common to jump to the wrong conclusions and, in effect, waste large amounts of time which, in the long run, would have been saved through a more thorough diagnosis.

In both the over-extended diagnosis and abbreviated diagnosis, the lines of danger are elusive; each examiner is being forced to the best of his ability, to make judgements in these matters.

4. *Overstepping professional boundaries*

There is a tendency for educators to make statements concerning a child's problem which are beyond the professional boundaries of their preparation. The diagnostician must refrain from playing psychiatrist or medical doctor; instead, knowing the signs of referral, he must refer willingly.

5. *Unfounded statements of fact*

In direct relation to the preceding pitfalls, it is common to find positive, factual statements being made by educators on evidence which does not justify this strong a statement. The couching of terms to indicate areas of suspicion, areas where more testing may be needed, or areas where referral is necessary, will be beneficial to all of those who are attempting to arrive at a true indication of the child's problem. The examiner must be certain that positive statements concerning the child's problem are backed by highly reliable data.

6. *Isolation of factors*

Isolated pieces of diagnostic data, test scores, etc., must not be examined without consideration for their relationship to the entire diagnosis. It is not unusual for the significance of a particular piece of data to be lessened when it is placed in the total picture of a child's reading problem. A single piece of data or a single test score used in isolation is likely to lead to a distorted picture of the child's problem. Even in the classroom, where time and materials are at a premium, this pitfall should be avoided.

7. *Previous bias*

The examiner must be alert to the possible interference of data which is tainted by bias. Bias is often found in the remarks of parents or teachers and can have a definite effect on the direction the diagnosis may take. To circumvent this effect, the examiner may intentionally avoid the evaluation of data from the parents and teachers until his tentative hypothesis is reached.

Summary

It is through mutual awareness of the specific diagnostic responsibilities of the classroom teacher and the reading specialist that both can perform their tasks most efficiently. The difference between having the child in a classroom group and having a child individually outside the classroom calls for quite different diagnostic responsibilities and approaches. The realization of these differences enables educators to effectively diagnose problem readers.

Following the observation of the child in reading situations or following testing, the diagnosis takes the form of questions which are designed to lead the classroom teacher and the reading specialist to adjustments in instruction in terms of the child's needs. The fact that clinical diagnosis goes further than the classroom teacher can go must not deter the teacher from doing what he can for the child in the classroom.

Diagnosis, to be most useful, must be properly recorded and interpreted to the individuals concerned, whether teachers or parents.

Finally, diagnosis does not terminate within a given period, but continues as long as an educator is working with the child. The continuous nature of diagnosis enables the educator to determine the precise program which will best help the child toward improved reading.

Suggested Readings

1. Betts, Emmett A., *Foundations of Reading Instruction,* pp. 438-85. New York: Book Company, 1946. In this section of his book, Betts presents in detail the concepts and techniques involved in the con-

duction and interpretation of informal reading inventories. The student who desires to use this technique should check this source.

2. Bond, Guy L., and Miles A. Tinker, *Reading Difficulties, Their Diagnosis and Correction.* Chaps. VI, VII, IX. New York: Appleton-Century-Crofts, Inc., 1957. Another of the basic texts which must be considered required reading for those who are involved with the diagnosis of reading problems. The chapters recommended refer particularly to the diagnosis of educational problems.

3. Harris, Albert J., *How To Increase Reading Ability,* 4th Ed. Chaps. vii, viii. New York: David McKay Co., Inc., 1961. These two chapters present rather interesting discussions of the topics discussed under educational diagnosis. Harris's book is considered required reading by all those seriously interested in the diagnosis of reading problems.

4. Kolson, Clifford J., and George Kaluger, *Clinical Aspects of Remedial Reading.* Chaps. iii, iv, vi. Springfield, Illinois: Charles C. Thomas, 1964. These three chapters discuss diagnosis of reading problems from the most difficult to the not so serious. This book limits itself to clinical diagnosis and would be most interesting to the reading specialist.

5. Strang, Ruth, *Diagnostic Teaching of Reading,* p. 8. New York: McGraw Hill Book Co., 1964. In chapters three through seven, diagnostic techniques are presented which have application to classroom as well as clinical situations. There are specific suggestions for working with older children in diagnostic situations.

5

Remediation - A Place To Start

Remediation of reading problems is not, as many believe, based upon mysterious techniques which are impossible for the classroom teacher to understand. Rather, it is based upon sound instruction, pinpointed toward the needs of a given child or group of children who, on the basis of a careful diagnosis, have been termed "deficient." Remediation of problem readers assumes that the person conducting the remediation has a knowledge of sound teaching techniques and that he has either conducted a careful diagnosis or has information from one.

As previously discussed in diagnosis, there is seldom *one* cause of reading problems; therefore, there is seldom one approach to the solution of such problems. On this point the public has often been led to believe the contrary, causing pressure to be placed upon the educators to teach more of certain methods. That there is seldom one satisfactory remedial approach, however, in no way justifies using a little of all known teaching techniques; this is called the "shot-gun" approach. Rather, remediation must be in direct response to the diagnostic conclusions, necessitating the use of the most suitable educational techniques as solutions to the diagnosed deficiency. With this philosophy as a base, the principles of remediation are viewed with reference to the diagnostic findings.

Principles of Remediation

Certain aspects of remediation may be considered as principles to guide the educator. The first three principles of remediation apply equally well to the reading specialist and the classroom teacher. They are to be considered unalterable, for without them the remedial program is likely to fall short of efficient operation.

Remediation must guarantee immediate success.

In the remedial program, the child's first instruction should be at a level we are certain will result in a successful, satisfying experience. In this manner, the child who has experienced frequent failure in reading begins a remedial program with the attitude that this educational experience will be both different and rewarding. Without this attitude, the best remedial efforts are often ill-spent. Successful learning situations are also assured by directing activities toward learning experiences which the diagnosis indicated were the child's strengths and interests. Ultimately it is desirable to instruct in areas of weaknesses, but we start with strengths to develop favorable attitudes.

Remedial successes must be illustrated to the child.

It is not enough that a child be started at the right level and experience a successful situation; for him, successes must be real and must be presented in such a manner that he is acutely aware that *he has been successful.* This principle remains in effect during the entire remedial program, for we shall always be interested in accentuating the child's growth and success.

Remediation must provide for transfer to actual reading situations.

There will be occasions in a remedial program where isolated drill in various areas will be required; however, drill sessions must always be transferred to a reading situation in which the child has an opportunity to use those skills upon which the drill was conducted. The overlearning of all skills takes place best in actual reading situations.

The remaining principles of remediation, although important, are not unalterable, as occasions will arise when they will not completely apply.

Remediation should result in skill development.

It is not unusual to hear of remedial programs which are tutorial in nature, implying that the instruction is designed to enable the child to be successful with a given material in a given classroom situation. Although we are interested in the child's success in the classroom, the remedial program should be designed to develop the reading skills in which the child has demonstrated a deficiency, not merely to help him get through tomorrow's class session. The child should not become solely dependent upon remedial sessions for his daily school success.

Remediation should be flexible.

While applying the remedial program prescribed by the diagnosis, the teacher should remain willing to adjust to the occasionally changing needs of the child. His original procedures may be found to be less effective than desired, creating a further need for flexibility. Since diagnostic findings are not completely formulated until after remediation has commenced, flexibility is required.

Remediation should be conducted in terms of established goals.

This principle is based upon the diagnostic conclusion that the child has an area of weakness and that the goal of remediation is to correct that weakness. Regardless of the flexibility in technique, the ultimate goal should be retained and a conscious effort made to achieve it. The immediate goals of remediation are usually stated in terms of desired skill development. Normally, remedial efforts will cease when a child demonstrates that he has overcome his skill deficiency.

Remediation involves cooperation.

The remedial program is seldom the responsibility of one person. More commonly, it requires an interaction between the reading specialist, the classroom teacher, medical personnel, specialists outside the educational field, parents, and school officials. One-man programs, particularly for the severely retarded child, are unnecessarily limiting.

Types of Remediation

Remediation falls into the same three categories as does diagnosis. The reader will find his remedial role more clearly defined as he gains an understanding of each category.

On-the-spot remediation. The type of adjustment made daily by a teacher to the needs of his children is on-the-spot remediation. Based upon informal diagnosis, its characteristics are: 1. It is conducted immediately; 2. It is pinpointed to a directly observable limitation; 3. It does not involve major adjustments in classroom instruction. On-the-spot remediation is a daily occurrence in effectively handled classrooms and is not to be emphasized in this chapter since it is an integral part of good teaching.

Classroom remediation. Educational adjustments in the classroom resulting from classroom and/or clinical diagnosis are included in this type of remedial program. Although instruction is directed to the child with an established problem, the child remains in the classroom during remediation and continues to participate in normal classroom activities although instruction is often individualized. It differs from on-the-spot remediation in that it is a more formal, directed effort.

Clinical remediation. The child is removed from the classroom for instruction by the reading specialist in clinical remediation. It assumes individual or small group (one to five children) instruction directed towards problems that appear too difficult to cope with in a normal classroom situation. In this type of remediation, instructional efforts allow for more individualization.

Some clinical situations require the child to be removed from the school, as well as the classroom, to receive even more extensive analysis. Multi-disciplinary approaches are often used involving cooperation between the reading specialist, the medical doctor, the psychiatrist, the social worker, and others.

Clinical remediation in the following chapters refers only to the removal of the child from the classroom. While many of the approaches and materials discussed are appropriate to clinical situations in which the child is removed from the school, multi-disciplinary approaches are not discussed.

Remediation — How Does it Begin?

In remedial situations a frequent question is, "How do I begin?" For an answer to this question, the relationship of diagnosis to remediation must be clearly discerned. In order to *pinpoint* the problem reader's difficulties, the four major skill areas (orientation, sight vocabulary, word attack, comprehension) were carefully scrutinized and evaluated through a classroom or clinical diagnosis. In order to *correct* the problem reader's difficulty, these same four skill areas are re-examined, now in terms of the specific techniques and materials which may be effective in alleviating the deficiencies found in these skill areas. It is in this manner that a remedial program is established.

In initial remedial instruction, it is highly important to establish rapport and maintain the child's self respect. For these two reasons we suggest that one start remediation in the area of the child's strength, permitting him initial success and satisfaction. A lesson or two on strong skills can easily be developed into lessons in the area of weaknesses determined in the diagnosis. Time spent developing strengths should not be regarded as wasted, for it is through strengths that attitudes and interests are developed to assist the child when working on his weaknesses.

On the following pages, each skill area identified in chapter 4 is analyzed, providing suggestions for remedial techniques, materials, and motivation. Remedial suggestions for both the classroom teacher and the reading specialist are given, although oftentimes they apply equally to both classroom and clinical remediation. It must be understood that in this overlapping of techniques, clinical remediation continues to require that the child be removed from the classroom and that the instruction be intensified and personalized in small groups and/or individual situations.

Based on diagnosis, remediation must begin with emphasis upon a technique which the teacher feels will be most effective. The materials which a teacher has available to him must be adapted to the technique which he has chosen. Note that the approach is not reversed, i.e., the materials are not the first consideration and do not control the technique. If teachers permit materials to control their techniques, there is little use in a diagnosis and little opportunity to provide adequate remediation. The following remedial suggestions emphasize technique and are illustrated with materials that work well with the technique being suggested. Teachers will, no doubt, find other materials that work equally well with these suggestions. When the teacher does not have an appropriate material for use with a suggested technique, the alternatives are: (1) to adapt a material that is available even if it is not designed for such a purpose; (2) to construct materials, such as experience charts, which will suit the technique; or (3) to request that the school officials provide the necessary materials. In any case, the diagnosis and the resulting remedial suggestions are based upon techniques, not materials.

Summary

Once the classroom teacher or the reading specialist has the principles of remediation well in mind, he must formulate a remedial program. Once rapport has been established by working with the child in the area of his strengths, the remedial program will attempt to eliminate the child's skill weaknesses that have been indicated by the diagnosis.

6

Remediation Of Orientation Difficulties

It is generally acknowledged that children's orientation errors cannot be corrected by simply calling the errors to their attention. Remedial procedures in the area of orientation skills are most effective when they (1) help the child to feel the comfort and success that accompanies correct orientation and (2) provide practice to extend the skill into a habit.

Remedial Techniques

The following remedial techniques are designed to correct specific deficiencies in the orientation skill area. The answers to the following questions established the precise skill area deficiency in diagnosis; therefore, attention to these same questions leads us to the appropriate remedial techniques.

1. Does the child exhibit visual difficulty in following the print from left to right?
2. Were the orientation errors basically ones of habitual reversals?
3. Were words habitually omitted without destroying context?
4. Was the symptom one in which the child habitually lost his place?

The reader will recall that the symptoms suggested by these four questions are highly related at times in that they all pertain to the organizational attack of the page of print. As a result, remedial techniques are often quite similar. We have differentiated these areas in an effort, however, to make remediation as precise as possible.

The *failure to move left to right* is a problem that can normally be traced to a faulty habit and, therefore, is usually alleviated by concentrated practice to correct the habit. Many suggestions for improved left to right movement across the printed page are available in the manuals of the basal readers. The following specific suggestions have worked well with children who need more practice than that suggested in these manuals.

Classroom remediation. All opportunities for writing experience should be utilized with children who have this difficulty. It is through writing that a child can clearly see the necessity of the left to right formation of words across the line. The child should observe the teacher as he writes on the board, and for those children able to write for themselves, every opportunity should be given for them to do so.

Illustrating to the child that sentences themselves involve a left-to-right progression of words is an excellent means of reinforcing orientation concepts. An initial approach would be to have the child reproduce sentences containing his own sight words, thereby actively involving the child in developing effective left to right sequence. An understanding of this concept is demonstrated when the child is able to create his own sentences from his resource of sight words. The *Rolling Readers**, which present basic sight words in a game-like situation, are readily adaptable to this technique.

Although it is generally considered undesirable for a child to point to words as he reads, there is some advantage to permitting a child with this type of difficulty to follow a line of print left to right across the page with his finger. In this respect, the finger is used as a crutch until the *habit* of left to right eye movements can be more fully developed.

Another opportunity in the classroom to work with children with this type of problem is through the utilization of choral reading activities. A dividend added to obvious advantages of choral reading is the child's opportunity, in a group, to experience a feeling for the flow of words from left to right.

Clinical remediation. Each of the above mentioned techniques, readily usable in the classroom, is of equal value in clinical situations.

---

*See Appendix B.

Specifically appropriate for clinical use are various instruments which may be used to control the child's visual exposure to printed material, thus regulating his left to right eye movements. The *Controlled Reader,** one such device, has a setting which exposes the film upon which a story is written in a carefully regulated, left-to-right manner. Although practice with this type of device develops a feeling for proper eye movements, it must be followed with reading in book-type material, for the reading situations created by such devices lack normalcy.

The Controlled Reader. *(Photograph Courtesy of Educational Developmental Laboratories)*

The *Leavell Language Development Service** and the *Delacato Stereo-Reader Service,** are stereoscopic devices which can be used to assist the child having an orientation difficulty complicated by confused hand-eye

*See Appendix B.

dominance to develop more systematic left-to-right movements. Both of these devices force the child to use the eye which corresponds with his dominant hand, creating a situation in which better hand-eye coordination may be developed. Although these devices have gained considerable clinical acceptance, children with certain visual defects should be permitted to use these techniques only with the approval of the visual specialist. The child who has symptoms of visual difficulty should, of course, be referred, and this type of remediation must await the pending report. (See Non-Educational Diagnosis, page 47, for visual symptoms.)

Tachistoscopic* devices, designed to flash words and groups of words at a pre-determined rate, also have value with children with this type of difficulty. Prepared tachistoscopic materials generally have figures, letters, or words which permit non-readers, as well as children with some reading skills, to participate in these activities. The words are flashed at a rate of 1/5 to 1/10 of a second and the child must react to the word, signifying that he knows it. As has been mentioned before, all drill of this nature must be transferred to context for effective utilization.

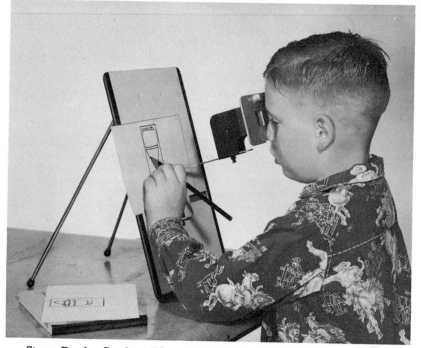

Stereo-Reader Service. *(Photograph courtesy of Keystone View Co.)*

The *Tendency to Reverse Letters, Words, and Phrases.*
This is one of the common orientation difficulties, particularly with young problem readers. Different from following left to right across a line, reversals involve appropriate left to righ progression in words and phrases within a line. The child must not only consciously attack words left to right but develop it into a habit.

Classroom remediation. Kindergarten and first grade teachers should emphasize directional progression both directly and subtly. Through writing on the board in front of children and calling their attention to the direction that the letters flow to make a word, children have opportunities to grasp this concept. The children may also write on the board for there is less tendency to make directional errors when doing board work. The correct response may be reinforced by permitting the child to write very large letters at his seat. It should be noted that this is a more difficult concept for some children to grasp than the left to right movement across the line of print, especially when the whole word techniques have been stressed in initial instruction.

The writing of easily confused words either at the board or at the child's seat, reinforces with a sense of touch the left to right progression within words. Phonics lessons also provide opportunity for the reinforcement of proper progression through words, particularly in initial and final consonant substitution activities where the position of the letters in words is emphasized. In phonics lessons where stress is being placed upon the initial sounds in words, it is often possible to place words on the board illustrating the similarities or differences in the initial sounds. This, of course, emphasizes the left-to-right concept as it applies to word attack.

Spelling class, where the concept of the position of the letters in each word is of primary importance, is considered an excellent time for reinforcing the proper image of the word for children with this deficiency. Through the spelling of confused words the teacher is able to reinforce the proper sequence of letters in a silent situation.

These children may also be encouraged to trace the words that are missed so that they may feel the left-to-right progression. When groups of children display this difficulty, imaginary tracing of the letters in the air can achieve much the same results. As the children trace the word, they are expected to pronounce it properly; if they cannot do this, the problem is more likely one of an inadequate sight vocabulary.

Clinical remediation. Familiarization with the left to right progression concept within words and phrases is extended through more individualized efforts in clinical remediation. A child dictating an experience story to the reading specialist can watch as the words are written; then, as the child reads the story, there is opportunity again for the left-to-right reinforcement of words missed.

In the preceding situation, it is quite often advisable to apply the *Kinesthetic Technique*[1]. In short, this technique involves the following:

1. The child is exposed to the word symbol and its pronunciation. (The fact that these words are usually taken from the child's experience stories implies that he knows their meanings.)

2. The child is directed to trace the word while saying it. (This tracing procedure is to be repeated until there appears to be confidence within the child that he actually has mastered the word. The teacher demonstrates as often as necessary when beginning this approach.) Fernald notes that finger contact with the letters is essential, especially in these early stages.

3. The child then writes the word with the copy in sight. Again he is instructed to say the word as he writes it.

4. The child is then directed to reproduce the word without the copy, again pronouncing it as he says it. When starting with a situation involving an experience story, the child returns to attack the word properly in his own story. It should be noted that this technique is not one in which the child spells the word or sounds the letters; rather, it is a whole word technique where the child pronounces the word as a unit. The advantages of the tracing technique are not limited to orientation skills; other uses will be seen under sight vocabulary and word attack where a more detailed explanation is presented.

The reading specialist may find several variations of this technique useful depending upon the materials available. Some prefer that all tracing be done in sand; some prefer to use the blackboard; others feel that tracing the word in large copy is entirely adequate. Regardless of the system, the left-to-right progression of the words is reinforced, and the child, sensing the total results of his efforts, does pronounce the word properly when it is transferred to context.

Three-dimensional letter blocks are available commercially or can be made in a woodshop. The blocks should have one rough surface (the top

---

[1]Grace Fernald, *Remedial Techniques in Basic School Subjects* (New York: McGraw Hill Book Co., Inc., 1943), Chap. V.

side) made of sandpaper or the like. The child is told to examine the block letters and build words from printed copy, trace them, and pronounce them, thus having the reinforcement of touch added to his learning skills in this manner.

*The Delacato Stereo Reader Service** has a set of prepared cards which are of particular value when used with children who have a combination of mixed dominance and reversal tendencies. In this situation the reading specialist places the appropriate card on the side of the Stereo Reader which corresponds to the child's hand preference. The child then reads the card, indicating his knowledge of: 1. the placement of abstract symbols in various left-to-right positions; and 2. the placement of words in their proper left-to-right pattern.

The reading specialist, as did the classroom teacher, will find many opportunities in other reading activities to reinforce left-to-right progressions through words. It goes without saying that every opportunity should be explored.

———————————

Tendency to omit words without distorting context.

Omissions are generally made unknowingly. Therefore, the first remedial activity in the classroom and clinical remediation is to call the child's attention to the fact that although his error has *not* interfered with his comprehension, his reading has *not* been accurate. It should be understood that, in these cases, we assume that the children have read the words prior to pronouncing them and, while not distorting the context, have failed to recall the precise words of the author.

Classroom remediation. Effective utilization may be made of a tape recorder for children with this type of difficulty. Having taped a selection of oral reading, the child listens carefully to the tape while following the story with his eyes. He then marks each word he discovers that he has omitted. Children are generally surprised to find that they make the number of omissions that they do. A child then attempts to reread the story without omitting any words; again he listens to the tape while following the story; again he marks his errors. We often find that once alerted to this type of error, the child is able to make conscious corrections. This technique may need to be repeated several times to develop satisfactory performance.

If this does not seem to develop the desired understanding, the teacher can read and have the child follow in a book. In this case, the

———————————

*See Appendix B.

teacher is to make intentional omissions, and the child is to mark them. The taping of this reading provides an opportunity to go over the child's markings, calling his attention to the specific errors. Listening stations, designed to permit several children to listen to oral reading on one tape without disturbing others, have been used to great advantage for these purposes.

Many children who commit omissions read unusually fast, perhaps in an effort to conceal their errors. The classroom teacher may urge such children to slow their reading speed in an effort to be more accurate. This is one of the few situations in remedial reading in which children are asked to read more slowly.

Phrase flash cards, used in sight vocabulary development, have application to this difficulty in that a child is taught to become aware of the order of commonly used, small groups of words. These cards having a left-to-right aspect, enhance the child's orientation skills even when used for other purposes.

Clinical remediation. The above mentioned approaches are all applicable to clinical remediation with particular stress on the use of the tape recorder. The tape recorder is popular in clinical situations because there is generally more opportunity for closer teacher assistance.

Prepared *Tachistoscopic Slides* of the most commonly used words, (based on Dolch's list)*, are available in phrases and may be used with children having this specific deficiency. Flashed at rates of 1/5 or 1/10 of a second, the child is provided practice in accurate word identification of common groupings. An omission in this area calls for more practice followed by transfer of the learned skills to the printed page.

Controlled exposure devices, such as the *Controlled Reader,** are useful in these cases also. By controlling the amount of print exposed, the eye-voice span is also controlled, facilitating emphasis upon the words as they appear sequentially in the story. Omission errors will usually decrease with the use of these materials; however, activities must again be developed to provide the transfer from these types of devices to normal reading from books. As a rule, we would say that every controlled reading exercise should be followed by reading from a book. This transfer step is extremely important, and over-learning is inherent in the process.

Habitual losing of one's place in reading might be a visual problem; therefore, it would first be advisable to check for signs of ocular difficulty

---

*See Appendix B.

manifested by other symptoms (see page 115). If there is not indication that the difficulty is visual, the child should be given instruction in techniques to help maintain his place while reading.

Classroom remediation. Many children who habitually lose their place are aware of having done so; however, if the child remains unaware of his difficulty, instruction will likely be ineffective. A child's failure to maintain his place while reading may be illustrated by the use of the tape recorder as it was used in noting omissions.

There is a tendency for children who have this difficulty to point with their finger to the words while they are reading. This is normally considered an undesirable crutch; however, if it keeps the child from losing his place, it is better than having him floundering. The classroom teacher should attempt to assist the child to break away from *unnecessary* finger pointing. First, he can have the child point to each line in an attempt to break away from the emphasis on words. Secondly, he can permit the child to hold the line with a card until he develops the habit of reading through the line without losing his place.

Clinical remediation. Although it is possible that the techniques mentioned above can be used in clinical remediation, it is more likely that the reading specialist will make a direct attempt to correct the child's problem without such crutches.

Pacing devices, which control the child's exposure to the page, have some usefulness with this type of problem, for they give the child a feeling for fluent, uninterrupted reading. For older students, films such as those provided with the *Controlled Reader** and *Iowa Films** are also available. Using these, the student is able to concentrate more fully on the concepts in the story because the controlled exposure lessens the possibility of his losing his place. The limitation of both of these types of devices is that, in the actual reading act, the child alone is responsible for keeping his place; he will not have a mechanical instrument to assist him.

Pacing devices can be used with the child's books by regulating his reading through the movement of a shield down the page to cover the print. It should be remembered that these machines are basically designed for speed reading exercises, and since that is not the objective in this case, the rate of operation of the machine should be at an easy pace

---

*See Appendix B.

for the children to handle. The *Reading Accelerator** and the *Rateometer** are two popular examples of pacing devices.

Rateometer. *(Photograph Courtesy of Audio-Visual Research)*

A modified pacing device, the *Delacato Stereo Reader,** may provide the child with a similar type of controlled experience. The modification in this case is the child's control of the pacing device. He can stop it, reread the passage, and practice the type of reading he will eventually be expected to do in other reading situations.

Extended remediation

The extension of diagnosis by the reading specialist establishes two additional areas for remedial consideration. Normally this remediation

---

*See Appendix B.

is conducted by the reading specialist and occasionally by the classroom teacher, upon the recommendations of the reading specialist. These two areas are eye motion in the act of reading and confused lateral dominance.

When physical disabilities have been ruled out and eye motion difficulties prevail, the reading specialist must evaluate whether the faulty eye motion results from a lack of orientation skills which have developed into faulty habits or whether they are due to weaknesses in sight vocabulary and/or word attack skills. Excessive fixations and regressions are the symptoms of orientation difficulties, which concern the reading specialist.

Specific suggestions to improve fixations have been given above; however, upon the completion of the diagnostic evaluation, one must give more careful attention to situations in which eye motions can be controlled and developed. Basically, every effort will be made to develop the ability to fixate upon words properly and to minimize the habit of unusual numbers of regressions. It has been found that regressions tend to diminish as maturity in reading skills develops. Specific information concerning the number of regressions found in normal reading can be found in the manual for the *Reading Eye*[2]. When the child indicates symptoms of visual discomfort, the task of analyzing the cause of his difficulty with fixations and regressions falls to the vision specialist. Remediation, in these cases, will be based upon the report and recommendations of the vision specialist. Again we must be aware that the child, not likely to be aware of his faulty eye motion, needs first to develop the feeling of proper eye motion. For these purposes, the controlled exposure devices previously mentioned are of particular value. When diagnosis points to visual directional confusion as the basic limitation, the program that has been designed by Frostig[3] may prove to be very helpful. In this program the visual perception skills are divided into five developmental stages, with exercises designed to lead the child through these stages. Of particular importance are those skills relating to directional confusion. According to Frostig, approximately twenty to twenty-five percent of children starting the first grade are deficient enough in directional confusion to profit from the experiences that this program provides. Older children of any grade level can use these materials when the diagnosis warrants.

Confused or mixed lateral dominance causes problems of consider-

---

[2]Stanford Taylor, Manual, Reading Eye, *Eye Movement Photography with the Reading Eye* (Huntington, N.Y.: Educational Developmental Laboratories, 1960).

[3]Marianne Frostig and David Horse, *The Frostig Program for the Development of Visual Perception* (Chicago: Follett Publishing Co., 1964).

able controversy. Avoiding this controversy, we simply say that it is the remedial obligation of the reading specialist to establish as comfortable a reading situation for the child as possible; therefore, when mixed lateral dominance is accompanied by other symptoms of orientation disability, efforts should be made to establish comfortable dominance situations, i.e., situations in which the child has the habit of using the same hand and eye. This does not involve the changing of hand or eye dominance, nor does it cause a situation in which the child should be overconcerned about this characteristic; rather a child can be exposed to brief periods of training with either the *Leavell Language Development Service** or the *Delcato Stereo Reader Service** in each remedial lesson. The remediation conducted with either of these instruments should be correlated to work in the other three skill areas whenever possible. The whole purpose of this type of exercise is to permit a child to sense the comfort that a strongly dominant person normally senses in reading. This theory has, in our experience, produced desirable results. It is particularly important that the reading specialist not conduct extended remediation in this area without the approval of the vision specialist, who may be able to provide another reason for the child's apparent mixed dominance. The application of these techniques by the classroom teacher is generally considered impractical.

Motivation

The classroom teacher and the reading specialist must be alert to the fact that the child needs to have a sense of accomplishing something worthwhile during orientation exercises. In fact, many of these drills are at a very elementary level and may hold little appeal to older remedial students. Therefore, the child should be led to understand the possible results of this type of activity. We have found that older children readily accept this type of mature approach, but one must show the child that desired outcomes are possible. Other techniques for motivating the child to work diligently in this area are: to devise charts denoting progress to illustrate to the child his skill improvement; to establish measures of the child's efficiency for a pre and post comparison; to use the tape recorder at regular intervals throughout the program; and, in general, to comply with the first three principles of remediation.

---

*See Appendix B.

Summary

It is imperative in the initial stages of the remedial program that the classroom teacher and the reading specialist see their respective roles as complementary. The principles which guide remediation have been established through experience; to disregard any of these would render instruction less effective.

Orientation deficiencies should be dealt with before remedial work in other skill areas is undertaken, for the patterns developed in the orientation program are basic and carry over into the other skill areas.

Suggested Readings

1. Fernald, Grace, *Remedial Techniques in Basic School Subjects,* Chap. V. New York: McGraw Hill Book Co., Inc., 1943. The advantages and specific techniques of the tracing technique are presented on these pages by Fernald. The reader will find this presentation interesting and complete.
2. Monroe, Marion and Bernice Rogers, *Foundations for Reading,* Chaps. I-V. Chicago: Scott Foresman and Co., 1964. The author's have presented a series of chapters relating to the beginning processes of reading. The educator who is attempting remediation without a thorough understanding of this initial process will find this reading very profitable.
3. Kephart, Newell C., *The Slow Learner in the Classroom.* Columbus, Ohio: Charles E. Merrill Books, Inc., 1960. The reader will find interesting reading, covering completely the motor readiness needs of youngsters. Particular attention is given to motor skills, which the author sees as related to success in learning.
4. Roach, Eugene, and Newell C. Kephart, *The Purdue Perceptual-Motor Survey.* Columbus, Ohio: Charles E. Merrill Books, Inc., 1966. A survey to help identify non-achiever problems of a perceptual-motor nature.

7

Remediation Of Vocabulary Difficulties

Remediation for children with vocabulary deficiencies will be considered under the two broad categories of sight vocabulary and word attack. The decision as to which category applies to a specific child will have been determined by specific diagnostic considerations.

Remediation of Sight Vocabulary Difficulties

Sight vocabulary involves the skills of instant word pronunciation and word meaning. While the remedial approaches in the area of sight vocabulary deficiencies are presented in terms of the questions asked in diagnosis, it must be remembered that the end goal of sight vocabulary is the decoding and association of the word in a line of print, in a sentence or in a paragraph, not in isolation.

In direct reply to the questions asked under the diagnosis of sight vocabulary difficulties, remedial procedures will be developed. Specifically, those questions were:

1. Does the child miss small, similar words, or does he falter on words that are obviously different?
2. Do the words missed represent concrete or abstract concepts?
3. Does he know the word in isolation but not in context?
4. Does he pronounce the word properly but fail to associate it with the correct meaning?

5. Is the error one in which the child eventually pronounces the word but not without due hesitation?

These deficiencies seldom appear alone; rather, they are inter-related. The purpose in establishing the answers to the questions is to determine in which areas the inter-relationship has taken place and to emphasize those areas in remediation. Through examination it can clearly be seen, for example, that words of minimal meaning differences are often words with abstract meanings, requiring dual remedial considerations.

The language experience approach

Throughout this and the following chapters, considerable emphasis will be placed upon the language experience approach. An understanding of the facets of this approach will assist the reader as he works through the various remedial suggestions. It operates as follows:

1. An experience upon which the child is to develop a story is selected. This experience may be personal, derived from the group, or extrinsic to him based upon a motivating picture, object, or selection of music. As the child's conceptual background is developed, the child finds a need to express these ideas in words.
2. So that the child is not handicapped by having to write the words he pronounces, the teacher may perform this task, leaving the child free to use any words in his speaking vocabulary.
3. Through a cooperative teacher-student effort, the story is read and changes are made only if the student feels they are necessary.
4. The resulting product should be typed or printed clearly for the child to use immediately.
5. Of primary interest is the child's ability to decode his story and read it with expression. As the story contains his words and concepts, it is assumed that he is able to relate them to his experiences. Troublesome words and phrases provide opportunity to develop meaningful word attack and sight vocabulary exercises.
6. These stories may be collected and formed into a booklet for the child to use in future activities. Parents often appreciate reading and discussing the stories with their children.
7. Opportunities for the enrichment of these stories should be used. Related materials can be used to enhance the child's concepts and reinforce his sight vocabulary. The use of adjectives can be devel-

oped, for example, by asking the child to describe an object or incident more fully.

The reader will want to check the suggested readings at the end of this chapter for more information concerning this approach.

Does the child miss small, similar words?

Or does he falter on words that are obviously different? Quite often problem readers will miss small words which are minimal in configuration differences, e.g., *when, where,* while effectively attacking larger and more obviously different words, e.g., *elephant* and *Christmas.* The former is considered a problem in sight vocabulary, while the latter is normally considered a problem in word attack, especially if the large words missed are at or below the institutional level.

Classroom remediation. Special efforts must be made to be certain that the child receives instruction in the discrimination of words that are minimally different. Most appropriately, these exercises should be conducted in phrase and sentence form, so that the child's attention is called to the fact that the minimal difference distorts not only the pronunciation of the word but the meaning of the words as well: "We took the dig (instead of "dog") for a walk." To clarify these similarities and differences in minimally different words, it is sometimes feasible to pull these words from context for study. (*dig-dog*). Any exercise, however, which concludes with the word in isolation is in error, for drills should always be followed by return to context.

Programmed materials which are particularly adaptable to the classroom for use in this type of skill deficiency have been prepared. When formulated by qualified persons, these materials can lead the child to observe the differences made by particular words which are alike except for minimal differences, e.g., *hat* and *bat.* An example of these materials, *Programmed Reading**, contains a series of exercises through which the child can develop skill with a minimum amount of teacher supervision. The child is forced into a closure activity by these exercises. Note the sample page below. The child must look at the pictures, read the sentence or partial sentence, and use closure to obtain the correct code and message. These exercises develop from the elementary type seen below to complete stories. The forced choice closure concept is maintained at all levels.

---

*See Appendix B.

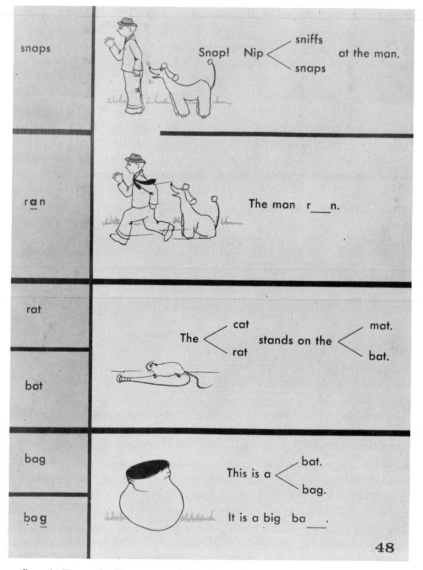

Sample Page of a Programmed Reader. *(Photograph with Permission of Webster Division, McGraw Hill)*

The child is further reinforced by the correct answer after each frame or after each page, depending upon how much material the teacher feels the child can handle without reinforcement. The skills developed in the workbooks are transferred to reading from prepared *Storybooks**, containing stories with minimally different words. Although it is unlikely that these materials will satisfy the total reading needs of the child, they are particularly useful in the correction of this type of skill deficiency.

In the early grades, the teacher may utilize opportunities while working with experience charts to illustrate the need for careful visual discrimination of minimally different words. In these situations, the teacher will take every opportunity to emphasize how words of similar configuration actually differ in both form and meaning, using the child's own language contributions. It may be noted that this is a desirable technique for all children to experience; therefore, it should not be limited to a child with this deficiency alone.

Clinical remediation. Due to the adaptability to individualized instruction, it should be obvious that the techniques utilized in the classroom are equally usable in clinical remediation.

For children with this deficiency, the concepts inherent in the linguistic approach have definite advantages. Adaptations can be developed to almost any type of material. The programmed materials mentioned above illustrate adaptations of the linguistic approach. The *Let's Read Books** and *The Merrill Linguistic Readers** are carefully prepared linguistic materials for beginning reading, appropriate for individualized instruction for children with serious reading problems. Both of these approaches have in common: (1) a controlled vocabulary of minimally different words; (2) the controlled initial presentation of words with consistent vowel and consonant sounds; and (3) no pictures, therefore requiring correct visual perception for accurate decoding. Another similar approach, *The Linguistic Readers**, varies somewhat from those mentioned above but does maintain the necessity for visual perception of minimal differences. If the use of these particular materials does not appeal to the reading specialist, it should be obvious that the *concept* of the linguistic approach has advantages for certain children and adaptations of it may be made.

_____

Do the words missed represent abstract concepts?

It is common for children to find it particularly difficult to remember words which represent abstract concepts, e.g., *when, these, if, those.* Emphasis in remediation for children with this type of difficulty should

_____

*See Appendix B.

focus on the word as it appears in context, for it is from context that the function of these words can be understood. Furthermore, since there is seldom a reading situation in which these words are used in isolation, they should not be taught in isolation.

Classroom remediation. Once again, experience story approaches are of particular value in the development of this type of reading sight vocabularly. Children use these words to formulate their experience stories, providing a natural opportunity for instruction in the service and function of these words as the child uses them. Although the experience story approach will probably be used more frequently with the younger problem reader, considerable success with this type of approach may be found with older students as well, particularly if they have this skill deficiency. It is in experience story reading that we can be certain that all words used have a meaning for the child since they are his contributions. Through these materials, the use and nature of abstract words can be effectively illustrated to the child.

Due to the nature of these words, it is advisable that the initial introduction take place in a contextual situation. Applicable to the teaching of all children, this phase of classroom remediation will not require that the child be instructed alone.

Sight vocabulary drill with abstract concepts are most effective when in phrases, e.g., *in a good spirit.* Prepared phrase cards with the more commonly used word combinations are available in the *Dolch Game** series. There is little or not justification for sight word drill with these words in isolations, for when they are extracted from context, any meaning the word contains is lost.

Clinical remediation. In clinical remediation, individualized emphasis will be placed on the same techniques used in the classroom. A particularly useful technique for clinical remediation with this type of child is the experience story; the resulting activity is used as it is in the classroom. However, in clinical remediation, a more direct teacher effort can be made to obtain maximum results.

After a certain amount of sight vocabulary has been developed, children with more serious reading problems may build sentences from word cards. Here, emphasis should be placed upon the function of the abstract word as created by the student. With this activity the unknown word is not placed in a definition situation; rather, it appears in a functional situ-

---

*See Appendix B.

ation, the sentence. Intentional distortions of these types of words in context may be used to illustrate their importance. Here a child is directed to substitute so as to distort the author's meaning and then to indicate an awareness of how the author's flow of meaning and ideas have been changed.

Does the child know the word in isolation, but not in context?

A word which appears in isolation on the chalkboard may be recognized more accurately than is the same word when it appears in context surrounded by other words.

ran

The child *ran* to the store.

However, the reading act requires use of the latter example. With this type of deficiency, remedial approaches in the classroom and in the clinic do not differ, for the emphasis is on placing sight vocabulary exercises in context. Whether through the use of experience stories, sentences obtained from prepared materials, or sentences created by the teacher, *all* drill for children with this deficiency must begin with the word as it appears in context and end in the same manner. Children who are seriously crippled by this deficiency may have the word in question highlighted or emphasized in some manner, but it would be the exception which would justify taking this word from context to develop sight vocabulary, for it has already been established that the child knows the word in isolation. For the emphasis desired, the word may be framed by the hands, underlined, marked in different color, or some such technique; but since it remains in the sentence, the child is ever alert to that function of the word. Most of the difficulty with this type of reading problem can be prevented by the application of all drill to context, even in the earliest reading instruction. If, from the beginning, the child obtains the concept that words are learned to be used in sentence, this difficulty is less likely to arise.

A group technique for these children can be of value to all. Each child uses a given word in a sentence and places the sentence on the back of a card. These are collected and redistributed providing other children a chance to read a given child's responses. Activities of this type develop an active feeling for the use of the word in context.

Can he pronounce the word he sees in print but fails to associate it with the correct meaning?

Remedial instruction in this very important area must be precluded by the following two considerations:

1. There are situations in which children, for one reason or another, fail to develop a background of experiences which permits them to associate properly the meaning with the word they have pronounced. If this deficiency is chronic, remediation will of necessity consist of experiential language development, rather than instruction in sight vocabulary.

2. We find numerous children who have little trouble pronouncing the words they see in print. Although they know the meaning of the word and can use it in a sentence, these children fail to associate the word with the correct meaning due, apparently, to preoccupation with word pronunciation. Remedial activities with these children, then, are in the area of sight vocabulary where they must be taught to be conscious of what the word *says* as well as how it *sounds*.

Classroom remediation. As has been stated previously, every word drill should end with the word in context. In this way, the precise meaning and function of the word are best understood; children with this deficiency must have context emphasized even more precisely.

The child begins by reading easy material which allows him to demonstrate his knowledge of the word in question by paraphrasing the author's words. Specific mention of this technique will be discussed under the answer to the question (p. 170) on paraphrasing in comprehension remediation.

It is often useful to establish whether the child knows the meaning of the word through definition. If he does, it is not the meaning of the word as such that is causing the problem, but the use of the word in a particular contextual situation. The presentation of the word in various settings is then appropriate.

Since children already understand the meaning of the pronounced words, experience stories using the child's own wording again play an important role in remedial efforts. We hope that teachers of elementary school children will provide numerous opportunities for group experience stories in which there is an association between the experiences of the group and the words which represent those experiences. This is a golden opportunity to create the situation so often observed in which children learn from other children better than they do from adults. Frequently we find other children reacting better to the responses of their peers than to teacher efforts. Competition must be held to a minimum and, although children will learn from each other, efforts must be made during remediation to be certain that there is peer group rapport and that differences between the children do not become the issue.

There are numerous opportunities for the classroom teacher to provide directed exercises in word meaning through a study of synomyms and antonyms. Drills of this type usually involve the collection of lists of synonyms and/or antonyms and their usages. Emphasis, of course, is upon the similarities in the meanings of the words, and children with association skill deficiency will find this drill to be particuarly profitable.

Although frequently not included as a remedial technique, the use of the dictionary is of particular assistance to older students. Their knowledge of the correct pronunciation of the word in print permits them to use the dictionary to find meanings efficiently; it may, incidentally, develop a habit of consulting the dictionary for unknown words. Techniques for use with the dictionary are discussed under the heading of word attack skills.

It is well to talk about building a child's experiences to develop listening and speaking vocabularies, but it is another thing to build such a program. The *Peabody Language Development Kits** contain programs for 180 lessons in language development. The teacher may find this type of program to be a guide for the entire school year. The experiences included with this kit are: following directions, brainstorming, critical thinking, memory, rhyming, listening, etc. Pictures, objects, and tapes are used to enrich the child's experimental background.

The *Ginn Language Kit* A* provides the teacher with another program for language development. The Ginn Kit consists of pictures through which language can be stimulated.

Clinical remediation. For the child seriously handicapped with this type of deficiency, the *Non-Oral Reading** approach may contain the requisites for initial clinical instruction. This approach by-passes completely the vocalization of the printed word and emphasizes instead the word's association with a pictured concept. The child's task is to match the printed symbol with a picture representing the concept for that symbol. This direct association from print to concept minimizes pronunciation for children who have been over-drilled in it.

The reading specialist will also find it useful to have the child respond directly through physical activity to printed word commands—"jump up,

*See Appendix B.

shake hands," etc. This approach also minimizes vocalization of the printed word, emphasizing again the meaning of the word through the child's response. The *Nichols Tachistoscope Slides**, developed for this purpose, appear to be effective in establishing the concepts of word meaning.

The reading specialist may also use initial sight vocabulary exercises consisting of nouns, adjectives, and verbs which can be pictured. The *Dolch Picture Word Cards**, containing 96 of these types of words, may be used. Several matching-type games are available, in which a child is physically involved by matching a picture with a printed word, indicating his understanding of the meaning of the word. A game-like activity, this approach is self-motivating. *Picture Word Puzzles** provides similar reinforcement with children having association deficiencies.

Active participation can be achieved by having the child build sentences from the words which he knows. After known words are placed on cards, the cards are scrambled, and the child is asked (1) to build a specific sentence or (2) to build a sentence of his choosing. The *Linguistic Block Series** can be used in the same manner, using the blank block for words in the child's personal vocabulary.

Is the error one in which the child eventually pronounces the word, but not without undue hesitation?

Remedial techniques used to correct this deficiency require some type of timed or flashed exposure of the word in order to illustrate to the child the necessity and possibility for instant recognition.

Classroom remediation. The major emphasis in the classroom is likely to be in the use of flashcards containing the sight words either alone or in a phrase. The classroom teacher, assured that the word is already known, is assisting the child to realize that the word can be recognized without undue hesitation. When instant recognition has been accomplished in flash card drill, the placement of the word in contextual situations is again desirable.

Many children appear to be hesitant when they are, in reality, not making a serious, concentrated effort as they work. With these children, reasonable time limits for the completion of the task should be set and adhered to as much as possible. It is often possible to set shorter term goals which will enable this child to see his way more clearly to the end

----

*See Appendix B.

of the established goal, thus permitting him to work more efficiently. Here, of course, our goal is not speed reading; it is merely the efficient use of time in the act of reading.

Clinical remediation. The reading specialist is likely to use mechanical devices such as the *Tachistoscope** or the *Flash X** to accomplish the same ends as the classroom teacher. This does not preclude the use of flashcards in any clinical situation, but we have found that children seriously limited in this respect seem to enjoy the motivation provided by machine-type devices. With both of these devices, it is possible to make slides from lists of words with which the child has demonstrated difficulty. These home-made slides are preferable for children with this deficiency. Again, it is best to place the words used in these techniques into context for quick recognition at the end of every lesson.

Because of the nature of clinical remediation situations, it is often easy to identify the child who is not working efficiently. Every effort should be made to help this child realize the need for efficiency in use of working time. Proper emphasis here may be placed upon the completion of a reading task in a reasonable time period rather than upon words per minute. It can be noted that children who are working to meet a words-per-minute criterion often make *that* their major goal and de-emphasize comprehension. Use of the *SRA Laboratory** (rate builders), in which a story must be read and questions answered in a relatively short period of time, provides useful practice of a desired type. Using easy material, the child should adhere to established time limitations.

When mechanical motivation is desired, another use for the *Controlled Reader** is found; however, the child must work with material he can recognize if he is to be able to perform within reasonable time restrictions. It is essential, therefore, that the use of the *Controlled Reader* to increase speed of recognition must be at recreational reading levels.

Additional Considerations in Sight Vocabulary

The following aspects of remediation in the area of sight vocabulary should be carefully understood by any person conducting remediation in this area:

_____

The need to tell the child the word. The teacher will find many situations in which it is advisable to tell the child an unknown word. Although

_____

*See Appendix B.

we would not normally suggest this with words upon which the child has worked, he will often be in situations where he simply does not have the skills needed to attack unknown words. In these cases, telling him the word will permit him to move along with the context of the story, focusing his attention on those words for which he has the skills to attack effectively. In such cases the teacher need not feel guilty about telling children words, nor should he make the child feel this way. Instead, this will be a needed technique in the situations described above and should be understood as such. In other situations, the remedial teacher is justified in being reluctant to tell children words.

The need for overlearning. The very nature of sight vocabulary (instant recognition and meaning) implies that it must be overlearned. Overlearning is not best conducted in isolated drill activities; rather, it is most effective when the child has opportunities to use the word again and again in context. Many remedial efforts fail because they do not provide for the overlearning of sight vocabulary words in context. Experience stories, trade books, game, and similar materials are available to facilitate transfer for children with the most serious limitations.

Motivation techniques

The often subtle development of power in sight vocabulary needs to be illustrated to the problem reader so that he may be encouraged by his progress. The following techniques have been found to be particularly motivating to certain types of children:

1. Transferring every lesson to contextual situations illustrates to the child that the work he is doing in sight vocabulary is, in effect, making him a better reader. Particularly with older children, this in itself is often ample motivation.

2. Recording of experience stories in booklet form is of interest to younger students, for they can see progress merely by the quantity of the material which they have been able to learn to read. The sight vocabulary implications of that quantity can be pointed out as needed to the child.

3. Charts illustrating the goals toward which the child will work in sight vocabulary seem to trigger some children to better performance. Ultimately it is desirable that intrinsic motivation fulfill the function of such charts.

4. Sight vocabulary cards maintained in a file or on a ring illustrate

visually to the child that he has accumulated a number of useful words through which he can become a better reader. These words should not be listed in isolation; rather, they should appear in a sentence with the word highlighted.

In several of the techniques above, games and mechanical devices have been suggested for teaching purposes. These appear to hold the child's interest and establish a degree of motivation, while assisting the child in learning his sight vocabulary.

Remediation of Word Attack Difficulties

Word attack skills include those techniques which enable a child to decode an unknown word so as to pronounce it and to understand it as it is used in contextual situations without teacher assistance.

Deficiencies in the area of word attack are the most outstanding weakness of problem readers. Consequently, there are many commercial materials available and many approaches recommended in the professional literature; the resulting abundance has often served to confuse, rather than to clarify, the preciseness of approaches in the area of word attack difficulties.

Children need word attack skills in order to read words without depending on teachers or parents. Remedial programs in word attack, then, should be designed to foster independence in reading, not merely proficiency in word attack drills.

Because there are various methods for attacking words not known at sight, educational efforts should focus on those word attack skills which assist the child to attack words most efficiently in terms of time, and most consistently in terms of application. Once overlearned, this efficiency should ultimately end with the same aim as did sight vocabulary, i.e., to decode the word and associate its meaning instantly to the context in which it occurs.

As indicated in the diagnosis of the problem reader, word attack falls into three major categories: phonic clues, structural clues, and contextual clues. The dictionary skills, the fourth category of word attack, not normally considered of remedial necessity, at times need development in remedial programs.

Phonic Analysis

Remedial efforts in the precise area of phonics will, again, be in terms of the questions asked following the establishment of word attack as the area of skill deficiency.

1. Is the problem basically the child's inability to discriminate auditorily?
2. When the child mispronounces or substitutes words, is there a pattern of vowel or consonant errors?
3. Does the child need instruction in the usage of known sounds?

Although in diagnosis the skills of phonics have been delegated to three precise areas (sounds of letters, syllabication, and blending), it is necessary that the remedial program combine these areas for instructional purposes. The functional use of phonic skills involves the ability of the child to divide the word into syllables, sound the letters, blend the sounds into a recognizable word, and check the derived pronunciation in the context from which the word was taken. Essential to the sounding of letters is the ability to discriminate auditorily the differences in the sounds. Remedial suggestions will deal with each of these areas in terms of questions presented in chapter IV.

Is the problem basically the child's inability to *discriminate auditorily?*

Classroom remediation. Precise speech patterns of the teacher are requisite to the proper learning of auditory discrimination skills. One of the first considerations in this program, therefore, will be a conscious attempt on the part of the teacher to vocalize her speech patterns as accurately as possible. In the event that the child has a speech deficiency, the classroom teacher may want to call upon the services of a speech therapist to assist in the development of proper speech patterns. Assistance from the speech therapist will normally include diagnosis of speech deficiencies, suggestions for the classroom teacher, and, perhaps, tutoring the child.

Rhyming games, in which the child is directed to listen to the similarities in word beginnings and endings, have long been popular in the development of auditory discrimination skills, and suggestions for such are found in the manuals of the various basal series. Game-like in nature, these activities can be conducted in the classroom to the advantage of all students, eliminating the necessity for individualizing instruction.

More formal word drills, presented in most basal series manuals, are designed to assist the child to discriminate auditorily words of minimal differences. These lessons generally include exercises which are designed to identify those areas of auditory discrimination most often confused by children and are usually quite helpful.

Many of the phonic approaches which are commercially available have auditory discrimination exercises built into them. Programs such as *Speech to Print Phonics** and *Phonovisual** include considerable auditory training along with the identification of the sound as a printed symbol. In such systems, a small amount of time preceding each lesson is devoted daily to auditory discrimination until those skills have been mastered. In the event that the teacher who uses these materials feels that there are not ample exercises of this nature, more of them may be easily devised.

Clinical remediation. Children with severe phonic disabilities quite often need an auditory discrimination program which is clearly related to the phonic technique to be used. It is, therefore, recommended that the child with this deficiency be instructed with a phonic technique which has auditory discrimination as an inherent part of the program. In this manner, it can be assured that no child is introduced to sounds which he cannot discriminate auditorily. *Speech to Print Phonics** and *Phonovisual** are examples of these types of materials.

Several of the *Dolch Games** provide exercises in auditory discrimination. As in other cases, games can provide the reinforcement needed for the overlearning of skills without the aspect of routine, monotonous drill. The games in auditory discrimination require considerable teacher supervision with problem readers, for there is no point in having the child reinforced by his errors. Under teacher supervision, errors can be turned into valuable learning situations.

When the child *mispronounces or substitutes words, is there a pattern of vowel or consonant errors?*

The diagnostic conclusions should have established whether this weakness is basically one of total unfamiliarity with the sounds of letters or if there is a specific vowel or consonant pattern in the error. This pattern should have been precise enough to establish the position of the error; i.e., initial, medial, or final, assuming, of course, that the problem is not one of auditory discrimination.

The process of teaching the child the unknown sound will not vary in classroom or clinical remediation in most cases. The decision as to how to teach this sound is basically reserved for the teacher. There are two

---

*See Appendix B.

basic approaches to instruction in this area: to teach the sounds from whole words or to teach the sounds in isolation. The suitability of either approach depends upon the following:

1. The teacher's familiarity with a given technique combined with the availability of materials and results obtained through its use. Although we recognize that teachers generally work best with familiar techniques and materials and we encourage them to do so, new methods and ideas should not be overlooked. Inflexible and stereotyped teaching can result from the failure to adapt. It is therefore very important for the teacher to be as objective as possible in her assessment of the materials and techniques which she can use most effectively.
2. The child's previous experience and his reaction to that technique. If, after good instruction, a child fails with a given technique, developing a negative attitude toward it, another approach may be more desirable.

Approaches to teaching vowel and consonant sounds. If information is available concerning the child's initial introduction to phonics (a whole word method, for example), and if it can be determined that this instruction was of satisfactory quality, it is quite correct for the teacher or reading specialist to select the other approach (sounds in isolation), for it can be assumed that, even with good instruction, the first technique was not effective. This type of selection requires that there is an awareness of the techniques used in both approaches. Caution is again advised, for if it can be determined that the child has profited to some degree by a previous method, it is justifiable to build upon that which the child has learned. In these cases, a reteaching of a previously taught method may be called for, or it may be appropriate to teach the same method with minor modifications. These assessments are difficult and can often be best made only by placing the child in instructional situations and evaluating his performance. Reference is made to the suggested reading at the end of this chapter for several sources of recommended techniques for the teaching of the sounds of the various letters and letter combinations (see p. 154).

Regardless of the approach employed, each lesson should be concluded with the child's being placed in the situation where he can attack: (1) the sound in a word and (2) words containing the sound in a sentence. The difference between clinical and classroom approaches will likely be

due to the type of material appropriate for follow-up activities to facilitate overlearning. A conscious effort on the part of the teacher and reading specialist must be made to keep the child alert to the fact that each
time he decodes a word, the sounds which he utters should be associ-
ated with a meaningful concept. As part of each phonics lesson, techniques must be used to facilitate this alertness. The child should be required to place the pronounced word in a sentence, or the teacher may
present words in which classification is possible, such as: things we do
at school; names of animals, etc. In either case, the child's attention is
called to the fact that the pronounced word has meaning as well as sound.

Classroom remediation. Materials have been designed to provide
systematic follow-up for the instruction mentioned above. Such materials
as *Phonics We Use**, *Phonics Skilltext**, and the workbooks of various
basal series can be adapted to meet this need. It is indefensible, however,
in remediation to start a child on page one of such material and force
him to work through the book; rather, those activities which will effectively reinforce the sound which has been taught should be selected and
utilized.

Placing children in game situations for the overlearning of these skills
has proven effective. In these situations, children work together without
the pressure of scholastic failure toward the overlearning of the desired
sound. The *SRA Word Games Laboratory** has particular usefulness in
these classroom situations, for it has game attractiveness and does not
require constant teacher supervision. Included in this material are ample
reinforcement exercises needed for the various consonant and vowel
sounds and sound combinations.

Consonant Lotto* and *Vowel Lotto** can also be used to provide reinforcement activities in game-like situations. These games may be best
used after the sounds have been taught to reinforce the learned skills;
they are of little value in the initial instruction of a sound.

Clinical remediation. The reading specialist will provide follow-up
activities which are either commercially available or are of his own design to appropriately comply with the basic approach he has decided to
use. He may, as a result, choose one of the techniques listed under classroom remediation. He must also be aware of the packaged programs
which are commercially available and have found popular acceptance

---

*See Appendix B.

with reading specialists. The following annotated list may serve as a guide:

1. *Speech to Print Phonics** provides for auditory discrimination; teaching of the names of letters, sounds of letters, and letter combinations; and the application of these learned skills to word attack situations. Context and meaning as well as sounds are stressed. It is structured for group work by way of every-pupil response cards.

2. *Phonovisual** carefully presents initial sound identification followed by final sounds and leads to the "tucking in" of vowel sounds for whole word identification. Consonant and vowel picture word chart are included for initial instruction.

3. *Gillingham** presents a system of teaching and reinforcing the sounds through kinesthetic techniques. Spelling and phonogram identification cards are featured.

4. In *Phonetic Keys to Reading**, techniques and materials starting with pre-basal reading are continued with reinforcement and more advanced skills as the basal stories are brought into use. These materials are in workbook form but differ from other workbooks in that they are designed to be used at specific times during the basal program.

5. Workbooks: A variety of workbooks are available to guide the child through the various sounds of the letters. Not directly related to any basal series, these programs are intended as suitable replacements of the skills taught in the basal program. The *Phonics Skilltexts**, *Phonics We Use**, *Diagnostic Reading Workbooks**, *Working with Sounds**, and *Herr Phonics** are examples of these materials.

Vowel and consonant exercises designed for use with secondary school students are not as plentiful. For the most part, these students are expected to profit from the materials used with elementary school children. It is not uncommon, however, to find that these students do not care to work with elementary materials. The specialist will find materials such as *Tactics for Reading** more acceptable to secondary students. Of course, if the student has no phonic skills, he will find little satisfaction from the use of materials designed with the assumption that the basic skills have at least been developed to a small degree.

Does the child need instruction in the *usage of known sounds?* Remedial efforts in answer to this question include instruction in syllabica-

---

*See Appendix B.

tion, blending, and pronunciation. Since these skills are quite often either neglected or handled poorly in the classroom, the child has an awareness of sounds but no system of applying this awareness to the attack of larger words.

Syllabication

It is imperative to remember that the child will need to use syllabication when he comes to words of two or more syllables which he cannot pronounce at sight or through the use of other word attack techniques. An illustration of the difficulty of this task may be seen when an adult looks at the following nonsense words and attempts to pronounce them:

sogtel	sog-tel
akot	a-kot
sognochest	sog-no-chest

It should be realized that when one attacks words which he does not know at sight, his procedure is likely to be: (1) divide the word into syllables and (2) pronounce the syllable without intensive phonic analysis, due to his ability to associate a given syllable with a familiar syllable. A highly valuable word attack technique which meets the goal of efficiency, syllabication is of particular value to older students. The teaching of the generalizations necessary for accurate syllabication is similar for the classroom and clinic.

For children who have had this instruction in their normal classroom situations and have failed to respond to it, we would suggest the use of Botel's *Discovery Technique*[1] which includes the following four steps:

1. The teacher provides accurate sensory experiences.
2. The students examine the structural pattern with the teacher's guidance.
3. Students collect words that fit the pattern.
4. Students generalize the pattern.

The effectiveness of this technique depends primarily upon the teacher's preparation of patterns from which to work and his understanding of the generalizations to be made, including their exceptions (see *Suggested Readings*, p. 154). The number of generalizations necessary may vary

---

[1]Morton Botel, *How to Teach Reading* (Chicago, Ill.: Follett Publishing Co., 1962), pp 40-42.

with the needs of the child in relation to the types of words he meets at his instructional level.

The following three generalizations are *essential* for all children in syllabication of words:

1. The vowel-consonant-vowel generalization: When a word has the structure v-c-v, syllable division is usually between the first vowel and the consonant.

    Example: (over = o/ver)   (akot = a/kot)

    However vowels which are followed by a consonant "r" form an exception to their generalization, the "r" going with the preceding vowel.

    Example: (carol = car/ol)

2. The vowel-consonant-vowel generalization: When a word has the structure v-c-c-v, syllable division is usually between the consonants.
    Example: (picnic = pic/nic)   (sogtel = sog/tel)
    However blends and digraphs are treated as one consonant.

    Example: (achieve = a/chieve)

3. The consonant — le generalization: When a word ends in the structure consonant plus "le", those three letters form the last syllable.

    Example: (ankle = an/kle)

Once the generalizations are made, it remains necessary to reinforce the learning through activities in which the child can use syllabication for word attack. This reinforcement is most effectively conducted through activities designed by the teacher to correspond to the material from which the child is reading.

Again it is possible to reinforce introduced skills through game-like exercises. Some of the *Dolch Games** are useful for reinforcement of this type. These exercises will help the child to realize that words can be divided into syllables rapidly and effectively. Once this awareness has been developed, he should be placed in situations where he is expected to use this skill when meeting words in a line of print.

For children who fail to understand syllabication at this point, use may be made of the *Fernald Technique*[2] with a modification for

---

*See Appendix B.

[2]Fernald, *Remedial Techniques,* Part II.

emphasis on the syllables of words. This change would demand that the child substitute the pronunciation of *syllables* in all steps that require him to pronounce the *word*. Although this technique will not teach the child how to divide words into syllables, its value is in assisting the problem reader to grasp the concept of syllabication.

Blending and pronunciation

Once the word has been dissected, either through syllabication or through the actual sounding of each letter of the syllable, the child must be able to blend these sounds and obtain a pronunciation with which he can associate a meaning. Again classroom and clinical techniques are similar.

When difficulty with this process arises, the child must be given ample opportunity to divide known words into syllables and then to blend these sounds and obtain a feeling for blending. It is clear that the blending of sounds and syllables is an inherent part of each lesson in which the child learns the sound or divides the word into syllables. Again the stress in remediation should be on giving the child material which will permit him to use his newly developed skills and to overlearn them until they become a reading habit. In phonics instruction, this cannot be accomplished without practice in syllabication and blending.

There are several phonic approaches which simplify the problem of blending and pronunciation by teaching the sounds as units, rather than in isolated pronunciation. In the following case, for example, the sound of "b" will be taught in the initial position as it relates to the various vowels: ba, be, bi, bo, bu. This then is immediately substituted in word building exercises:

bad	*bit*	*but*
beg	*boss*	

*Cordts** presents in detail the techniques and philosophy of this type of approach.

Structural Analysis

Do the words which are substituted or mispronounced contain prefixes, suffixes, or compound words?

---

*See Suggested Readings.

After having experience in diagnosis, a teacher will likely note that the most serious difficulty in these three *structural areas* is in suffix usage. Deficiencies in the ability to attack compound words are generally not too serious, for children can easily be taught to pronounce the words if they know the parts. If they do not know the parts, the problem is inadequate sight vocabulary. Although prefixes cause more difficulty than compound words, the fact that they are: (1) at the beginning of the word; (2) usually a separate, easily pronounceable syllable; and (3) concerned with a meaning which directly alters the base word, makes them easier to learn, and causes less difficulty in remedial reading. However, in the case of suffixes, where the above three factors are usually missing, many children experience difficulty. It is with suffixes that the service of the base word is most likely to change, but a precise difference in meaning is not evident. Note that in the following words when the suffix is removed, the spelling and configuration of the base word is distorted, causing an additional complication in the study of suffixes.

run	*running*	*runn-ing*
hope	*hoping*	*hop-ing*

Classroom remediation. Basal series teacher's manuals contain specific suggestions in the area of structural analysis, which, if followed, will be of great assistance in classroom remediation. These manuals are generally followed by recommendations for specific skill activities in the accompanying workbooks.

For a child who fails to respond to this technique, the *Discovery Technique*[3] is again suggested for its advantage in making the child generalize structural patterns from known words. This technique is equally applicable to difficulties with prefixes, suffixes, or compound words. In teaching the decoding and interpretation of the suffix "un," for example, it may be best to follow a procedure similar to this:

1. Present the word happy in a sentence. *John is happy.*
2. Change the word happy to unhappy. *John is unhappy.*
3. Have the child generalize what the difference in meaning is.
4. Present several other words in a similar manner.
5. Have the child generalize, "What does "un" generally do to the meaning of a word to which it is prefixed?"
6. Collect word patterns of this type, and see if they apply to the generalization.

[3]Botel, *How to Teach Reading*, p. 40.

7. Note that "un" has a sound which is consistent and that it changes the meaning of the words to which it is attached.

8. As the child reads, his attention should be called to words prefixed by "un." He should determine if these words fit the generalization.

Word wheels can easily be made which contain the base word; upon moving the wheel, the child adds either the prefix or the suffix. Suggestions for these are found in Russell's *Reading Aids Through the Grades*.[4] The teacher is cautioned in the construction of such reinforcement devices: (1) to be certain that the problem is not one of the child's not knowing the base word and (2) to be alert to the spelling changes which occur when the suffix is added. Prepared exercises of this type are found in materials such as the *Classroom Reading Clinic*.* In this kit word wheels, upon which base words are altered by prefixes and suffixes, provide ready-made reinforcement exercises.

Clinical remediation. Assuming that the child has been exposed to instruction in structural analysis and that the results of that instruction were, for the most part, unsatisfactory, the child is led to make the basic generalizations necessary for attack on unfamiliar words. Through the *Discovery Technique**, the child is encouraged to make generalizations and become an active learner.

The reinforcement of this instruction is quite often done in connection with instruction in other areas; for example, when an experience story is formed to aid sight vocabulary or comprehension, words which have structural analysis possibilities can be attacked in that manner. Similar reinforcement can be applied during the free reading that the child will do during remediation.

Children find the game approach an easy way in which to overlearn these skills. The *SRA Word Games Laboratory** has several well-developed games for the reinforcement of the initial instruction in prefixes, suffixes, and compound words. These are usually interesting to the child and contain an inherent motivational advantage, as well as the peer group learning advantage which has been previously discussed.

Supplementation of instruction can be accomplished by the use of the film-strips *Goals in Spelling** which have been carefully prepared to present the concepts of structural analysis in a meaningful, motivating

---

[4]David H. Russell and Etta E. Karp, *Reading Aids Through the Grades* (Bureau of Publications, 1951).

*See Appendix B.

manner. Further reinforcement can be provided, especially for older students, with the materials from *Tactics in Reading** and *Basic Reading Skills.** Note that these materials direct older students to structural analysis exercises designed to encourage the student with more mature interests.

When the child made his contextual errors, were *contextual clues* available which, if observed, could have prevented the error? (Context clues are words or phrases used by the author to assist the reader in attacking unknown words.)

This difficulty is twofold: First, the child may not know what a contextual clue is and may need basic instruction toward making him aware of the function of such clues; secondly, the child recognizes such clues when directed to them but does not normally anticipate them. For contextual clues to be useful in word attack, the child must anticipate the author's use of them. Finding that the child's difficulty is in not knowing the clues, the teacher, besides simply teaching the clues, must provide instruction in how to anticipate them. However, if the child already knows the clues, instruction may be limited to anticipation.

Classroom remediation. Necessary for the anticipation of contextual clues is experience with various types of literary styles; therefore, remedial efforts should include free reading in the various types of contextual situations, i.e., the novel, the biography, etc. Based upon these experiences with various types of literature, the child is able to anticipate the type of context that a style normally presents and, therefore, to have better opportunities for using context clues when they are available.

The next step in anticipation of context clues is to assist the child in the technique of previewing material before reading it. This helps him to determine the type of literature and the general direction of the author's writing, as well as possibly locating some specific context clues prior to reading.

Again the classroom teacher will find use for directed activities in the manuals of basal series which will show, within the material the child is using, the classroom techniques for the use of context clues.

Specifically prepared exercises, such as *Using the Context**, provide the child with experiences in drill type situations which require the type of thinking necessary to use context. Using a forced-choice incomplete sentence arrangement, these exercises place the child in the position of

---

*See Appendix B.

necessarily justifying his choice in terms of the available information. One of the early exercises reads as follows:[5]

Dick's picture was very funny. The children looked at it and began to
(1)........................... .

(1)   find   laugh   little

Removing the pure contextual guess from reading and replacing it with contextual inferring helps the child to develop the proper attitude for using contextual clues. Exercises of this type help to establish attitude and habit, but the ultimate effectiveness of the use of context must be in normal reading situations, not drills.

Clinical remediation. An emphasis on free reading in a variety of types of materials must precede direct instruction, with attention to the author's style and use of context clues. Drill activity has not proven useful with children who are seriously limited in this skill; in fact, it appears that excessive drill may be one of the reasons that the child does not make use of contextual clues. Because drill activities are normally out of context, over-use of drill places the child in a situation which denies him the use of the context and sabotages our aim in remediation for children with this deficiency. Therefore, although not outlawed in clinical remediation, drill type activities are unnecessarily limiting.

In place of drill, it is best to use the contextual situations in which the child is placed at one instructional level and to teach the use of context in directed activities while striving for other desirable goals. This may be easily done in clinical remediation due to the individual nature of the program. Suppose that a child is working in a Directed Reading Activity (DRA) with the purpose to look for the main idea. The child can be directed to context clues which will assist him to develop the main ideas of the story. In this manner, the child is not so likely to obtain the impression that the skills being presented are isolated and to be used one at a time.

For older students, stressing of the importance of context may be done through the use of books which they are expected to study in school. More attention to this aspect of the use of context is discussed under the comprehension skill area. *Tactics in Reading** and *Basic*

---

[5]Richard A. Boning, *Using the Context,* Book A (Rockville Centre, New York: Barnell Loft, Ltd., 1962).

*See Appendix B.

*Reading Skills** provide directed activities with context clues for these older students.

Did the child's error result from failure to observe *punctuation clues?*

Punctuation errors are often found to be due to the frustration level of the material rather than the failure to observe punctuation. If this is true, directed activity to observe the markings will be useless, and time will more wisely be spent on other skill areas with materials of the proper level. However, if the error is due to the child's lack of knowledge about the use of punctuation marks, instruction is in order.

Classroom remediation. Choral reading is again found to be an effective, subtle way for the child to obtain a feeling for punctuation marks. Following choral reading, the child's attention should be called to the fact that punctuation marks have different functions and call for different inflections.

Listening to good oral reading placed on a tape recorder will also assist in helping the child become aware of the need to observe punctuation marks in their reading materials.

Opportunities for the child to follow the teacher as he reads to determine whether or not he observed punctuation marks properly, may be used effectively. When the teacher intentionally distorts the punctuation, the child is directed to explain what this does to the ideas of the author. When used sparingly, this technique works well with youngsters having trouble hearing their own punctuation errors.

Clinical remediation. The above mentioned procedures may be supplemented by the experience story approach, which places the child in the author's shoes and makes him more aware of the need for punctuation to express how he feels and what he says. Generally, the reading specialist will add the punctuation necessary to indicate the expression which the child has made. This procedure can be varied by asking the child to indicate the appropriate punctuation and then intentionally distorting the punctuation to change the meaning of the child's contribution. The child must then recognize the error and correct it. Note that both of these techniques place the burden upon the child for awareness of correct punctuation.

----

*See Appendix B.

Extended remediation

Due to the thoroughness of clinical diagnosis, several additional considerations must be made when the child begins remediation. Again, these considerations are in terms of the diagnostic conclusions.

Are the child's errors made when he knows the proper word attack skills in isolation but not when they are needed in context?

This particular diagnostic conclusion was reached in clinical diagnosis. It is accentuated in clinical remediation because readers with severe problems have this difficulty in common, complicating other weaknesses. In these cases the child has been exposed to at least one system of phonics instruction and has learned the phonic skills involved. It becomes important, therefore, for the child to be placed in a reading situation where the skills can be applied and, through individualized instruction, directed toward their most effective use. Of course, these children will have all isolated word attack drills discontinued since drill is not needed.

Techniques for the application of word attack skills to context have been mentioned under each skill category. Children with this deficiency will be placed in many situations in which a word attack skill will help him to attack unfamiliar material. Since each is a highly individualized instructional situation, the child must be provided with direction as to the effective technique. Gradually, he will develop the ability to attack unfamiliar material with less and less teacher direction.

Special Considerations in Word Attack

Several comments will further the teacher's understanding of her total role in the area of word attack. First, dictionary skills are excellent, indispensable word attack techniques. Children with reading problems may benefit from dictionary instruction; however, asking for special help for problem readers does not usually result from a limitation in dictionary skills alone. Work in programming has produced two publications which may be of use in either classroom or clinical remediation, *Lessons for Self Instruction in Basic Skills* *and *David Discovers the Dictionary* *. The appeal of these programs to remediation is their individualized approach, requiring a minimum of teacher supervision to assist the child in the skills necessary to use the dictionary.

---

*See Appendix B.

Secondly, although many children can be taught the various word attack skills and know how to use them in context, the efficient use of word attack skills must be understood. Specifically, which word attack skills should be used first? A child comes upon an unknown word, e.g., *debating*, and must make a decision about how to attack it. Should he start with sounding the first syllable "duh-eh," should he first detach the suffix, or should he start elsewhere? The following suggested procedure is based on the belief that the child should start with the largest unit in the word so that he can attack it quickly and with the least possibility of distortion. The child follows this procedure to the point at which he pronounces the word. The procedure is:

1. Start with the context and examine it for contextual clues.
2. Look carefully at the word, left to right. Although this step may appear to be elementary, we find it is often all that is necessary.
3. Examine the word for structural characteristics: prefixes, suffixes, and compound words.
4. Divide the word into syllables and try to pronounce it. As stated earlier, this technique is often sufficient for older readers.
5. Establish the vowel sounds and attempt to pronounce them.
6. Sound out all letters and attempt to pronounce the word.
7. If at this point he is again unable to derive the word pronunciation or meaning, he should: first, be referred to the dictionary; secondly, be directed to word attack skills which will unlock the word; or thirdly, be told the word.

Certainly not an unalterable approach to unknown words, the above system enables the child to practice efficient word attack techniques and generally leads him to the quickest, most satisfactory pronunciation and meaning of the unknown word. Now when the child comes to an unknown word, e.g., *debating,* the teacher can direct him through the steps mentioned above. The handy placement of these steps in printed form, easily available to the child, will facilitate quicker independent usage. Reinforcement activities in context will be necessary for the child to develop such a technique and retain it as a habit.

Motivation

By far the strongest motivation for the child in the study of word attack skills is to be able to see how this knowledge and skill enable him to become more independent in his reading. It is essential, therefore, for the child to be placed in the situation of transferring learned skills to context in every lesson, if possible.

Game type activities, as suggested above, place the reinforcement of these skills in a more informal situation creating an atmosphere of pleasure in the process. When used for this purpose, an effort should be made to assure the child of an opportunity to win the games. It is obvious that a constant failing situation with these games will discourage the child. The motivation inherent in the pleasant interrelationship with children supplies the desired outcomes.

It has been our experience that the *Discovery Technique* has motivational appeal, especially to some of the older students who need work in word attack. The idea of generalizing the concepts of word attack with a minimum of teacher supervision usually turns into a highly motivating situation.

Graphic illustrations of a child's progress usually offer some assistance. Teacher-made materials designed to illustrate established goals and achievement within the scope and capabilities of the child are most effective.

Programmed materials with immediate feedback are interesting to children and contain a good bit of inherent motivation appeal. These materials, designed to reinforce correct and incorrect responses, establish situations in which the child is eventually going to be successful . . . an aspect which is desirable in all types of remedial programs. A special section has been included at the end of Chapter 8, p. 182 for discussion of the child with no specific skill deficiencies and who may be, for all practical purposes, labeled a non-reader. Included in that discussion will be a combination of word recognition and comprehension techniques.

Summary

The remedial techniques to be used in the area of vocabulary deficiencies, whether sight vocabulary or word attack, are based on precise diagnostic findings. Once these are determined, the educator has a variety of approaches in remediation from which to choose. Starting with those which he believes will serve the child's needs most adequately, the educator remains alert, during instruction, to the possibility that his original approach may need to be modified as instruction continues. The goal of diagnosis is to make efficient use of instructional time; therefore, changes should be made only to insure maximum effectiveness.

Constant awareness of the value of incorporating skill activities into contextual situations is the responsibility of both the teacher and the reading specialist. Continued drill, without well-developed transfer opportunities, is of little value.

Suggested Readings

1. Botel, Morton, *How to Teach Reading*, Chaps. III and V. Chicago: Follett Publishing Co., 1962. In this well-written book, Botel presents the "discovery" and "spelling'" mastery techniques for use in sight vocabulary and word attack lessons. The reader will find this to be a practical guide to developmental as well as remedial activities.
2. Cordts, Anna D., *Phonics for the Reading Teacher*. New York: Holt, Rinehart and Winston, Inc., 1965. This entire book is devoted to a description and explanation of a method of teaching phonics which reduces the necessity for extra blending of isolated sounds. The reader will find this technique of value with many problem readers.
3. Fries, Charles C., *Linguistics and Reading*. New York: Holt, Rinehart and Winston, Inc., 1963. One explanation for the linguistic involvement in the teaching of reading can be found in this book. For those who have difficulty in understanding the linguist, this book is a good introduction. Teachers of problem readers must acquaint themselves with the works of the linguists.
4. Herrick, Virgil E., and Nerbovig, Marcella, *Using Experience Charts with Children*. Columbus, Ohio: Charles E. Merrill Books, Inc., 1964. This booklet will provide the reader with many suggestions concerning the construction and use of experience charts. The classroom teacher should find these suggestions easily applicable to her group.
5. Heilman, Arthur W., *Phonics in Proper Perspective*. Columbus, Ohio: Charles E. Merrill Books, Inc., 1964. Heilman has combined an assessment of the place of phonics with a survey of the skills to be taught with examples and appropriate word lists. The educator who works with problem readers will find this book or one like it to be indispensible in working with phonics.
6. Lee, Doris M. and R. V. Allen, *Learning to Read Through Experience*. New York: Appleton-Century-Crofts, 1963. A combination of

philosophy and techniques, this book is a must for those who plan to work with seriously handicapped children. As we have indicated, this approach will be of particular value with many children, and this book presents the educator with a thorough background from which to work.

8

Remediation Of Comprehension Difficulties

Comprehension is a term which has come to include many aspects of getting meaning from the printed page, as well as relating this meaning to concepts which are within the realm of the reader. We have done a thorough job of testing children on their comprehension in various situations, especially with details, but our suggestions for instruction have been, for the most part, vague and idealistic. Perhaps this is due to the elusive meaning of comprehension; perhaps it is due to our failure to come to grips with the precise nature of instruction in this area. In either case, we have large numbers of children who demonstrate apparent knowledge of sight vocabulary, word attack, and orientation skills, but fail in comprehension situations. For them, we must tackle this skill area and provide the necessary remedial instruction.

Note that sight vocabulary and word attack are separated from comprehension, although they are concerned with the meaning of the words. This separation is made on the assumption that comprehension involves the meaning of words as they relate to each other and that it requires both sight vocabulary and work attack to be effective. It also involves reading as an active, thinking process. Pure memory will be an asset, but the act of comprehension involves purposeful reading during which the reader brings his ideas and those of the author together to form new meanings through association.

Comprehension, being a complex concept, involves progressive experiences in the reading act. Therefore, the more a child reads, the better he is likely to comprehend because his experiences with the printed page are enhanced. Since problem readers do not usually care to read, they fall farther and farther behind. Remedial programs should be designed to allow for many opportunities to read easy, interesting material of many varieties (fiction, science, biographies, animal stories, true adventure, etc.). It is partly through the awareness of authors' styles that a realistic feeling for comprehension can be developed. Without this feature in a remedial program, progress in the concepts of comprehension will be limited.

The Directed Reading Activity

As the techniques for teaching comprehension are discussed, repeated reference will be made to the *Directed Reading Activity* (DRA). It is assumed that the reader is aware of the basic steps in a DRA; however, they are presented here in summary for convenient review.

1. Readiness. In the readiness step, vocabulary familiarity, experience and concept development, and goal setting are established.
2. Silent reading. In the silent reading step, the child reads to obtain answers to questions set by the goals.
3. Recitation. In this step, the child is provided an opportunity to demonstrate the knowledge which he obtained from the reading by reacting either orally or silently.
4. Reread. The child rereads, either orally or silently, checking to ascertain specific information pertaining to the questions asked.
5. Enrichment. All opportunities to enrich this reading experience should be employed. It is here that concept formation can be accentuated, leading to depth and permanency of understanding.

Allowing for flexibility, the above mentioned procedure will be the basis for instruction in many of the remedial techniques employed with children weak in the comprehension skill areas. Specific variations will be mentioned.

As in other skill areas, the remedial efforts in the comprehension area will be in terms of the questions which led to diagnostic conclusions in the last chapter. These questions are:

1. Do the child's comprehension difficulties appear to increase as he encounters larger units of material?

2. Are the child's errors due to the type of comprehension expected?
3. Was the child able to paraphrase the author's ideas, or was he able to relate them only in the words of the author?
4. Can the child recall the author's ideas, yet remain unable to perform in content areas?
5. Is there a total failure to respond to comprehension situations?
6. Was the lack of response due basically to speed?

It is unlikely that a child will be limited in only one of these aspects of comprehension. The merging of the following techniques is clearly possible and highly desirable when the occasion demands.

Do the child's comprehension difficulties appear to increase as he encounters larger units of material? The improvement of reading skills depends on the ability to respond to units of print of increasing length. In diagnosis it is easy to note whether the child's comprehension is limited basically to sentences, paragraphs, or to even larger units. In these cases the problem is one of being able to recognize the relationship between units of varying size and the flow of ideas created by the author.

Classroom remediation. All remedial approaches must start at the instructional level or lower. When the difficulty is related to the size of the unit being attempted, the instructional level is the largest unit the child can handle with fair effectiveness. The DRA is then used by the teacher to help the child approach the next largest unit. The teacher must carefully direct the child toward desirable comprehension goals. When skill in comprehension has been attained, the child is then provided experiences to enable him, in the future, to set his own goals. More material is then attempted using the same general procedure to facilitate overlearning.

Many commercially prepared materials are available to assist the teacher in this effort. Note that the *SRA Reading Laboratory**, for example, numbers the paragraphs in the easier materials for direct reference to small units of print. Many other materials take similar approaches to quantity of material expected to be understood.

The structure as well as the length of sentences and paragraphs causes trouble in textbook reading and in free reading, especially with older children. *Tactics in Reading** provides specific exercises in sentence

---

*See Appendix B.

and paragraph meaning. These are designed for students in the secondary grades and contain sufficient interest for motivation and a variety of sentence and paragraph structures. *Basic Reading Skills** provides this reinforcement in workbook form with emphasis on shorter passages for older students.

Clinical remediation. Again the approaches used in the classroom are applicable; however, they are intensified and personalized in clinical remediation.

Paragraph comprehension and the inter-relationship between paragraphs appear to be difficult for many of the older students. The reading specialist, therefore, must have materials available for various reading levels and interests, upon which to direct the reading activities of these children. The *McCall Crabb Standard Test Lessons**, *The Reader's Digest Skill Builders**, and the *SRA Reading Laboratories**, as well as a wide variety of workbook type materials, provide clinical remediation with a large supply of appropriate materials.

Experience stories of increasing size may be used for the child limited in this area. The experience stories may appear as lines of print, short paragraphs, or larger units as the need demands. Again, it is the placement of the child in the role of the author that creates a receptive atmosphere for effective instruction in the concepts of comprehension.

Are the child's errors due to the type of comprehension expected? All too often, in the classroom, comprehension is limited to questions on items for which there is but one correct response; consequently, they measure only the ability to recall details. However, in real reading situations, obtaining details is but one of several vitally important comprehension skills which must be developed. Instruction in these skill areas calls for specific changes in the DRA Readiness, Recitations, Rereading, and Enrichment steps. These changes are explored under each type of comprehension skill.

The types of comprehension skills can broadly be classified as:
   a. Recalling directly stated facts.
   b. Understanding the main idea.
   c. Recalling sequence.
   d. Making inferences.
   e. Evaluating reading.

*See Appendix B.

The abilities to follow directions and organize the author's ideas, although types of comprehension, will not be discussed here. They will be discussed under the topic of study skills.

Remediation of comprehension deficiencies is based on the diagnostic findings in relation to these five areas. Remediation presumes: 1. that the diagnosis was conducted with instruments which will provide some measure of these different types of comprehension and 2. that the diagnostic conclusions were based upon an inner-analysis of these measures to determine the precise nature of the deficiency. Comprehension, a thinking process, needs to be taught with an eye toward guiding and developing the thinking processes of the child to anticipate the type of comprehension desired.

Recalling directly stated facts

This is the area in which the child has likely had the most instruction prior to his identification as a problem reader. From his first reading experience in school, the child is asked to repeat the details of the material which he has read. If he cannot do this, it is obvious that he will not recall details any more effectively now by simply being asked to repeat them. A quite different approach will be needed, for it can be assumed that he has had considerable opportunity to develop this skill. It is in the first and fourth steps of the DRA that attention can best be focused to develop this skill. First, the child must always be aware of his purpose for reading this particular material; and second, if upon recitation the child is unable to understand the details, he should return to the specific section of the material in which the answer can be located. The problem then is twofold: 1. What types of goal setting experience are the most helpful? 2. What types of directed rereading best illustrate to the child a method for obtaining details?

The thought process involved in the recall of directly stated facts involves encouraging the child to pay attention to important details, remember them, and relate them to the larger ideas of the author. Names of people, places, dates, and major events should be emphasized during reading. Some prefer to underline or otherwise highlight the directly stated facts to be remembered; others take notes. Regardless of the technique, the process is the same, i.e., the child is expected to indicate through action an awareness of the fact to be recalled, thereby triggering his mind to remember that fact.

Classroom remediation. Besides normal reading exercises, many available classroom situations may serve to focus attention on obtaining details. With direction, the child can come to realize that details have definite importance in certain reading situations. To facilitate this realization, the teacher should start remediation with materials which are vitally interesting to the child, creating motivation for the effort which will be expected of him.

This may need to be followed by pointing out the information which the author feels is important. Italicized print, boldface type, information repeated for stress, and illustrated information are all clues to important details to be remembered.

Perhaps more subtle, but equally useful, are clues which words contain. Descriptive adjectives, proper nouns, action verbs, and the like, call attention to those types of details which should receive more careful attention. For example:

The *large house burned* in the middle of the *night*.

Most basal material is well designed to develop skill in this area. The classroom teacher, using these types of materials, must first be certain that the child is working at the appropriate level and then select those lessons which appear to be most useful.

The reinforcement of these learned skills should occur daily in all reading situations; this task is more clearly the responsibility of the classroom teacher since he has these opportunities regularly, especially in the content areas. Although a child with this deficiency is likely to have reading for details stressed to the exclusion of other types of comprehension, efforts should be made to call the child's attention to other types as soon as possible; otherwise, the child may obtain a mistaken impression about comprehension.

Clinical remediation. Using the same techniques as the classroom teacher, the reading specialist focuses his attention on the Readiness, Recitation, and Reading Steps in the DRA. During Readiness, the child is assisted in obtaining certain types of interesting background which will prepare him for the information to be read. As the child develops skill in this step, there will be less and less teacher direction, until finally the child is in a position to direct himself to attack the passage purposefully. During Recitation some check will be made on the effectiveness of the child's attempt to recall directly stated facts. When recitation indicates that reading for details was ineffective, rereading is used for instruction. Here the reading specialist directs the child to the section of the passage in which the desired information is contained. The child is asked to reread this section orally or silently and locate the section which contains the desired details. These then should be paraphrased by the child to show his understanding. The child is then redirected to the question and asked for the appropriate response. Immediately, another situation should be created requiring the same performance on new material, so that the child is aware of his ability to handle this step unassisted.

Due to the numerous test-like situations that call for the recall or recognition of details, the reading specialist will, particularly with older students, attempt to provide test-like exercises in which the preciseness of response depends upon the selection of the proper answer from several possible correct answers. Particularly useful in these cases is the multiple choice question technique and, at times, the matching question technique. An awareness of the necessity for satisfactory performance on these types of questions is useful for children who appear to have this deficiency.

Although initial instruction in this area is wisely conducted at easy reading levels, it is necessary to move to the instructional level as rapidly as possible, for it is at this level that the child is most likely to see the necessity for concentration in order to reach desired goals. We often find that full attention is lacking when children are limited to working on easy material which does not require concentration. For it is only with concentrated reading that directly stated facts can be recalled accurately. The *Reading Skilltext**, *Reading for Meaning**, and the *Standard Test Lessons in Reading** are examples of the type of readily available materials on obtaining details. Most of these materials are best used for reinforcement since careful teacher direction and instruction are necessary in a child's initial efforts. It is a mistake to drill children in these materials without immediate teacher follow-up to evaluate and redirect, since, in the case of continued failure, they can soon become burdensome and disinteresting to the child. By correcting errors immediately, the likelihood of reinforcing correct responses is enhanced.

Understanding the main idea

The ability of the child to understand the relationship between the details and to draw one or two central ideas from a series of sentences

---

*See Appendix B.

or paragraphs is a high level skill. Part of the instructional problem is that the question is as difficult to ask as the answer is to evaluate objectively. We have found that it is seldom effective to simply ask the child to try to find the main idea. If it has been determined that he is weak in this area, he obviously does *not* go through all the thought processes required for performance in obtaining main ideas. The task, then, is to direct the child toward those types of thought processes which will enable him to understand main ideas.

Classroom remediation. The classroom teacher will first need to consider exactly what processes *are* involved in this task. All reading should then be preceded by stimulating discussions and questions to direct the child through these thought processes. One technique which has been used successfully is to tell the children that they are about to produce a play or a movie based upon this story. Naturally, the movie will need a good title, so have them read the story and determine an appropriate title (the main idea). Similarly, the children may be asked to rename the story since the name as given is not appropriate. As answers are provided (all should be tentatively accepted), discussion should follow as to why a particular title was chosen. Does it contain enough information to direct a person's thinking to the central ideas in the story? The creative child will often contribute ideas which, at face value, appear to be far from appropriate, but which, upon discussion, reveal an understanding of the main ideas. These are the types of thought processes which help to direct the child's thinking toward larger ideas in a portion of print. Sometimes it will be advantageous to work with smaller units of print to develop the ability to search for main ideas with a minimum of extraneous material to confuse the child.

Authors often use clues to assist the reader to obtain the main ideas and to direct the child's attention to appropriate clues. An awareness of the skeleton of the sentence or of the topic sentence in a paragraph is particularly useful. In certain types of materials, the table of contents, pictures, and summaries are equally useful. If the child continues to have difficulty in this area, more direction from the teacher in the recognition of these clues, followed by similar work on unfamiliar material of the same type, gives the child a sense of being able to perform on his own as soon as possible.

Clinical remediation. We often find failure in obtaining main ideas to be directly related to the amount of material being read; therefore, in clinical remediation, we generally try to establish the concepts involved in smaller units of print and move to the larger ones as awereness of the skill is indicated. (See page 159.)

In place of directed instruction in the use of main idea clues, the reading specialist utilizes each reading situation to illustrate the use of these clues as they appear in the reading which the child is doing, thus eliminating the necessity of transfer from drill to context, for context is always used.

Several of the prepared materials have made special efforts to emphasize the main idea as a comprehension goal. The *Standard Test Lessons in Reading** emphasize recognition of main ideas as well as detail-type questions. The *SRA Reading Labs** and the *Reader's Digest Skill Builders** also contain numerous opportunities to reinforce concepts of main idea after the initial instruction in that concept has been completed.

A useful technique is developing experience stories to enable the child to realize how an author writes with a main idea in mind. As the author, the child must grasp the main idea and state it in his own words. He may be asked to paraphrase his own words to make better sentences. As he does this, he should be directed to activities which will help him to recognize his mental processes. Opportunities must then be made available to him for this same process when reading the writings of others.

Recalling sequences

A highly desirable but more advanced skill, recalling sequences, causes considerable difficulty with many children. When deficient, the child is limited in his ability to handle content type materials and to fully appreciate reading of longer units. Both types of remediation should emphasize a direct awareness for this type of comprehension.

The thought processes needed here involve perceiving groups of items that are related in time, i.e., one comes first, then the next, and so on. Initially, children must get this practice from such activities as following oral directions, doing work at their seats from oral and written instruction, or recalling events from a story which has been read to them by another.

Classroom remediation. During the DRA, the teacher will indicate to the child, prior to actual reading, that the material to be read has sequen-

---

*See Appendix B.

tial information in it and that it will be in terms of sequences that a comprehension check will take place. When the child is deficient in this skill, it is normal to start with a sequence of two events and, after that is understood, to advance to more involved sequences.

Directing the child's attention to the types of clues used by authors for emphasis on the importance of sequences is usually of some value. Items that are numbered, steps in a process, dates, the mention of time, as well as the use of sequence words, e.g., *afterwards, before, during*, are all indications that the author feels the sequence of events is of particular importance.

As in obtaining an understanding of the main idea, the development of sequence consciousness is often best done by a more subtle means. We might attempt to direct the child to the idea of making a movie, again, in which three or four scenes are to be produced. "What is the order of scenes so that the audience will understand the story?" Many teachers have successfully used the technique of asking the child to retell the story. However, it is important to realize that the child who is deficient in this skill may experience considerable difficulty in telling the story in sequence and may, instead, merely relate the details indiscriminately.

Clinical remediation. It must first be established that the child is interested enough in the material to feel that the sequences are worthwhile and that he is reading material which is not too difficult in concept and vocabulary. For this reason, we often start with experience stories in which the child is asked to explain how to do something, such as build a model airplane and then is directed to analyze the techniques which he used to indicate sequences. From this, of course, he will be directed to unfamiliar material of a similar nature to see how another author accomplishes the same task.

Again, the quantity of the material upon which the child is expected to recall sequences will be carefully controlled so as to keep the situation a potentially successful one. We want to be certain that the child's limitations are not due simply to poor memory.

Organization skills are closely related to the skill of sequence reading and should be considered as remedial techniques. They will be discussed more fully on page 171.

Older children seem to respond quite well to the materials in *Tactics in Reading**, which provides directed activities suitable for the reinforce-

---

*See Appendix B.

ment of sequence skills. The use of outlining to establish sequences has been used effectively as a means to develop this skill. The *Reading for Meaning** exercises emphasize this technique for children able to read at and above the fourth grade level. A partial outline is suggested for children displaying serious difficulties with the concept of outlining. Completion of the outline develops the concept of what an outline should be, as well as a feeling for the sequence of ideas. As competency develops, the child's contribution should constitute more of the outline; the ultimate goal is that the child, unassisted, will be able to construct an outline of his own.

The reinforcement of sequences is quite often not available in prepared materials, so it is necessary to draw upon every opportunity to correlate and reinforce sequence skills in the context areas.

Making inferences

Even more difficult, yet of great value, is the ability of the child to make correct inferences from the words of the author. Again, due to the problems in question construction, we are plagued with indefinite, non-objective answers. The task here is for the child to obtain information which is not directly stated and yet not to read into the print concepts which the author did not intend.

The thought processes here are similar to those that the child uses to read for contextual clues. He must be willing to see implied ideas in the print for which there is substantiating evidence. Children can be encouraged to think this way by making character judgments based on the incidences in a passage or by making judgments of time and place of occurrence when they are not directly stated. As with remediation in the area of context clues, the child should not be encouraged to guess on items for which proof is not available.

Classroom remediation. Carefully conducted exercises based on the fourth step of the DRA (Rereading) can help the child to make simple inferences. Often best done in a group of children who can reread a portion of a story and conduct a discussion about what the author meant, the child with a weakness in this area senses the processes that the other children are orally going through. The child then attempts these same

---

*See Appendix B.

processes on unfamiliar materials upon which inferences can be made. The teacher can start with questions concerning how a certain character in the story must have felt when this incident happened to him or questions about the character qualities of certain people presented in the story. Once the child understands, the author does not necessarily write down every-thing that he wants to be obtained from his writing, the child is ready to progress to more subtle types of inference work. To illustrate the problem encountered in making unjustifiable inferences, the teacher may decide to make inferences that are not justified and have the child show, from the words of the author, how the teacher is wrong. Note that the amount of mental activity that is required in this type of comprehension is one of the most desirable outcomes of helping children to develop this skill.

Although authors make inferences in all types of material, it may be best to limit initial instruction to fiction since it is here that inferences have their greatest usage.

Clinical remediation. The above mentioned program is equally useful for clinical remediation situations, and it should be intensified and di-rected more precisely to the diagnosed needs of the child.

Students who use context clues well are quite often capable of making inferences. It is recommended, therefore, that those types of exercises mentioned under context clues be applied to this comprehension skill. Taking context-inferring to the next step can be accomplished with exer-cises such as those in the *Reading for Understanding** materials. These exercises are appropriate to various grade levels, starting with very simple materials which require the child to draw meaning from what the author has said without repeating directly stated facts. One of the first exercises in this material reads:[1]

> Susan did not play outside when it was raining because she did not want
>
> a. to get wet   c. the rain to stop
> b. to stay indoors   d. the sun to shine

Starting at the child's recreation level, these materials require active re-sponse from the child and have been found to assist in establishing the attitude necessary for successful reading.

Other prepared materials provide occasional opportunities to respond

---

[1]Thelma G. Thurstone, *Reading for Understanding* (Chicago: SRA, 1959), p. 1.

*See Appendix B.

to inference questions. When examined in advance, these materials, such as the *SRA Reading Labs**, can be used for directed activities to derive inference in interesting, easy-to-read materials. *Tactics in Reading** provides appropriate reinforcement exercises for inferences with specific direction toward older children of the junior and senior high school age level.

It is essential for the reading specialist to understand the active role which the child must play, for it is an unnatural role to many of these children. To find that they are expected to engage themselves actively in meeting the author's words and project themselves into the material in this manner at first creates a feeling of discomfort and may require much supervision. As the child initially develops these concepts, he must immediately be made aware that this is not to be interpreted as license to read unintended meaning into the author's words.

Evaluative reading

Not normally a deficiency in which a child creates enough of a problem to be referred for diagnosis or remediation, remedial efforts in this area will be attempted when the child, referred for other reasons, has symptoms of difficulty here. Although in evaluative reading the dividing lines of correct and incorrect responses are not so sharp, the child must understand that his reasons for making various evaluations should be substantiated by the print. For example, if you ask a child if he thinks that this is a good story for third grade boys, you cannot tell him he is wrong regardless of his answer, for you have asked him what he thinks, and he has told you. What you must do, however, is to be certain that he has a valid reason for making his evaluation as he has made it.

Initially, the efforts in both classroom and clinical remediation are restricted to those types of questions which direct the child to conclude whether or not he enjoyed the story and why; whether the story is most likely true or untrue and why; whether or not the author seems to have been thorough in his descriptions and why. From these elementary observations, the child is placed in a situation which can result in a feeling for evaluation as he reads. Using the Readiness Step of the DRA, the child is directed to read for some type of evaluative purpose. Evaluative reading, encompassing all other comprehension skills, should be used whenever possible. Again it is appropriate to start with fiction type ma-

---

*See Appendix B.

terials which lend themselves best to these types of reactions.

Many of the *SRA Lab** materials and the *Reader's Digest Skill Builders** call for evaluative reactions to the reading based upon discussion questions framed by the author to evaluate various aspects of the material. However, the teacher and the reading specialist must create questions and discussions centered around materials which are appropriate for evaluation.

Complicating instruction in this area, as in inferences, is the necessity to make certain that the child does not take license to criticize everything written by the author; therefore, all questions must require the child to explain how he arrived at his reaction. It must further be understood that evaluative reading need not be reading in which the student reacts negatively to the ideas of the author; on the contrary, he will find that his evaluations are often positive in nature and that they reaffirm the author's ideas and concepts. This type of evaluative reading must be developed and understood just as is the negative type.

Was the child able to paraphrase the author's ideas, or was he able to relate them only in the words of the author?

There are numerous situations in which the evaluation of the child's comprehension can be measured only in terms of his ability to interpret the author's ideas in his own words (to paraphrase). Although paraphrasing is highly desirable, it is discouraged in many children by the type of comprehension situations into which they have been placed. The child sees no need to think of the author's ideas in his own words; rather, he need only repeat the exact words of the author.

Classroom remediation. For the child to develop the concept of paraphrasing, we find it useful to start with recognition type response questions (multiple choice, true-false, etc.) in which the words of the author are changed slightly while retaining the same meaning. This forces the child to select the answer which he feels most closely parallels the ideas of the author. At this time he should be directed to notice the lack of exactness of the response choices and that an acceptable response can be correct without using the author's precise words.

The child will then be placed in recall situations in which he will be asked to think of the ideas of the passage in his own words in response to questions which are open-ended in nature and which require this type of

---

*See Appendix B.

thinking. For example, following a reading selection in which the Civil War has been the topic, the question may be formed around such topics as summarizing the events of a battle or relating the most noticeable characteristics of the hero. Older children will be expected to write some brief summaries of material which they have read. Each of these activities lead to the desirable goal of paraphrasing the words of the author.

All teachers have, at one time or another, had the unfortunate experience of hearing a child read or recite from memory a report from a reference source in which the exact words of the author have been reproduced. It is a disappointing experience, it is usually read poorly, and it is seldom understood by the person relating it. These situations must be avoided in the classroom program for a child (and all other children) with this deficiency by insisting that reports be presented in the child's own words. In this manner, the child sees the relationship between paraphrasing and success in other school subjects.

Clinical remediation. It has been found that students with this skill deficiency can often obtain the idea of paraphrasing by being asked to do so with their own experience stories. We direct the child to a small unit in his experience story and ask him if he could say this another way without changing his basic meaning. When dealing with his own ideas and his own words, the child can readily see the possibilities of this type of response. He is then directed to unfamiliar material and asked to do the same thing. Many children require much experience in these tasks before they are able to do them without teacher direction.

An additional technique is to have the child react to a picture in the story after he has completed his reading. Questions which direct his attention to the purpose the author might have had for using the picture, the part of the story being illustrated, and/or the description of the action in the picture lead the child to the desired paraphrased response.

All reading activities in clinical remediation will be followed by situations in which a child is expected to paraphrase; however, as in other comprehension situations, it is not desirable to use this technique to the exclusion of other types of comprehension checks.

Can the child recall the author's ideas, yet remain unable to perform in content areas? The child in this case seems to be able to perform in reading class but does not transfer those skills to his reading in content areas. The first consideration for this child must be in terms of the readability of the material upon which he cannot perform. It is often possible to notice extreme differences between the books used in reading class and the books used in content areas in terms of readability. On an informal basis the teacher should note the differences in: (1) the size of print; (2) the length of sentences; (3) the vocabulary load in terms of difficult words; and (4) the difficulty of the concepts. If any of these factors varies noticeably, the problem is probably one of material difficulty. *Yoakham*[2] and *Gunning*[3] present some of the more formal readability techniques which may be used to determine readability. These methods generally involve a formula used to obtain a grade level of readability but do not evaluate the concept load. A technique has been developed which will enable teachers to determine the ability of the child to handle materials; it will also indicate the ability to handle concepts as well as word and sentence structures. Named the "cloze procedure," Taylor[4] claims it is of value in determining readability. We have used this technique with the materials we expect children to read in the clinic and find it to be most helpful. It involves:

(1) Select at random a passage containing an adequate sampling.
(2) Retype this passage, leaving out every eighth word. (Authorities differ on which word to omit, but we have found the eighth to be effective.) As a rule the first word in a sentence should not be omitted, nor should proper nouns. An example of a clozure test on easy material would appear as follows:

   Nancy was anxious to have her birthday .... this year. She had invited some children .... her room at school. She hoped that .... would all be able to attend.

(3) Have the child read the incomplete sentences, filling in the missing words. To close properly, the child must know the words and understand the concept, thereby anticipating the author's ideas.

As the teacher gains familiarity with this technique he will find it a valuable aid in determining (1) whether a child should read a certain book and (2) how much help the child is likely to need with the book he had selected.

The second consideration is that reading problems in content mate-

---

[2]Gerald A. Yoakham, *Basal Reading Instruction* (New York: Prentice Hall Inc. 1955), Appendix I.

[3]William A. Jenkins, ed., "The Educational Scene," *Elementary English,* XXXVII:6, October 1960, p. 411.

[4]W. L. Taylor, "Cloze Procedure—A New Tool for Measuring Readability," *Journalism Quarterly,* 30, Fall, 1953, pp. 415-33.

rial do not usually become pronounced until the child has reached the fourth grade. It is at this point that content reading becomes a regular part of the school program and the child with this deficiency is clearly handicapped.

Classroom remediation. The teacher should use the DRA with materials in content areas. The child who fails to see the need for a similar attack in unfamiliar material must be directed to it in the same manner that we use in reading class. Each step of the DRA must be carefully used in the development of skill in reading content materials, gradually permitting the child to guide himself through the steps.

Older children may find it beneficial to follow a specific study technique in their reading of content materials. Several of these are available, the most prominent being SQ3R[5] (Survey, Question, Read, Recite, Review). The effect of this type of technique is the same as a DRA except that the student is to apply it to his studies without supervision. Independence in reading content material is the desired objective of this system.

Activities in which the child organizes and classifies ideas are useful in remediation of this deficiency. Children who cannot read in the content areas usually are deficient in outlining skills. Beginning with completed outlines of material recently read, the teacher illustrates the method of following the author's train of thought. An outline format is then presented for the child to complete, followed by simple outlining of clearly organized material with little or no direction. The *Reading For Meaning** workbooks, designed for the intermediate and secondary grades, have practice exercises to develop the child's ability to organize material through a gradual exposure to outlining techniques.

The ability of the child to follow directions has a direct relation to his ability to perform in study situations. Composite in nature, this skill depends upon the child's ability to follow the sequence and organization of the author's thoughts, as well as to obtain the main idea. The *Specific Skill Series** includes sets of intensive exercises in following directions at the various grade levels. Once the ability to follow directions is mastered, remedial sessions should provide further experiences with this concept at regular intervals.

---

[5]Francis P. Robinson, *Effective Study* (New York: Harper & Row, Publishers, 1961), Chap. ii.

*See Appendix B.

Clinical remediation. The reading specialist uses the techniques mentioned above and adds to them the individualization of instruction through the use of certain materials designed for classroom use having particular application to remedial cases with this skill deficiency. The *Be a Better Reader** books provide specific suggestions for study in the major content areas, particularly for older students.

The *Study Skills Library** which provides specialized instruction in developing the same type of concepts is useful with younger children. Individualized for clinical use, these materials can serve a highly useful function with children who are deficient in this skill.

The *SRA Organizing and Reporting Skill Kit** has individualized exercises which gradually introduce the concepts of note taking, reporting, and outlining. The adaptability of this material to clinical remediation can assist in meeting the skill deficiency of these children.

Another SRA study aid is the *Graph and Picture Study Skills Kit.** Designed to be adapted to any subject area, these materials are useful in developing a type of useful reading often overlooked in remedial programs.

Each of these four materials must be followed by practical work from text type materials similar to that used by the child in his work in the classroom. Without the adaptation of newly formed reading skills to the study areas, one is likely to find remedial efforts less effective than desired in terms of scholastic improvement.

Is there a total failure to respond to comprehension situations?
For the child who does not respond to any type of comprehension check, even at relatively easy levels of performance, remedial techniques are difficult to apply, for there is no place to begin. For these children, the level of material must be easy, the interest of the material must be high, the quantity of the material must be small, and the type of comprehension expected must be the simplest.

Classroom remediation. Again the use of experience stories permits a start with relatively easy, interesting material of as small a quantity as desired. Again, the child is directed to demonstrate an understanding of the experience stories which, containing his own concepts, can usually be done without difficulty. Once a feeling for this type of directed activity is developed, the child is exposed through the DRA to similar, yet unfamiliar material.

---

*See Appendix B.

Placing the child in reading situations which call for action and re-action is often successful for a child with this deficiency. Signs, posters, and flash cards which can be presented to him with directions for his re-action are developed from the opportunities which appear daily in and out of the classroom.

We often find that the child with a total comprehension deficiency will react to a basal reading program which uses books not used in pre-vious school situations. When the teacher is able to provide these, major emphasis, of course, is placed upon comprehension situations which in-volve a reaction to the reading so that the student may demonstrate an awareness of meaning. Specifically, the type of story in which the student is asked to follow directions has particular merit.

Clinical remediation. Beginning exercises and instruction through the DRA are prescribed for a total comprehension deficiency. Clinical pro-cedures use the same materials discussed in the various comprehension deficiencies but are highly individualized to prohibit the development from step to step without a thorough understanding of the meaning. Of specific value are: experience stories, *Non-oral reading**, basal pre-primers, and *Programmed Reading**. All of this material must be made interesting and must include reading goals which are clearly understood by the child. By carefully leading the child to small quantities of interest-ing, meaningful material, it is possible to develop the basic skills needed in reading for comprehension.

Vocabulary exercises which involve the child in nonverbal responses to the printed symbol have considerable usefulness here. The *Nichols Slides**, mentioned on page 134, or their equivalent, can be used starting with the very simple, direct commands and progressing as the child de-velops the skill. (Example: Start with words such as *sit, stand,* and *jump* and go to more complicated combinations of words such as *stand and sing now* or *jump three times.*)

Certainly, with this type of child, all drill without context would be discontinued until the desired awareness of meaning was developed.

Extended Remediation

Again the extension of diagnosis by the classroom teacher and the reading specialist established two additional areas for remedial considera-

---

*See Appendix B.

tion. Normally this remediation will be conducted by the reading specialist and occasionally by the classroom teacher upon the recommendations
of the reading specialist. These two areas are speed and distraction.

Was the lack of response due basically to speed? It is not unusual to
find, after clinical diagnosis, that the responses of the child are, in fact,
due to slow speed. In these cases the child has been asked to read a selection (ample time must be alloted) and asked to give comprehension type
responses. Not having completed the material, the child's comprehension
responses appear to be short of satisfactory. Upon more careful examination, it is often found that the child has responded properly to those
responses which were related to the material which he has read and
missed those which were concerned with material which he has not read.
Remediation, then, should be not in terms of the child's responses but
rather in terms of the reasons for the child's slowness. It is in this manner
that we become involved with the problem of reading speed in remediation, not by evaluating words per minute or by employing specific speed
drills.

Using the first step in the DRA, the child reads for a specific purpose and is instructed to be flexible in his approach.

Practice is accomplished on easy, interesting material, so that we can
be certain that the child's slowness is not basically due to poor sight
vocabulary or word attack problems. (Slow reading caused by these
types of deficiencies is corrected by direct remedial efforts in the skill
areas of sight vocabulary and word attack.) The child is then placed in
pressure situations which limit the time permitted for reading of small
passages. This pressure can be gradually increased or reduced as the reading situation demands, and the child gains a sense of what we mean by
"flexibility of reading rate."

Most of the devices mentioned under Orientation Remediation are
useful in developing more efficiency in reading speed. The controlled exposure devices such as the *Controlled Reader** and the *Rateometer** are
useful here; however, it must again be noted that these devices should be
used on easy, interesting materials and that the child should be directed
through step one of the DRA to the type of comprehension expected.

Prepared materials are available for children to use for practice exercises in reading within certain time limits. The *SRA Laboratories**, at

---

*See Appendix B.

the fourth grade level and above, have rate building exercises in which the child must read and answer the question in three minutes. The emphasis here is on efficiency in relatively easy material of high interest. The *Standard Test Lessons in Reading** also has the three minute time limitation.

Other available exercises permit the child to establish the time he desires to use in reading yet keep track of his rate. Designed to motivate improved time performance, such exercises generally place more emphasis upon measures of reading rate, such as words per minute. In remediation, none of this emphasis should be stressed without equal or greater emphasis on the quality of comprehension which accompanies the rate. The *Better Reading Books** are an example of this type of material, providing charts for easy motivation to better speed and better comprehension.

Charts or graphs which illustrate the child's progress are always helpful. These should be constructed so that the child can note small gains in improved rate, so that the aspect of comprehension is charted as well as the reading rate, and so that the goals for which he is striving are realistically within reach.

Was the poor performance due to the fact that the child was easily distracted? In many cases, the child's performance on any exercise or in any book may be more basically due to his distractability than to a lack of skills. When such a diagnosis is made, the remedial procedures should be adjusted to reduce as many distractable elements as possible. Recommendations should also be made to the classroom teacher to facilitate learning situations in which the child can perform with a minimum of distraction. Specific suggestions are:

1. When working with other children, this child should be placed so that the actions of other children are no more distracting than necessary. In the classroom this would normally involve a front corner seat.
2. The person conducting the remediation should dress plainly, wearing clothes which do not call unnecessary attention to the teacher. We have found that the dress of the teacher appears to distract these children.
3. Remediation should not be conducted in physical surroundings in which pictures and other distracting objects are prominent. In clinical remediation this would be a plain room where a child's total efforts

----

*See Appendix B.

can be directed to the book before him. In the classroom, this child should take his reading instruction in an area of the room without extensive decoration.

4. When this difficulty is recognized as a serious limitation, it is often helpful to use books which contain a minimum of pictures, permitting the child to focus his entire attention upon the print and the skills necessary to read it.

5. This child will need to have skill exercises in periods of shorter duration. He should understand that his entire attention will be expected for a short period of time, after which he may move to another activity and return to his reading skill activity later. In the clinic we have found that it is good to vary the child's activity as much as possible. This type of adjustment is difficult and at times impossible in the classroom, for it disrupts the activities of the other children. The classroom teacher should, however, make every effort to provide a variety of activities for this child and at least refrain from punishing him for distractability over which he has no obvious control. In the more extreme cases it is desirable for the child to run, jump, and play actively in other ways between his periods of skill activities in reading. With these children, opportunities should be used to get them to be active in class as well as out of it. For example: have them come to the board for some of their work; let them pass out materials to other children; provide them with opportunities to stand. In these ways their tensions are released, and they become more receptive to the required silent work at their seats.

6. Children who are easily distracted generally enjoy a program which has as much consistency as possible. When they can anticipate an interesting routine, they are more likely to be able to concentrate on it to its completion. In clinical and classroom remediation, efforts should be made to develop program constancy.

Motivation

In each of the comprehension areas, motivation was discussed as an inherent part of the remedial program. In the general area of comprehension, motivation is most appropriately inherent, for here the child most readily senses his accomplishments. Comprehension, the goal of reading for teachers and for students, is a rewarding experience in itself. Specifically, we note that motivation in comprehension includes:

1. Improved performance in the content area in school.
2. Charts and graphs of progress.
3. Free reading of enjoyable material.
4. The enjoyment of reading for inferences and reading for evaluation.
5. The creating of successful comprehension situations.
6. Experience stories which permit the child to assume the role of the author.
7. The mental alertness which is generated by many comprehension situations.
8. The active role required of a child in most reading.
9. Genuine appreciation of discovering the unknown.

Other Structured Remedial Program

The reader's attention is directed to several carefully structured remedial programs which involve a new system for learning. In each of these the teacher, once committed, is expected to follow the program to a transfer stage where the child returns to reading traditional print. Of particular interest may be the remedial programs being conducted with *ITA** and *Words in Color**. The reader is directed to the noted sources for further study.

Remedial Techniques for the Reluctant Reader

The third type of problem reader, the child who has the reading skills but gives all indication of reluctance to use them, can be found in almost any classroom. Normally, this child will not be referred for clinical remediation on the basis of this deficiency alone. However, most children who come to the clinic are reluctant readers. The major responsibility for remediation in this area is with the classroom teacher, for the development of attitudes and habits can only *begin* in clinical remedial programs; their continuation and development must take place in the classroom.

Classroom remediation. It is first important for this child to develop the attitude that free reading is an activity which the teacher feels is worthwhile. Therefore, free reading opportunities should occur periodically in all classrooms. Free reading in this case implies reading which is

---

*See Appendix B.

not followed by question and answer periods and reading in which the child is relatively free to choose the desired materials. As this child develops the understanding that free reading can be fun and is important enough to take school time, gradual changes of attitude are likely to be noted.

The development of an attitude of willingness to read obviously involves the availability of books. The problem reader must have books available to him for free reading at his seat, in the classroom library, in the school library, and at home. There is little chance to develop attitudes and habits towards reading when books are difficult or impossible to obtain. School administrators should note that attempts to be thrifty by cutting appropriations for classroom and school libraries place teachers in the position of being unable to encourage the reading habit.

Every opportunity should be utilized to promote free reading through the use of peer group recommendations. The child who has read an interesting book and wants to share it with a class can often create more interest than can the teacher. This sharing may be done through brief voluntary oral reports, through a classroom card file including the name of the book and the reasons that the child enjoyed it, or through a school book fair where interesting books are displayed.

The teacher can develop interest by reading to the children from books which would be too difficult for them to read themselves but which contain stories and ideas of interest. If he takes the time to read some of the children's books, he too will be able to provide book summaries and develop interest in new books as they appear in the library. He also develops this attitude subtly by showing enthusiastic interest in his own personal reading.

The teacher may find it useful to consult book lists prepared by authorities to facilitate his guidance of children and the recommendations he will be expected to make. *Teacher's Guide to Children's Books,*[6] *Children and Books,*[7] *your Children Want to Read,*[8] and *Good Reading for Poor Readers,*[9] are four examples of these listings. Through the use of

[6]Nancy Larrick, *A Teacher's Guide to Children's Books* (Columbus, Ohio: Charles E. Merrill Books, Inc., 1960).

[7]May Hill Arbuthnot, *Children and Books* (Chicago: Scott, Foresman & Co., 1947).

[8]Ruth Tooze, *Your Children Want to Read* (Englewood Cliffs, N.J.: Prentice Hall Inc., 1957).

[9]George D. Spache, *Good Reading for Poor Readers* (Champaign, Illinois: The Garrard Press, 1960).

such resources, the teacher may also recommend to parents books which would be appropriate gifts for this child. Teachers should encourage parents to consider a book a valued, highly desired gift.

We often find that this child is reluctant to select a book which, to him, is a threat in terms of volume alone. Perhaps due to pressure from adults in his past, the child has developed an attitude that taking a book from the library commits him to read the book from cover to cover. The teacher, of course, must discourage this attitude, for we have all been in situations where, after starting a book, we feel no desire to finish it. Nevertheless, too many false starts tend to discourage the child from any start at all. Materials are available which enable the child to sample brief portions of books prior to selecting the books from the library. Two such materials which have been well received are the *Literature Sampler** and the *Pilot Library**. Both of these materials provide the teacher with a guide to the readability of the book and the interest factors involved, assisting him to direct the child to the books to which he will most likely respond favorably.

Clinical remediation. The type of activities mentioned above are required in clinical remediation as often as they can be applied. Extensive use is made of book series which, while maintaining high interest, have low vocabulary levels and facilitate interesting reading for problem readers. Without these books to reinforce the skills that are being developed in clinical remediation, the chance for transfer of these skills is seriously limited. The following list of high interest, low vocabulary books have been used effectively in programs of clinical remediation.

Series	Vocabulary level	Publisher
About Books	2-4 —	Children's Press
All About Books	3-6 —	Random House
American Adventure Series	2-6 —	Wheeler
Bucky Buttons	1-3 —	Benefic Press
Cowboy Sam	1-3 —	Benefic Press
Dan Frontier	1-3 —	Benefic Press
Deep Sea Adventure Stories	1-3 —	Harr Wagner
Dolch First Readers	1-2 —	Garrand
Interesting Reading Series	2-3 —	Follette
I Want to Be Books	1-3 —	Children's Press
Sailor Jack	1-3 —	Benefic Press

---

*See Appendix B.

Books such as these are inexpensive and readily available for clinical remediation. For a more complete list, see Botel, *How to Teach Reading* (*Suggested Readings*).

Free reading may be permitted in clinical remediation by using materials such as the *SRA Reading Laboratories** and the *Reader's Digest Skill Builders**. When used for free reading, these materials should be used without requiring the child to answer questions or to do the vocabulary exercises and, of course, should be selections at the recreational reading level.

Of particular value to the clinic are the *Literature Sampler** and the *Pilot Library** which, as in classroom remediation, save time in book selection.

Remediation for the Non-reader

Diagnosis occasionally uncovers a child who does not have a specific skill deficiency and might be termed a non-reader (see p. 95, chapter iv). Remediation for these children involves all of the best that has been discussed in the preceding pages. However, in these cases, instruction must be more precise and more thorough. The major characteristics of this instruction may well follow these recommended procedures:

1. Build upon the experiences of the child using the language experience approach. (See page 125.)
2. Develop basic sight vocabulary by using the Fernald or VAKT techniques. Reading specialists have found these techniques to be particularly valuable, although when used as a basic approach they are reserved for the seriously handicapped. Since these children normally profit most from a consistent approach, it is important that the reading specialist follow these sight vocabulary approaches with careful consistency. *Fernald*[10] and *Kolson*[11] provide detailed descriptions.

   The following version is one which we have found to work effectively:
   a. A word is selected from the context in which the child is working. This word will be printed on a card, in sand, on the chalkboard, or on the paper from which the child will work.

---

[10]Fernald, *Remedial Techniques in Basic School Subjects*, Chap. V.

[11]Clifford J. Kolson and George Kaluger, *Clinical Aspects of Remedial Reading* (Springfield, Illinois: Chas. C. Thomas, 1963), pp. 44-6.

*See Appendix B.

b. The teacher then demonstrates how to trace the word while pronouncing it. Using the fore- and index fingers, he traces the word left to right, and pronounces it.

c. The child then does the same. If he makes an error, he must be directed to start from the beginning of the word and try it again. Remember, he says the whole word as he traces it.

d. After several accurate tracings, the child is directed to reproduce the word while saying it. This reproduction is done with the copy in sight.

e. When he reproduces the word successfully, the child is then asked to reproduce the word without the copy in sight. Of course, he says it as he writes it.

f. When mastered, this word is placed on a card with a sentence contributed by the child.

g. The word can be reviewed as the teacher sees the need, and it can be used in future works for reading. It is quite possible that the child will come to this same word in context and claim to not know it. He should be asked, "How does the word feel? Trace it." He will usually find this to be successful.

At any step in this process, the child may fail. The procedure then is to go back to the preceding step, for it can be assumed that the preceding step has not been mastered.

Talmadge and others[12] have found this tracing approach to be the most successful technique to use when teaching children with cerebral dysfunction. The reader is cautioned that the technique is time consuming, must be accomplished precisely, and requires overlearning. As a result, there is no suggestion that these procedures be used over a long period of time in less serious cases. In fact, as soon as the child can learn words effectively by taking short cuts, we encourage him to do so. Once learned, this technique can be accomplished by the child, without teacher supervision, except for the pronunciation of the unknown word.

As the child builds sight vocabulary through tracing, he should be placed in reading situations constantly. Initially the reading will consist of the language experience approach using the concepts and vocabulary of the child. As the child progresses, easy, interesting

---

[12]Max Talmadge, Anthony Davids and Maurice W. Laufer, "A Study of Experimental Methods for Teaching Emotionally Disturbed, Brain Damaged, Retarded Readers," *Journal of Educational Research*, LVI:6, February 1963, p. 312.

material can be used from other sources. As a rule, it is desirable to have this child experience much success at each step in the program. It will be necessary, therefore, to limit word analysis exercises until the child starts to indicate confidence in a learning situation.

3. Many children who are classified as non-readers demonstrate difficulties in visual discrimination. Carefully working through the types of visual discrimination exercises found in most readiness programs is often helpful. The Frostig* exercises may be required for children who are more seriously handicapped in this area. For the experienced reading specialist, the language experience stories will provide many opportunities to stress both auditory and visual discrimination.

4. Because this child needs as many stimuli as possible, the teacher may pursue oral reading further than usual. Note that the Fernald Approach makes optimum use of available stimuli.

Survival program

Older children, ages 15-20, particularly in clinical situations, are often so seriously retarded in reading that there is little chance of their ever using reading for anything but the essentials of life. These young people can often profit most from sight vocabulary instruction which is directed towards their survival in our society. Normally dealt with in clinical situations, the pupils are often found in classrooms where clinical remediation is not available. What these people need is strong motivation and good teaching techniques to learn the sight words and concepts necessary for functioning in our society. The materials used for this type of instruction may consist of:

1. Driver's manuals
2. Road signs
3. Menus
4. The Essential Driver's List[14]
5. The Essential Vocabulary List[15]
6. Various sight words used in the occupation in which the child has an interest

---

[13]Corlett T. Wilson, "An Essential Vocabulary," *The Reading Teacher,* November 1963, pp. 94-6.

[14]*Ibid.*

*See Appendix B.

7. Rochester Occupational Series*
8. Ads in newspapers
9. Employment contracts
10. Income tax forms

The words and concepts involved with this material, necessary for survival programs, may be taught in any manner that seems efficient.

The *Non-Oral** technique, the *Nichols Tachistoscope Slide** concept, and the *Fernald** technique have all been used effectively in these programs.

The young person involved in a survival program should understand the goals which we assume are self-motivating and should not normally be placed in other types of reading situations. He will not enjoy sitting down with a book, nor will he be attempting occupations which require regular reading. It is through the learning of the essential sight vocabulary that he will receive the most benefit. This type of work often encourages him to continue to strive for reading skills beyond "survival," in which cases the remedial program may be continued toward some other short term realistic goals.

When survival types of programs are desirable for the classroom, the child should be placed in learning situations of minimum pressure. Specifically, he should not be expected to be responsible for reading assignments in his text and should not be required to fail on written tests. Rather, text assignments can be read to him or placed on tape for his use. Tests may be handled in much the same manner. We recommend that this child have a text and be permitted to use it as he desires if for no other reason than the status which is involved. With this child the classroom philosophy is one of having him learn as much as possible via listening, pictures, and demonstrations, while reading instruction is initially limited to the above mentioned survival programs.

Remediation for the Culturally Disadvantaged

From diagnosis the reader will recall that certain groups of children, due to experiential backgrounds which are quite different from those of the average child, do not make normal progress in reading. Remediation must be designed to permit (1) development of experiential background,

---

*See Appendix B.

(2) success in decoding activities, and (3) personal success in the total reading act.

Both the classroom teacher and the reading specialist must take every opportunity to develop language experiences throughout all remedial sessions. When opportunities do present themselves, they should be structured. For example, if this child who is reading about the zoo has never been to the zoo, either a trip to the zoo, a film, or pictures must precede a reading lesson that has to do with those types of animals that one finds in a zoo. It can be assumed that in a normal school situation, the child has experienced considerable frustration by being placed in reading situations for which he has not had sufficient experiential background. There is no justification for this child to be continually frustrated for these reasons. For those who desire a systematic program of language experiences, the *Peabody Language Development Kit** and the *Ginn Language Kit A** mentioned previously can serve as guides.

Decoding activities for these children should always be in terms of language involving concepts which they possess. This then assures motivation, for the child sees that the system actually does help him decode words for which he has concepts.

Although motivation is an important part in all remediation, for these children it is extremely important. Remedial sessions should have an aura of excitement about them, and the values of reading should be subtly stressed.

Beyond these suggestions there should be a program which is developed according to the precise needs of the individual child.

Pitfalls of Remediation

In concluding the discussion of remedial techniques, the classroom teacher and the reading specialist should consider the following pitfalls, which, when not avoided, disrupt the efficiency of many remedial programs.

Isolated drill.

Perhaps the major pitfall in remediation is the abundance, in a remedial session, of isolated drill activities in which the child obtains the impression that satisfactory performance in the drill itself is the reading act.

---

*See Appendix B.

Failure to establish a program which complies with established goals.
Another common pitfall in remedial programs is for instruction to become sidetracked into areas which do not meet the goals as they were established on the basis of the diagnosis. This quite often occurs when isolated drill (pitfall #1) appears to have become the goal of remediation. A conscious effort must be made to establish goals which are realistic and which can be understood by the person conducting the remediation, the child, the parents, and the child's classroom teacher. These goals then should serve as a guide to remedial approaches.

Failure to illustrate progress.
As educators, we are quite often satisfied with the child's progress as he develops his reading skills. This progress, however, is not always clear to the child. It is important that the child have this progress illustrated to him through any techniques available. When this does not occur, it is common for the child to become discouraged and lose interest, even when working up to his full potential.

Failure to share information about remedial progress.
This pitfall is particularly directed at clinical remediation in which the child has gone through an extensive and successful remedial program. If the results of such programs are not readily available to the classroom teacher or to the parent, false assumptions may be gathered concerning the child's reading skills based upon previous performance. Therefore, effective communication lines must be maintained between the various people concerned with the remedial program.

Summary

The development of comprehension skills is generally based on the Directed Reading Activity. Modifications are made, however, to adjust to the particular diagnostic needs of the child. Special programs will be required for students who have been diagnosed as having particular types of overall reading deficiencies. The ultimate goal, regardless of the program, will be to develop successful reading situations for all children. The educator is further reminded that remediation can be conducted most successfully when the educator is alert to certain pitfalls which must be avoided.

Suggested Readings

1. Botel, Morton, *How to Teach Reading,* Chap. II. Chicago: Follett Publishing Co., 1959. Botel's practical guide for teachers will again be useful to the educator who wants specific techniques for teaching comprehension as a thinking process.

2. Robinson, Francis P., *Effective Study.* New York: Harper & Brothers, 1961. The teacher of older students who desires to stress study skills in remedial sessions will find the SQ3R technique well-defined and explained in this book.

3. Tinker, Miles A., and Constance M. McCullough, *Teaching Elementary Reading,* Chaps. VIII and IX. New York: Appleton-Century Crofts, Inc., 1962. Excellent suggestions are provided in this book for the teaching of comprehension skills to elementary school children. The reader will find these suggestions specific and practical.

9

Evaluation in Remedial Reading

Instruction which has been directed through effective diagnosis to meet the needs of the child stands a good chance of being successful. Following remediation, be it classroom or clinical, the child is likely to show signs of being an improved reader. It is also likely that a post-test in most cases will be the evaluation technique used by the educator to determine how much gain has been made by the child. While the assumption is logical and the technique acceptable, post-testing is not itself the entire answer to the problem of evaluation in remedial reading.

Has the pupil made *useful* progress? Post-test comparisons with performance prior to remediation measure how well the child has improved but only in those areas measured by the test. Has he improved so that his classroom performance will be better? Will he read more at home? Has his attitude toward reading changed? Are the gains which are indicated by the test of a permanent nature? Has the test measured the child's ability to perform in non-test reading situations? Are the gains a significant change in the child's reading skills? These types of questions concerning the measuring instrument provide a still clearer picture for evaluation. Although the pupil has made real progress, were the gains made as a result of efficient diagnosis and remedial techniques? Could the child have accomplished more with less or more diagnosis, less or more remediation? Was this progress in terms of the educational goals which were established? Was the teacher able to direct the child toward useful goals, and was his progress a result of that effort? When answers to these types of questions have been obtained, we are closer to a true evaluation of the effectiveness of a remedial program upon the child. The evaluation of teacher efficiency in the use of diagnostic and remedial techniques is essential, for it is in this manner that one can more clearly see the effectiveness of the reading program as contrasted with the educational gains normally expected over this period of time.

When evaluation is conducted following clinical remediation, additional complications which are not present in the evaluation of classroom remediation arise. First, the child has been taken from the classroom, tested and tutored by someone other than the classroom teacher and sent back to the classroom to use his newly developed skills. This transfer from clinical to classroom situations is not always automatic, for many children in clinical situations perform for reasons that do not necessarily carry over to the classroom. We have experienced cases in which the child worked and improved during clinical remediation and was returned to the classroom with "adequate reading skills." However, upon returning to his classroom, the child was unable or unwilling to use these newly formed skills effectively. Upon investigation we found that the child had enjoyed the individualized attention, responded to the motivation of the tutor, and was willing to work to please this particular educator, but lost this desire upon returning to the classroom to be one of 33 children. To facilitate an effective transfer of skills learned in clinical situations to the classroom, we have made it a policy to culminate all clinical work in group instruction. That is, prior to the release of the child from the clinic, he will be expected to perform within a group of peers for a period of time long enough to satisfy us that he can work satisfactorily in a group.

Another complication of evaluation in clinical remediation is to determine just how much of the child's improved skills performance has been due to work in the clinical situation and how much would have occurred if he had remained in the classroom. Although it is not always feasible to measure precisely, consideration must be made for improvement outside the remedial program. Classroom and clinical evaluation have much in common, however, and the reader will find a use for many of the following suggestions, be they applied to the classroom or the clinic.

Principles of Evaluation in Remedial Reading

The following principles, common to all education, have particular application when evaluating the effectiveness of remedial reading programs:

Evaluation must be continuous

Actually evaluation is the final act of continual diagnosis. It involves many of the same processes as diagnosis, i.e., an evaluation of the child's skill development and reading effectiveness. Evaluation of past performance can be considered diagnosis for future instruction; therefore, evaluation is continuous.

Evaluation must be objective

Objective measures of performance should be used in an effort to control bias. One often reads evaluation reports which state that the teachers and pupils were enthusiastic about the progress which had been made. Although this enthusiasm is a factor which is highly desirable, it cannot be the basis for evaluation of program effectiveness. Non-objective evaluation techniques are certainly valuable and are not to be precluded by this principle. However, the principle that the basis of the evaluation must be as objective as possible in nature, still holds.

Evaluation must be in terms of established goals

It is desirable and natural for considerable progress to be noticed in areas for which instruction had not been planned. This progress, however desirable, cannot be considered in an objective evaluation of the basic program, for the program must be evaluated in terms of the goals for which it was conducted.

Evaluation must be broad in base

Ample allowance must be made for factors such as improved medical attention, relaxation of home pressures, and reaction to diagnosis by the classroom teacher. If a child has been provided with glasses as a result of physical screening and has then been tutored, a proper evaluation must give consideration to the effect of the glasses as well as the instruction. In an examination of our clinic cases, for example, we have found that children who were referred for inadequate visual screening performance made better progress (as a group) if the parents followed the referral advice than did children whose parents did not follow referral advice. Apparently, attention to the visual needs of these children had an effect upon the progress which they made. The appropriate importance to be applied to each factor is extremely difficult to determine; however, this principle insists only that it be considered in the evaluation of the child's progress.

Aspects of Evaluation. Broadly, the aspects of evaluation in reading can be considered in terms of pupil growth and educator efficiency. In order to be clearly seen as separate aspects of evaluation, they are discussed below individually; however, the reader is reminded that the two aspects of evaluation are closely related and evaluation of one, exclusive the other, is often not possible.

Pupil Growth

The questions which arose at the beginning of this chapter indicate several aspects of evaluation in terms of pupil growth. An examination of several of these aspects will assist the reader to become more effective in pupil evaluation.

Changes in classroom performance

Of primary importance is the child's performance in the classroom. If there are not noticeable changes of behavior in terms of classroom performance (grades and attitudes), there is cause to doubt the effectiveness of the remedial program. This aspect of pupil growth, although of basic importance, is quite often not considered in evaluation. Does the child make better grades in school following the remedial program? Does the child read more willingly, more often? Has the child gained independence in reading? Improved school grades are usually a satisfactory indication of pupil growth, particularly for the child and his parents. Grade improvement might be best noticed in the subjects which are language-centered. This author studied successful remedial reading cases and found considerable scholastic improvement in terms of school grades.[1] Subsequent to this study, it was found to be of value to conduct follow-up studies of groups of remedial students periodically to determine our effectiveness. Short questionnaires can be used to obtain this information, preferably from the classroom teacher. If scholastic performance has not improved, most parents will consider the remedial program to have been ineffective, regardless of other indications of improved skill performance.

---

[1] Robert M. Wilson, *The Scholastic Improvement of Successful Remedial Reading Students* (unpublished Doctor's dissertation, University of Pittsburgh, 1960).

The classroom teacher is in a favorable position to obtain information concerning changes in classroom performance, for he has school records available to him. He can follow a child's scholastic performance on a rather informal basis, while the reading specialist will generally be required to use questionnaires to obtain this information. In either case, the educator will be obtaining important information concerning the growth and development of the child after remedial efforts have been successfully terminated.

Changes of pupil attitude are of utmost importance to the teacher, the parents, and of course, to the child. In most cases, attitude changes are the most obvious indication to the classroom teacher that the program was effective. Parents often feel that attitude changes prove the worth of a given program. It goes without saying that, if the child can improve in his attitude toward reading and school in general, it will be obvious to him that the remedial program has made a difference.

Further evaluation must be made to determine if these changes in classroom performance were temporary or permanent. Temporary changes may indicate a lack of communication between one classroom teacher and another or between the classroom teacher and the reading specialist. Either case results in ineffective transfer from remediation to classroom work. A program which produces only temporary improvement may need to be evaluated, for it would appear that it is tutorial in nature, i.e., it prepares the child for a reading situation but does not develop skills which can be applied to all reading situations.

A study of a child's grades over a period of several years can be conducted in the same manner as can a study of immediate scholastic performance, i.e., through the examination of school records or questionnaires. When the evaluation findings are positive, the educator will find this type of evaluation to be a rewarding experience. It is most assuring to know that the child has not only responded to the teacher's efforts, but also has used his newly developed skills without his constant attention.

Changes in reading skills

1. *In terms of grade level improvement*

Evaluation of improvement in reading is usually determined by test performance. Bleismer[2], in sighting three basic post-remediation evalua-

---

[2]Emery P. Bliesmer, "Evaluating Progress in Remedial Reading Programs," *The Reading Teacher,* March 1962, pp. 344-50.

tion techniques calls this a simple pre- and post-test comparison. If a child enters a remedial program reading at 4.5 grade level and concludes the reading program at 5.5 grade level, it can be concluded that he has gained 1.0 years in grade level. Obviously, the adequacy of the test instrument used to determine grade level performance limits this aspect of evaluation. It does not account for the child's chronological age increase, nor for changes which would have occurred without remediation.

Reading skill performance as compared to grade level is of particular interest to the classroom teacher and the principal, for it has much to do with the placement of the child in a room and within a class. Once it has been determined that a child can perform at a certain grade level, it is necessary to create situations that require this performance of him.

2. *In terms of reading potential*

Evaluation in this area attempts to determine whether the child is working up to his potential. Bleismer[3] claims that potential will change with age and that estimates must be adjusted for effective evaluation. Regardless of the child's grade level performance and ability to perform in an assigned classroom, growth up to potential is generally considered a desirable goal of remediation. If a child had an estimated potential of 5.0 and a reading level of 3.0, he could be considered deficient by 2.0 years. If, after a semester of work, his reading level raises to 4.2, his potential will have to be re-estimated before growth can be measured.

January			May		
Potential	Reading	Difference	Potential	Reading	Difference
5.0	3.0	2.0	5.8	4.2	1.6

Note that in this case, the child's reading potential increased as he grew older, thereby lessening the apparent effect of the difference in reading grade level changes. Remedial sessions accelerated his growth over his potential by .4 years (found by subtracting the differences). This technique will be of more interest to the reading specialist than to the classroom teacher or the parent.

3. *In terms of past performance*

Evaluation of skill improvement in terms of the child's previous performance rates is of some advantage with older students. Again Bleismer[4]

3*Ibid.*

4Bleismer, *Evaluating Progress.*

is asking that the identifiable variables be controlled. Suppose that a boy has completed six years of school and has scored at grade level 4.6 before remediation has begun. This indicates an average growth of .6 years of reading skill for each year in school (4.6 — 1.0 divided by 6). Note that 1.0 must be subtracted as all children start with a reading level of 1.0 (the zero month of first grade). If this child obtained a reading level of 5.5 by the end of one year in remediation, he would have gained .9 years of skill in one year (5.5 — 4.9 = .9). He is not reading up to grade level and may not be reading up to expectancy. He has not progressed one full year even under intensive remediation. *But* his improvement is greater than it has been in the past, and there is indication of an effective remedial program.

Years in School	Average Yearly Gain Before Tutoring	Gain During Yr. of Tutoring	Growth Attributed to Tutoring
5	.6	.9	.3

Note that the gain of .9 years is greater than could have been expected from an average of previous efforts. Of interest to the reading specialist and the classroom teacher, the rate of improvement during remediation is of little interest to the child or the parent, especially if the child remains limited in ability to perform in the classroom.

Evaluation of this type is limited by the assumption — an unlikely one — that past performance was evenly distributed. However, the older child who is seriously handicapped in reading is less likely to score effectively in terms of the other aspects of evaluation while making significant progress. This technique, then, provides an indication of his skill improvements, however slight.

The precise instrument used for the comparisons mentioned above deserve the reader's attention. In most cases it will be advisable to use a different form of the same test. Standardized upon the same population, alternate form evaluation can be interpreted more reliably. If different tests are used, the educator cannot be certain whether the differences are due to skill improvements or to the differences in the norms of the two tests. The reader realizes that some tests use norms which are higher than other tests. On the other hand, it is equally unreliable to use the same form of the same test, for the child's acquaintance with the test as well as his skill performance is reflected.

In some cases it is worthwhile to administer two post-tests. One of these may be selected for its ability to measure specific skill improvement; the other, selected for its ability to measure the use of the skill in a reading situation. In any case, the educator will want to take every precaution to assure himself that the gains are due to skill improvement and not the design or the norm of the test. When informal techniques have been used for the diagnosis, these same techniques can be used for evaluation. An effort should be maintained to keep the evaluation as similar as possible to the diagnosis so that skill improvements can be assessed without undue concern over the differences in procedures. If the educator attempts to make an evaluation based upon observations of the child's reading without a rather well-established device, the results are likely to be invalid and unreliable. It is important, therefore, for evaluation using informal procedures to be carefully planned and administered.

Changes of reading attitude in the home. We have often heard parents exclaim, "Now John enjoys reading!" or "He actually sits down and reads without our urging him to do so!" Certainly a desirable outcome of a remedial program, this aspect of evaluation is usually measured more subjectively and therefore must be done more cautiously; but, nevertheless, it must be considered. It is the child's desire and interest in reading that, when developed, can mean significant changes in the child's performance in school. Without changes in attitude, the gains made during remediation can usually be considered temporary, for it is with improved attitude that the child will continue to strive and improve.

Questionnaires or interviews are generally used for this type of evaluation. Information should be obtained from the child as well as the parents to assure the reliability of the responses. The inherent danger of this type of evaluation is the tendency for respondents to maintain a "halo" effect; therefore, it is important that the interview or questionnaire be structured so as to avoid pointing to obviously expected responses. Difficult at best, evaluation of this type will add to the total picture of the child's improvements as a result of remediation.

When possible, directed observations can be used for evaluation of student attitudes. When using observations in evaluation, the educator must have recorded evidence of observed attitudes prior to the remedial program. Lacking such evidence, observation as an evaluation technique will be of little use.

Educator Efficiency

The efficiency of the educator is evaluated with more difficulty and is therefore less likely to receive the evaluative efforts that pupil growth receives. Educator efficiency in programs should be evaluated in the following areas:

Adequacy of diagnosis. Due to emphasis placed upon the proper use of diagnosis and the time spent in accomplishing it, there is valid reason for its inclusion for evaluation. The educator must determine whether the diagnosis uncovered the remedial needs of the child effectively and precisely. Further, he must decide that the diagnosis, while not overextended, was complete enough to cover the areas of the child's deficiency. When there is a failure to evaluate in these areas, there is a likelihood that inefficiency will develop into diagnostic habits. We have known teachers to use tests which, for them, appear to supply essential information for the diagnosis; however, upon closer examination, these tests do not provide any information that could not be determined more easily by better techniques.

Adequacy of remedial approach. As educators become accustomed to working in remediation, specific approaches often develop into standard procedures with all children. The error developed here, without constant attempts at evaluation, is that diagnosis is relegated to a secondary position since a given remedial approach is used with all children. For example, if all children were to be tutored through the use of the experience story approach, then, although diagnosis has some importance, the diagnostic conclusions would take second place to the remedial approach. It is through evaluation of remedial approaches that the educator is led to develop a variety of effective approaches as prescribed by the diagnostic needs of the children.

Adequacy of remedial techniques. Similar to the difficulty described in remedial approaches, a prescribed technique used with all children, regardless of the remedial approach, is equally limiting and can be avoided through careful evaluation of remedial techniques. For example, a graph to illustrate progress is not needed to motivate all children in all remedial techniques. The evaluation of techniques will save time in remediation and lead the educator toward those techniques best suited to the needs of the child.

Adequacy of remedial materials. As educators became familiar with the manuals and contents of the wide variety of materials available in remediation, they are likely to select and use those that appeal to them. This is entirely proper when these materials are selected after an evaluation of their effectiveness; however, when selected by the teacher on the basis of familiarity alone, there is a need to evaluate their adequacy. As the flood of materials continues, the educator will need to do more material evaluation.

A variety of techniques is available to assist the educator in the various aspects of evaluation discussed above. It is desirable that more than one of these techniques be used in the evaluation.

When requested, the reading specialist should be capable of conducting evaluation of the total school efforts in the area of diagnostic and remedial reading. This assumes that the reading specialist is acquainted with research design and controlled experimentation techniques and has the ability to interpret research data. Austin and others[5] discuss the school survey in detail, with specific suggestions for its implementation. When the school is unprepared for this type of evaluation, it will be necessary to call upon other school or university personnel to assist. In many cases, evaluation conducted by persons not directly involved in the program is advantageous, for it lessens the role of bias.

Summary

A carefully planned program of evaluation should be included in diagnostic and remedial programs. Educators would do well to consider the goals in advance and then to plan evaluation as a portion of the program in which they work. Care must be taken to determine the occurrence and relevance of factors outside the program which may be accounting for the child's growth. For effective evaluation, all progress should be judged in terms of the educational goals, long and short term.

---

[5]Austin, Bush and Heubner, *Reading Evaluation.*

Suggested Readings

1. Austin, Mary C., Clifford L. Bush, and Mildred H. Huebner, *Reading Evaluation*. New York: The Ronald Press Co., 1961. This entire book is devoted to the subject of evaluation in reading. Not restricted to remedial evaluation, the authors have provided specific evaluation techniques and tests. The reading specialist will find this book to have particular value when he is considering an all-school survey.

2. Bleismer, Emery P., "Evaluating Progress in Remedial Reading Programs," *The Reading Teacher,* March, 1962, pp. 344-50. A detailed explanation of three basic techniques for evaluating remedial programs is provided in this article. Reviewed in this chapter, these techniques can be studied more thoroughly by a quick review of this excellent article.

3. Ahmann, J. Stanley, and Marvin D. Glock, *Evaluating Pupil Growth,* Chaps XIV and XVI. Boston: Allyn-Bacon, Inc., 1959. In chapter XIV, the authors discuss the aspects of evaluating personal-social adjustment. Chapter XVI is devoted to diagnosis and remediation. These two chapters as well as the entire book will provide the reader with an effective basis for evaluation.

4. Strang, Ruth and Donald M. Linguist, *The Administrator and the Improvment of Reading*, Chap. IV and Appendix B. New York: Appleton-Century-Crofts, Inc., 1960. This booklet, designed for the administrator, has evaluation clues built into each chapter. Chapter iv addresses itself to the evaluation of suitable reading programs. Appendix B is a guide of teacher self-appraisal. These two references will be of interest to the reader who desires more information on teacher effectiveness evaluation.

10

Parental Roles in Diagnosis, Remediation And Prevention

"Let your child alone!" or "Don't worry, we'll handle it," are quite often the only suggestions that teachers have to offer parents who are seeking ways to help their child with reading difficulties. Today such advice is inappropriate and will likely fall upon deaf ears, for parents want to help their child, can help their child, and will help their child! As the educational level of our adult population rises, as the emphasis upon education for success in life continues, as education continues to be examined in the public press, and as commercial exploitations of parental concerns expand, it it no longer defensible to shut parents out of the role of assisting their child with reading, especially if he is experiencing difficulty. It is imperative that educators realize this and seek ways for parents to be most helpful in terms of the educational goals which have been established.

On the opposite side of the coin is the fact that, when left without guidance, the types of things that parents do to "help" their child may be inappropriate and often harmful. It is not uncommon for an uninformed parent, for example, to attempt to motivate his child through comparison with his brothers and sisters or playmates. More often than not, this merely compounds the child's aversion to reading and actually interferes with his progress in a remedial program. So, again, it behooves us to direct the parent to that role which will most effectively fulfill the educational goals which have been established.

Although not a hard and fast rule, it is our finding that parental anxiety is likely to mount as a child's progress in reading declines. There comes a point where this anxiety is felt by the child to such a degree that it complicates his reading problem. These parents, too, must have their concern and anxiety channeled into useful, helpful educational activities. It *does not* help to tell the parents not to worry; it is too late for this. The answer is to establish for them a role through which they can be most helpful.

Clinical and classroom diagnostic and remedial situations inherently demand that the parental role vary. The difference in roles is generally one of degree, for by the very nature of clinical situations, the parents are more actively engaged in what their child is doing. As the role of the parent is discussed in diagnosis, remediation, and prevention of reading problems, suggestions are termed in reference to the classroom teacher and/or reading specialist, so that they might direct the parent toward useful activities. It certainly is not assumed that all parents can perform all of the roles to be discussed. Final determination of the precise role of the parent is reserved for the educator who is working directly with the child.

Parents Can Help!

Parents teach their children to walk, to talk, and to do numerous other useful activities required in our society. As educators, we rely heavily upon the ability of the parents to do these jobs well. When they do not fulfill that responsibility, they leave the child ill-equipped for progress in school. As the child develops difficulties in his progress in reading, it is logical to call upon the child's *first teacher,* his parents, to assist us in any way that will be useful. The suggestions that follow, then, are based upon the following beliefs:

1. Parents can help.
2. Parents often know what makes their child react most effectively.
3. Children want parental support and assistance and strive to please their parents through school success.
4. Without parent-teacher teamwork, success with severely handicapped readers will be unnecessarily limited.

5. When directed toward useful roles, parents are usually willing to follow the advice of educators.

Parental Role In Diagnosis

Except for the classroom teacher, parents are most likely to be the first to recognize that their child is not making satisfactory progress in the development of his reading skills. When the classroom teacher fails to observe the signs of frustrated reading in a given child, one can be certain that it will not escape the parents for long. The responsibility for the initial identification of the problem reader then often falls to the parents. Parents may be properly directed to observe their child in reading and, when any of the following symptoms of frustrated reading occur, call them to the attention of the classroom teacher or the reading specialist. These symptoms are:

1. Avoidance of reading.
2. Inability to complete classroom assignments of home work.
3. Inability to discuss with the parent material which he has just completed in reading.
4. Habitual difficulty in attacking unknown words, especially if noticed after two or three years of schooling.
5. Word-by-word, non-fluent oral reading, especially when the child has practiced this reading silently before reading it orally.
6. Complaints from the child of visual discomfort in reading periods of fifteen minutes or more.

By directing the educator's attention to specific symptoms such as these, parents may identify reading problems before they become serious enough to necessitate the more formal types of reading diagnosis and remediation. Upon receipt of observations such as these from parents, the educator should conduct as much diagnosis as is necessary to inform himself and the parents of the nature of the problem.

That many parents will become overly anxious while observing the child for these symptoms must also be considered. However, it is just as important for this anxious parent to know that his child does *not* have a reading problem as it is for other parents to know the nature of their child's reading problem. In this way needless anxieties can be relaxed, creating better learning situations for the child.

Another important role of parents in diagnosis is to supply information in support of or in conflict with the tentative hypothesis which has been established in classroom diagnosis or initial screening techniques. The parents' role in clinical diagnosis, then, is to supply supporting observations concerning the child's work in school, his attitudes toward reading, his physical well being, etc. Without this information, frequently obtainable through either questionnaires or interviews, the reading specialist, making judgments based on relatively short exposure to the child, is likely to err. It is generally more effective to obtain information from parents after tentative hypotheses have been reached, lest the feelings of the parents tend to bias the examiner.

The parent has the complete responsibility for the follow-up in areas in which referral has been made. It is the right and the responsibility of parents to attend to the physical and emotional needs of their child; and it is the parent to whom we most often look for assistance in taking the child to the vision specialist, the neurologist, the psychatrist, etc.

As parents become involved in the diagnosis, it is important that they be consulted concerning the findings. Perhaps nothing is more frustrating to parents than to know that their child has undergone extensive study, and yet they have not been consulted about the findings. However, making diagnostic conclusions available to parents is far more than a courtesy, for quite often it is the parents to whom the suggestions for alleviating the problem most appropriately apply. A number of times we have consulted with parents concerning their child's problem, only to find later that the child, from that point on, improved and no longer needed remedial help. This is enough to convince us of the usefulness of this type of follow-up in diagnosis.

As parents are consulted concerning diagnostic conclusions, it is often wise to avoid the discussion of precise scores and specific findings. The tendency to overrate a score on a particular test without fully understanding the explanation of the test is a common difficulty of parents when they encounter test score results. It is usually preferable to provide parents with the general findings of the diagnosis, placing more emphasis upon the interpretation of these test scores than on the scores themselves. It may be better, for example, to indicate to the parents that the child reads well on about the second grade level and that he will need help in remediation in the area of word attack skills, than it would be to tell them that the child scored 2.6 on a given test and obtained a score of 75% on initial consonant sounds.

It is important that the parents have confidence in the findings of the diagnosis, for they are then more likely to adhere to the ensuing recommendations. Their confidence is, of course, going to depend a great deal upon the manner in which the diagnosis is explained; however, we have found that it often helps to explain or demonstrate a test or two upon which the child was evaluated. The parents then develop a feeling for the errors that the child has made and obtain the feeling that the educator really wants them to be informed in this area. When used as the only form of reporting, written diagnostic findings are of a limited value to the parents. Terms and implications are often not fully understood; questions arising from the reports are left unanswered. Parents can be better informed if diagnostic reports are explained in a consultation session with questions answered and understandings assured. Summaries of these sessions may be written and sent to the parents, but not without consultation.

Parental Roles in Remediation

For the parent to have any role at all in remediation, there must be a general understanding of the educational goals set by the person conducting the remediation. It is not only ethically appropriate for the educator to inform the parents of such goals, but it makes reaching the goal far more feasible when the parents are effectively involved. The first task, therefore, is to inform the parent of realistic goals and of the general approaches to be used in attaining these goals. It is extremely helpful if these goals are short-range and easily attainable so that the child, the parent, and the educator can see clearly that progress is being made. Of course, this will necessitate contacting the parent as the goals are readjusted and progress in the development of reading skills is made. Again, these contacts with parents are most effective when they receive the information in a consultation session.

The most appropriate role for the parent, after an understanding of the program has been made available, is to provide situations in the home where the skills learned in remediation can be *reinforced*. Although this task is time consuming, the parent should recognize the necessity of providing these opportunities as his foremost responsibility. Specifically this involves the parent in:

1. Providing a quiet, comfortable, and relaxing place for reading in the home.
2. Providing a planned time during the day when the household becomes suitable for reading: the TV is turned off; other members of the family pursue reading interests; and a pleasant feeling towards this time is created.

3. Assisting the child with material that is difficult for him in either word pronunciation or sentences and paragraph meaning. This, of course, involves the availability of one of the parents but should not be construed to imply that the parent must be "breathing down the child's neck." On the contrary, the parent (while reading something of interest to himself) may simply be in the same room and be available to the child, if needed.

4. Assisting the child with follow-up exercises which are sent home after a remedial session. The parent must understand that the child is learning a skill and will probably not be letter-perfect in these attempts. The parent must not become angry with the child when he fails repeatedly in these types of exercises; rather, the parent should contact the educator conducting the remediation and inform him of this difficulty. Neither the classroom teacher nor the reading specialist will send material home for this type of practice unless there is relative assurance that it can be completed with some satisfaction. However, there will be instances when, regardless of the care taken, the child will bring home materials which are too difficult for him to read without assistance.

5. Being available when an audience is needed or when discussion, following either oral or silent reading, is desirable. In this role, the parent should display an attitude of interest in what the child has read, permitting the child to feel a sense of doing something which pleases the parent.

It goes without saying that all of these activities will be conducted in co-operation with the reading specialist or the classroom teacher and that specific activities will be originated by these educators in terms of the goals which have already been explained to the parent. It is helpful to demonstrate these techniques to parents. Illustrating to the parents how effectively the recommended suggestions actually work with their child builds confidence in the recommendations.

On the negative side, it is important for the parent to understand what *not to do* as well as what *to do*. Depending upon the educational goals, the educator should anticipate the types of problems likely to arise and direct the parents away from them. For example, it is far better to have the parents in the role of reinforcing skills learned in remedial sessions, than it is to have them attempt to teach these skills themselves. If the parents feel that there is a great deficiency in a sounding skill, for example, the educator should be informed and the parents provided with an explanation of when that skill will become a part of the program. Furthermore, it should be made clear that no matter how great the temptation may be to have the child "sound out the word," it is the parents' job to tell the child unknown words until the skill is dealt with remedially. Note that these examples relate to phonics. We find that it is in this area that most parents feel anxious and in which they do the poorest job of assisting us. As a general rule, therefore, we direct their attention away from instruction in phonics while providing opportunities for them to notice the child's development in this area through carefully prepared home assignments.

Another role for the parents in remediation is to obtain books for the child to read. Normally, the educator will supply the first books from materials available in the remedial program; however, since the supply of books is often limited, the parents can be encouraged to assume responsibility for obtaining books. The educator, in these cases, will supply the parent with a list of appropriate books for the child to read at home, asking the parents to obtain these books from libraries, friends, book stores, etc. Consideration for the level and the interest factors of available books should be evaluated in the recommendations made to parents. It has been found to be worthwhile to recommend books to parents near the child's birthday or at Christmas so that books can be included on gift lists. More than simply supplying the child with a book, the attitude is being developed that a book is something of considerable value and worth, for it is given as a special gift. (See page 181.)

It is common to find parents who desire to supplement the efforts of the remedial program with commercially available materials. Unless these materials are in accordance with the educational goals which have been established and unless the educator knows of the materials and can recommend their appropriateness for this child, it is our feeling that they should be avoided. By placing the parent into the teacher's role, unsuitable commercial materials involve them to a degree which is not profitable for them, the child, nor the educational goals for which we are striving.

Parental Roles in Prevention

It is well to discuss the role of parents once the child has developed a reading problem, but it is far more important to reach parents before children develop reading problems. Next to the classroom teacher, parents can do more to prevent the development of difficulties than anyone else. Part of the problem here is to communicate effectively with parents who are *not* anxious about their child's lack of success in reading. When unconcerned, the parents are less likely to seek assistance, thus implying to the child that they do not care. Each school and each teacher should take every opportunity to present preventive information to parents. Programs during Educational Week, PTA meetings, individual conferences with parents, and notes sent to the home may be used to help parents prevent the occurrence of reading problems.

The following suggestions are designed to inform parents of activities which have been found to diminish the possibility of reading problems developing. They should be recommended by educators with discretion and for application when appropriate. No attempt is made here to supply a formula which will work with equal effectiveness with all parents.

Physical care

Parents who desire to avoid the complications involved with failure in school (reading, in particular) should reflect upon their child's physical needs. A visual examination prior to school entrance and at least every other year thereafter, is excellent insurance. An annual physical examination with follow-ups which are recommended by the family doctor eliminates the necessity of waiting until symptoms of physical disability are so apparent that they interfere with success in school. Many physical difficulties go unnoticed until the failure in school is so acute that remedial programs are grossly limited. If the child has refused to read for years because of visual discomfort, there is a void of reading experiences in his background for which, at times, it is impossible to compensate. From the number of children who come to school too tired to accomplish the expected assignments during a given day, it seems that parents might well consider the need for requiring ample amounts of sleep for their children. Since most teachers consider the first period of the morning to be the most effective instructional time, it is imperative that children be awake and alert. Parents who need suggestions as to the amount of sleep their children require may consult the family doctor. Hand in hand with alertness is the need for a substantial breakfast to replace an inadequate breakfast or none at all. Children who go without breakfast, fighting hunger long before the noon hour, are incapable of efficient use of school time. Recommendations for minimum breakfast requirements are readily available; however, when in doubt, the parents should consult the family doctor. If the parents send a child who is physically sound to school, the educational program has a greater chance for success.

Emotional climate

When the school receives a child who is secure, loved at home, and understood, interferences with success in school are further reduced. Parents can implant an attitude that learning will be fun and, though difficult at times, always worthwhile. They can develop an attitude incorporating: no threats for failures in school, e.g., withdrawing TV privileges; no promises for success in school, e.g., paying for good grades; respect and confidence in the teachers; and interest and enthusiasm for what is being accomplished in school. Parents should avoid criticism of the school and the teachers in front of their children. As parents, they have a right to voice their objections, but they should do so to the school authorities and the teachers, not the children. When children obtain the attitude that the school is weak and the teachers are incompetent, learning difficulties are compounded. Furthermore, parents can be directed to avoid, as much as possible, the direct and/or subtle comparison of their child to his peers. The reaction of the child who is striving to do as well as his sister is seldom effective or desirable. More concern should be demonstrated over the child's ability to perform as well as he can; performance which matches his sister's is not the goal needed to satisfy parents.

Setting an example

Probably all parents have heard that it is good for them to set an example for their children. In reading, this example should be one of reading for enjoyment. From the earliest years, the child who notices that both parents seem to enjoy spending portions of their leisure time reading can develop a favorable attitude toward reading before entering school. Some of this reading may be done orally for the child or for the family. Note that all oral reading should be accomplished with as much skill as possible; therefore, parents should be directed to first read silently all materials which they plan to read orally. Parents are inclined to discontinue oral reading as soon as the child himself develops skills in reading; however, oral reading by parents should continue taking every opportunity to read to children things which are of interest to them but which are too difficult for their developed reading skills. Children who come to school with these experiences have definite advantages in learning to read, for they realize the wonders that reading can unlock for them.

Providing language experiences

Parents are to be encouraged to use every opportunity to widen their child's language experience. Through such activities as reading to the child, taking him on trips, and discussing events with him, situations are created in which language can be developed through experiences. Parents should be encouraged to lead the child into discussions which will add listening and speaking vocabulary to the experiences. It is, of course, the listening and speaking vocabulary upon which the reading vocabulary hinges. Alerted to the potential of structured language experiences, parents can learn to use them more effectively.

Regulation of child's out-of-school activities

Parents who permit the child to do as he wishes with all out-of-school time indicate their lack of concern about what he does. First, parents must understand that a full school day takes a good bit of concentration and is mentally very fatiguing. Therefore, the child should be exposed to opportunities after school for active, expressive free play. Outdoor play, which physically releases the child, is desirable when possible. Secondly, the school program relies upon the interest and excitement which can be developed by the teacher and the materials from which the child is learning. Therefore, unusually large amounts of television viewing may interfere with the school program. After five hours of murder, passionate love, dancing girls, and the funniest of comedies, it is difficult to imagine that the child is going to fully appreciate a program which features the elementary school band or a story in the first grade reader which must be limited to his reading vocabulary. Although no formula is prescribed, we have found that limiting children to an hour an evening does not work undue hardships upon them. Of course, the parents cannot expect the child to sit in the living room and *not* watch the shows that the parents are watching. This suggestion then implies that television viewing for the family is restricted, especially during school days. Consideration can also be given by parents to the need for children to accomplish home assignments and have some quiet time. This can usually be best accomplished if these times are established and are held to with as much regularity as possible. Again, this of necessity involves the entire family.

Following advice

Parents must be encouraged to follow the suggestions of school personnel in matters concerning the education of their children. Most difficulty is experienced concerning the age at which the child should enter first grade and the decision to pass or fail the child in a given year. Each school system has its own method of determining whether or not a child is ready to profit from first grade instruction. When, after careful consideration, the school advises the parent to withhold the child from first grade for one year, the parent must be led to understand that it is foolhardy to insist upon entrance. A scene creates needless anxiety for the child, antagonizes everyone, and generally results in the entrance of the child into a program in which he will not be successful. Scores of children who have been referred to us are victims of early entrance against school advice; their parents all now realize their error and wish that they could share their mistake with others who might thus avoid it.

School advice in connection with the passing or failing of a child generally receives undue parental concern, which is passed directly to the child. Educators not only want the parent to comply with this advice but to embrace it with enthusiasm so that the child feels that he has not let the parent down. Unfortunately, in our pass or fail system, other children pick up the connotation of *failure* which will, unwittingly, create some disturbance within the child. This does not need be compounded in the home by parental anxiety. When parents choose to refuse school advice, they accept responsibility for the future failures of their child in the school program.

Willingness to follow referrals

Assuming that the school will overrefer to some degree (if they follow the procedure given in chapter iii), it is imperative that a maximum of parental support for the referrals be developed. Educators may develop a more thorough attitude and stimulate the parents through their own concern. It is not enough, therefore, to refer and then forget about it.

Follow-ups on referrals should be requested and expected. It is the parents' responsibility to see that their child's progress continues unhampered by obstacles which are non-educational in origin.

Reinforcement of learned skills

As was discussed under the parental roles in remediation, skills learned in school may be reinforced by understanding parents in the home. The suggestions made in the previous discussion apply equally well here, but with special emphasis on the fact that home reading situations should *always* end pleasantly with the child having a feeling of satisfaction. Parents who cannot control their anxieties and tempers should be led away from these types of activities. When the child reads orally to the parents, a difficulty frequently arises, regardless of the care the teacher takes to make sure that the child can read the book which she has sent home. That is, when the child comes to an unknown word, what should the parent do? In order to make the reading pleasant and meaningful, the parents should tell the child the word. If he misses it again, tell him again and again. Words missed with regularity should be noted and sent to the teacher for analysis of the type of error and the necessary instruction. We have found that parents are seldom satisfied with this limited role; thus we suggest the following. When a child misses a word again and again, it is helpful if the parent prints the word carefully on a card. When the reading is finished and the story has been discussed, a *few* minutes may be spent glancing over these cards. As each word is pronounced, the child should be asked to use it in a sentence, and this sentence should be written on the back of the card with the unknown word underlined. Preceding the next reading session at home, a little game-like drill can take place in which the child reads the sentence and the unknown word. Casey[1] makes further suggestions concerning the parental role in these cases. Her booklet is available for distribution to parents and may be effective when her suggestions match the philosophy of the teacher using it.

Pitfalls in Parental Cooperation

Obviously, there are numerous opportunities for parental cooperation

---

[1]Sally L. Casey, *Ways You Can Help Your Child With Reading* (Evanston, Illinois, Row Peterson & Co., 1950).

to go astray, creating more harm than good. Educators must be alert to these pitfalls and, when signs of their appearance occur, use alternate approaches.

Lack of contact

Perhaps the worst pitfall is to make no contact with the parent. As this entire chapter illustrates, since parental roles will be assumed, it is best that they be taken in terms of the school's program.

Underestimating parental love

Parents — even those parents who appear to be unconcerned — love their children. This love can easily be misdirected; for example, when the parents criticize the school in attempts to make the child feel more justified in his failures. When parental love is misjudged, it can result in lack of cooperation between parent and educator.

Needless anxiety

Educators are often forced to settle for the reactions and opinions of particularly true when they discuss a problem with the parents without any suggestions for a solution. As problems are discussed, they should be followed with sound suggestions for alleviating them, leaving the parent with a minimum of anxiety.

One parent

Educators are often forced to settle for the reactions and opinions of only one of the child's parents. One must avoid this pitfall, for the child acts to please *both* parents. Therefore, every opportunity should be made to involve both parents, even if a home visit is required. We have often reversed our opinion of the home and the learning climate upon talking with the other parent.

Coaching

That they should coach the child for his remedial sessions is an attitude parents often develop. This improperly involves the parent as a crutch and leads the educators to make false assumptions concerning the child's progress. The parent must be directed toward the roles mentioned in this chapter and away from coaching type roles.

Follow-up

When a remedial program is finished, the parents deserve a summary of the results. Without this follow-up, parental activities may continue as the educator has directed following diagnosis, creating feelings of discomfort and needless anxiety within the child. The summary, therefore, should include specific recommendations for future parental roles in terms of the changing needs of the child.

Teacher's role

Sending work books home in which the parent is placed in a teacher's role is seldom useful and often harmful. Educators must clearly see the difference between the parent's role as reinforcer of learned skills as opposed to the teacher of new skills — the educator's job. Workbook activities provide too many teaching situations for most parents to handle well.

Summary

Parents can help! The educator must evaluate the home situation and make specific recommendations to the parents of problem readers as to which roles are most appropriate to enable the parents and the educator to work as a team. All parental roles should be in keeping with the educational goals which the remedial program is attempting to accomplish. When the child's parent is not actively involved, needless limitations are placed upon the educator's effectiveness. Based on the premise that most parents are going to help the child with his reading, it behooves the educator to direct these efforts toward the most useful purposes.

Suggested Readings

1. Artley A. Sterl, *Your Child Learns to Read.* Chicago: Scott Foresman and Co., 1953. This book is a guide to parents to use with the Scott Foresman Series. It is obvious, though, that there are many practical suggestions for parents whose children do not happen to use this series in school. Of particular interest might be the graded booklist which is listed as a "Guide for Building a Home Library."

2. Casey, Sally L., *Ways You Can Help Your Child With Reading.* Evanston, Illinois: Row Peterson and Co., 1950. This excellent little booklet provides specific, practical suggestions for parents to help a child with his reading. Since it is inexpensive, educators may find this to be a valuable book to have available for parents.

3. Smith, Nila B., *Reading Instruction for Today's Children,* Chaps. XIX and XX. Englewood Cliffs, N.J.: Prentice-Hall, Inc., 1963. This book provides two thorough chapters with specific suggestions on how to advise and work with parents. Included are sections on materials, selections, and some critical *do's* and *don'ts.*

11

Professional Responsibilities and Programs

Emphasis upon reading and reading instruction continues to grow in our colleges, in the public, and in the press. Generally creating a favorable atmosphere for program development, problems are arising which must be evaluated. High school students (and in some cases even grade school students) are being recruited in various areas to assist children with reading problems. Tutoring needs are great and profits lucrative, but not all tutors should be working with problem readers. Commercial openings have been filled quickly by programs of a variety of caliber. It is for reasons such as these that consideration must be given to professional responsibilities and program development.

Professional Responsibilities

"Am I qualified to help problem readers?" "How will I be able to start a program in my classroom . . . in my school?" "To whom should I look for help?" These are questions educators ask when they realize that many children with a reading deficiency could be helped by the establishment of a remedial program. Preceding a discussion of programs, however, must be a clear understanding of the professional responsibility of the educator attempting to establish programs for problem readers.

The child

Regardless of the type of program or the competency of the person conducting it, first consideration must be given to the child who is to benefit from the program. Educators are professionally responsible to direct children toward those programs that seem to be best designed for the child's needs. This need not reflect negatively upon the educator if he decides that he cannot assist the child as well as another can; rather, it is to his credit. Clearly, many educators feel threatened when they become aware that they cannot help a certain child. To call for outside help seems to indicate a lack of competency. However, the diagnosis and correction of many of our reading problems cannot possibly be handled by any one person. Consequently, to call for assistance when it is needed is a sign of professional realism and maturity.

Cooperation

As mentioned in previous chapters, diagnosis and remediation are programs that cannot be conducted without full cooperation from all persons involved with the child. Programs which are conducted in an isolated manner are limited in their ability to offer the child the help that he needs. Therefore, programs should not be instituted without thorough communication, especially with the parents and with the child's classroom teacher.

Referral

All referrals, medical, psychological, and psychiatric, should be made prior to remediation and the final formation of diagnostic conclusions. When the child demonstrates enough symptoms of difficulties in these areas, it is inefficient to start a remedial program without a consultation. All conclusions should be tentative until final reports are available. This does not require the educator to refrain from working with these children; however, the fullest efficiency of remedial programs will not normally be realized without referral reports.

Qualification

Since the terms reading specialist, reading consultant, reading supervisor, reading teacher, and reading tutor appear to be defined differently within various states and school districts, a clear obligation remains with the educator to represent himself as honestly as possible. The International Reading Association has established suggested requirements for Reading Specialists, and these requirements may serve as a guide to the educator requirement of the IRA for reading specialist.[1]

When remediation is conducted outside the classroom, it is the professional responsibility of the educator to be certain that he does not cast unwarranted reflections upon the inadequacies of the school program, particularly to parents. However, in cases where the school program is suspect, the educator is professionally obligated to consult with appropriate school personnel in an effort to remedy the deficiency.

Here the reader's attention is called to the Code of Ethics approved by the International Reading Association as it appears in the Preface to this book.

The Reading Specialist in the School Program

The following suggestions are designed to assist the reading specialist in assuming the role which will best suit the needs of the schools for which he is responsible and the problem children that he finds within those schools. A reading specialist may assume responsibility for more than one of these program suggestions, for they are frequently related.

Diagnosis

Clinical diagnosis is a major obligation of most reading specialists as has been discussed in chapters ii, iii, and iv. When limited to diagnostic responsibilities, the reading specialist conducts the diagnosis and prepares the recommendations with directions for remediation. Many reading specialists feel that they can be most useful to the classroom teacher through diagnostic services; it may be difficult for the classroom teacher to find the time that clinical diagnosis requires.

[1]*Minimum Standards for Professional Training of Reading Specialists* (Newark, Delaware: International Reading Association, 1961).

Remediation

Following a diagnosis, the reading specialist can make a schedule and draw certain children from the classroom for the precise instruction which is needed. Naturally this program calls for a suitable setting in which this remedial program can be housed, for the materials which will accomplish the goals most effectively, and for the cooperation of all school personnel concerned. Due to the very nature of clinical remediation, groups must be small, instruction individualized, and the schedule flexible.

Supervision

Assisting the classroom teacher through observation of his classes, teaching sample lessons, and holding conferences has been the role of many reading specialists. As a supervisor, the reading specialist will often find himself assisting wth diagnosis and remedial efforts, making specific suggestions for further classroom adjustment, and evaluating the effectiveness of the program. When supervision is added to the responsibilities of the reading specialist, other dimensions should be added to the qualifications of such a person. He should have demonstrated an ability to work well with teachers; he should have had extensive classroom teaching experience; and he should have taken additional course work in the area of supervision. Without these requisites, the reading specialist is likely to find himself in an awkward professional position.

Clinic director

In larger school districts, the reading specialist may find himself directing a reading clinic in an attempt to serve children who are severely handicapped. Clinics are usually established in permanent buildings to which the children are brought for help. As director of the clinic, the reading specialist may assume all of the above roles, the administrative functions of the clinic, and the communication between clinic and classroom.

In-service education

Occasionally, the reading specialist will find it worthwhile to conduct in-service educational programs with teachers who have children in need of classroom diagnosis and remediation. Through demonstration, discussion, and consultation with authorities, the teachers will gain insights into effective methods of working with problem readers. The responsibility is closely linked to that of supervision when the supervisor finds a common lack of understanding among his teachers in certain areas.

Summer school

An increasingly large number of schools are establishing summer programs for children who have not made adequate progress during the school year. The reading specialist will likely be responsible for the program, with particular emphasis upon the screening and selection of children who are to be assisted. He might be responsible for the selection of teachers who will be involved. The financing of these programs, normally assumed by the school, may to a small extent be supplemented by a nominal fee paid by the parents. We have found that such a fee stimulates a more serious attitude toward the work being conducted. Through summer programs it may be possible to permit children to remain in the classroom during the year, providing them with the fullest opportunity to benefit from the classroom program. Of course, children with serious reading problems cannot always profit from summer programs alone. To avoid the stigma of failure which is often attached to such programs, summer facilities can be developed to provide for good readers as well. All types of readers, then, can be involved, making it no disgrace to be asked to attend a summer reading program.

Public relations

Included in this area are such situations as PTA meetings, conferences with parents, and home visits. During these, the reading specialist can explain the reading program, answer questions, and clarify any misinterpretations that may have occurred. At such meetings the school's reading program can be explained, questions answered, and misinterpretations corrected. The reading specialist can take full advantage of the suggestions mentioned in chapter ix, *Parental Roles in Diagnosis, Remediations, and Prevention* when provided with opportunities to meet with the public. Public relations opportunities such as conferences with parents

Diagnostic and Remedial Reading

and home visits as well as public speaking engagements will be available to the reading specialists.

Supervision of tutoring

Many schools ask qualified teachers to tutor problem readers after school hours and on weekends under the direction of the reading specialist. It is the reading specialist's responsibility to select the children, make available appropriate diagnostic and remedial materials, and, again, communicate with the classroom teacher, the parent, and others.

Pitfalls for the Reading Specialist

Complex as they are, the programs developed by the reading specialists are not without potential difficulties. Especially for those with little experience, there are certain pitfalls involved in establishing programs for the problem reader. To provide a brief consideration before beginning such programs may relieve the reading specialist of frustrating situations which can ultimately cause considerable difficulty.

Overloading

It is not uncommon to find the reading specialist assuming responsibilities which overload him to a point of ineffectiveness. First, he should not reasonably be expected to assume all of the roles which have been suggested in this chapter; rather, he should start where he can be most effective and slowly expand as he sees opportunities. Secondly, in the diagnostic and remedial role, he cannot be expected to carry the student load that a classroom teacher does. The very nature of the clinical situation precludes large groups. When overloaded, the reading specialist's effectiveness will be limited unnecessarily.

Inadequate housing

Teachers' rooms, damp basements, and worse have been relegated to the reading specialist to conduct diagnostic and remedial programs. Assuming that a program is worth having, the school district must make provisions for a well lighted, comfortable, undistracting environment for the children and the teacher. To be most effective, housing considerations should be built into the basic plans for the program's development.

Screening

Final responsibility for determining which children can be most effectively helped must be left to the reading specialist. Without diagnosis, a given classroom teacher is likely to select his dullest children for remedial attention. This alone is not sufficient criteria for program enrollment. The reading specialist should provide for the screening of all referred children, yet retain the right to reject any child which he feels cannot effectively profit from the established program. He will have to reject those children who add to the tutoring load, creating class sizes which cannot be effectively taught. Inter-school relations may be strained unless clear-cut systems are established concerning the final responsibilities for the identification of children to be accepted in the reading specialist's programs.

The image

Specific efforts should be made to keep from developing in the schools an image that the reading specialist is the educator who works with failures. As suggested previously, the reading specialist should find opportunities to participate in programs for all types of children. Such adjustment will help the children assigned to him by relaxing their anxiety about their failures. It will also prevent his getting a distorted opinion of the schools' reading program. (This easily occurs when one works hour after hour, day after day, with only the *problems* which a given system has produced.)

The Classroom Teacher in the School Program

With various degrees of competency, classroom teachers participate in school programs with problem readers in several ways. An understanding of the possibilities may assist each teacher to his most effective service function.

Classroom diagnosis

As the teacher develops skill in the techniques of classroom diagnosis, he is likely to find himself assigned to children who are in need of this service. The best teachers will perform this type of function as an on-going part of their teaching program. The administrator is cautioned that the overloading of excellent teachers is unwise, however, for excessive numbers of weak students will obviously hamper his efforts with all students assigned to him.

Classroom remediation

Using every opportunity, whether in a group or individually, the teacher's role is to help the child in the skill areas which have been diagnosed as deficient. When possible, flexible room assignments will permit the placing of children with common deficiencies with the same teacher, enabling him to use his time more effectively with the most children.

Tutoring

Having developed skills in diagnosis and remediation, through either in-service or formal course work, many teachers find opportunities to serve as tutors in school-established programs. The teacher's activities in these programs are usually supervised by the reading specialist and are directed toward the instruction of individuals and/or small groups.

Demonstration

When a teacher has been found to be particularly skillful in either classroom diagnosis or remediation, opportunities should be made for other teachers to observe him. This may be done in after-school in-service programs or through time in which teachers are released from their class-room assignment to observe this teacher.

Public relations

All teachers meet with parents and have the responsibility of inter-preting the school's program to them. Those who have studied the pro-gram more thoroughly will be expected to assist in such programs as the PTA in efforts to clearly illustrate the features of the program. We find that parents may better accept the classroom teacher in this role than they do the reading specialist, for they know that the classroom teacher works with their children each day.

Pitfalls for the classroom teacher

The classroom teacher must also be alert to several pitfalls in his roles as they have been presented.

1. Overloading: Teachers who are skilled in diagnosis and remediation are likely to become overloaded with poor readers. Ultimately, overloading is a detriment to his effectiveness with these children. Using free periods, short sessions before and after school, Saturdays, and summers, we have found many good teachers needing more time to do an efficient job. The healthiest teachers find that they must regulate their time so that relaxation and recreation are also part of their daily schedule. Their major responsibility continues to lie with the whole class and the education of all children assigned to them.

2. Short-cutting: Attempting to diagnose without using the suggestions in chapters ii, iii, and iv leads to inadequate classroom diagnosis. However, after limited experience, the classroom teacher will start to modify and refine these suggestions to his classroom and the needs of his children. After several diagnostic efforts, it is entirely understandable that a teacher will realize that his children are all proficient in one area or another and diagnosis in those areas is not essential in his classroom diagnosis. This does not justify excluding major portions of classroom diagnosis.

3. Cooperation: Regardless of the certainty with which a teacher operates and regardless of the feeling he has toward the total school reading program, the teacher must remain aware that he is a member of a team which is working toward the total education of the child. Gross distortions of the school program in an effort to satisfy his personal philosophy of reading must be avoided when it is found that they interfere with the overall school objectives. By cooperating and attempting to convince the school of the need of basic changes, this teacher will better serve his children and the school district. Needless to say, displeasures within the school should remain there and not be topics for community gossip.

4. Continued study: As changes occur in the field of reading, the teacher must have available to him a system for continued study. Some find that the subscription to and study of periodicals in educa-

tion serve this purpose. Specific reference is made to the journals of the International Reading Association[2], the National Council of Teachers of English[3], and the College Reading Association[4]. These organizations are striving to keep teachers informed of developments in the field of reading. Other teachers prefer in-service workshops and institutes; still others prefer formal course work in the colleges and universities. Of course, most teachers seek a suitable combination of each method. Regardless of his method, the effective classroom teacher must maintain an alertness to new ideas, lest he become too stale and fixed in his ways.

Out of School Programs

Many educators take part in "out-of-school" programs designed to assist problem readers. Some find themselves teaching in these programs, others have parents asking them for their opinions of the programs, and still others find these programs to be interfering with the educational objectives of the school. A brief look at the nature of some of these programs may assist the educator in making decisions concerning them.

Teacher education clinics: Many teacher education institutions operate reading clinics for the primary purpose of educating teachers. Children who are brought into these clinics for assistance are generally diagnosed and tutored by students doing advanced work in the field of reading. Normally the costs for services in teacher education clinics are slight since the programs are not expected to pay for themselves. The effectiveness of these programs is generally related to the effectiveness of the supervision which the students receive and the prerequisites for entrance of college students into courses of a clinic nature.

Some teacher education clinics limit themselves to diagnosis while others include remediation as well. Although the thoroughness of each program varies, it generally follows the lines of clinical diagnosis and remediation as presented in this book and is reliable.

---

[2]*The Reading Teacher* and *Journal of Reading* (Newark, Delaware: International Reading Association).

[3]*Elementary English* and *The English Journal* (Champaign, Illinois: National Council of Teachers of English).

[4]*The Journal of the Reading Specialist* (Rochester, New York: College Reading Association).

Privately-operated clinics: Usually available in large population centers are a variety of privately-operated clinics. Designed for financial profit, these clinics generally charge fees much higher than do teacher education clinics. The effectiveness of these clinics is clearly limited by the personnel and materials available for diagnosis and remediation. Referrals to this type of clinic should be made only after an acquaintance has been made with the personnel and the attitude of the clinic. Private clinics can accept this as a challenge: Work with the schools! Unless cooperation is achieved, the effects of privately operated clinics is limited indeed. The College Reading Association is constantly attempting to focus professional attention on the need for understanding and evaluating private clinics.

Private tutoring: Running from excellent to horrible, programs designed by private tutors are available everywhere. Generally restricted by the proficiency of the tutor and by the materials available for precise diagnosis and remediation, private tutoring programs are most effective with mildly retarded readers. Children with severe problems seldom benefit; however, it should be noted that there are many excellent, well qualified private tutors performing highly satisfactory services. Unfortunately, there are others who cause more harm than good. Private tutors are obligated to work closely with the school, which has the child in an instructional program every day. No justification can be accepted for programs which do less. Referral should be only on a personal evaluation of effectiveness.

Commercial programs for parents: Often advertised as panaceas, programs which feature these parents as teachers presume that all children have a common deficiency, and instruction with this technique may be done without diagnosis. Unless the educator is familiar with the contents of the program and unless a diagnosis has been conducted to pinpoint the remedial area, these programs are not recommended. Further discussion of these programs was mentioned in chapter viii. This does not imply that the programs are never successful and are inherently bad; on the contrary, some of them are well designed and have been used with considerable success. The educator is simply advised to study them closely. An assessment must also be made, in each case, of the parent's suitability as a teacher of his own children.

Temporary programs: Several private companies have organized crash programs designed to send materials and instructors into schools and industry to improve general reading skills. As crash programs, many of these are well designed and taught excellently; others are not. The long-term gains of such programs may properly be questioned, and these companies should be willing to answer questions and submit to research concerning these claims. The educator will have to evaluate the relative worth of any such program.

Out-patient, parental instruction: Several clinics have been established to diagnose children and then train parents to conduct remediation. Amazing results have been reported with this technique; however, the long-term gains are again in need of evaluation. These clinics handle large numbers of children and usually request periodic return for re-evaluation and retraining for the parents. Being out-patient in nature, the overall costs of these programs are not great although the per hour cost may be high. Note that these programs are generally designed for children with specific disabilities and should usually follow referral from medical personnel, psychologists, psychiatrists, or reading specialists.

Pitfalls of Out-of-School Programs

The basic limitations of each of these has already been mentioned. Specifically, however, the pitfalls of such programs are:

Goals: Do these programs assist us toward the most desirable educational goals, or do they, in reality, interfere? Once this question is answered, referral may be made more specifically. When it is established that the programs are not in agreement with the goals of the school, it is suggested that attempts be made to reconcile the differences. When reconciliation is not possible, it seems that the educators should strongly recommend non-participation by the parents of the children assigned to them.

Personnel: The effectiveness of all of these programs is dependent upon the supervisory as well as the instructional personnel. Weakness in personnel means weakness in the program. No compromise can be made by educators in demanding that out-of-school programs meet certain standards of quality. Again, efforts should be made to reconcile differences.

Intention: Since each of these programs has other aims beyond simply assisting children, it must be determined if assisting children is even included in their aims. Naturally they will claim to help problem readers, but do dollar signs or teacher education become so important that the child does not matter? When alternate aims prevail, the worth of the program is suspect.

Summary

Once the professional roles of the classroom teacher and the reading specialist are understood, programs can be effectively developed to incorporate them in the appropriate manner. An awareness of the types of programs available within the realms of the school permits educators to strive in developing those which the needs of their community demand. All facilities, county, state, college, and university, should be incorporated when it is felt that they can be helpful.

Out-of-school programs for children must be evaluated and cooperation should be encouraged, when possible. In areas where out-of-school programs proliferate, more concentrated efforts will be needed to assure educational programs of the most effectiveness for children.

Suggested Readings

1. Gans, Roma, *Common Sense in Teaching Reading.* Chap. xx. Indianapolis: The Bobbs-Merrill Company, Inc., 1963. The reader will find this chapter to be a stimulating adjunct to the material covered in this book. Dr. Gans has added many practical considerations which will be helpful to those who are attempting to develop programs.
2. Kolson, Clifford J., and George Kaluger, *Clinical Aspects of Remedial Reading.* Part III. Springfield, Illinois: Charles C. Thomas, 1963. In this section of their book, Kolson and Kaluger have provided excellent supplementary information to that presented in this chapter. On pp. 101-3, they have included what they consider to be the hallmarks of a good clinic. The reader will find these suggestions very beneficial.
3. Robinson, H. Alan, and Sidney J. Rauch, *Guiding the Reading Program.* Chicago: SRA, 1965. The reader will find this entire book to be an excellent source of information. Subtitled *A Reading Consultant's Handbook,* the emphasis is to develop for the reader insights into all aspects of the reading program from the specialist's point of view. This, it would seem, is required reading for the reading specialist.

APPENDIX A

Diagnostic Instruments

Appendix A, provided for the reader's reference, is based upon the tests which have been cited in this book. No effort has been made to include all known reading tests, nor have evaluations of the tests' merits been included. For that type of information the reader is referred to Buros' *Mental Measurements Yearbooks*.

The age range of each test is approximated. We realize, of course, that in diagnosis the use of a test will depend upon the instructional level, not the age, of the child. The educator must determine this instructional level and then select the appropriate test.

Administration time for tests often varies with the age of the child. The reader should accept these times as approximate — a factor which may determine the use of a test in a particular situation.

Publishers are coded. The key to the code is in Appendix C. The reader is referred to the publisher for the cost of the tests, the specific directions, and other desired information.

READING ACHIEVEMENT

Name of Test	No. of Forms	Type	Age Range	Approximate Administration Time, Reading Section	Designed to Assist in Evaluation of:							Publisher's Code
					Speed	Comprehension	Vocabulary	Word Attack	Spelling	Auding	Other	
Botel Reading Inventory	2	Group and Individual	6-18	20 Min.			X	X				FOL
California Achievement Test	4	Group	L. Prim. 6-7, U. Prim. 7-9, Elem. 8-12, Jr. Hi. 12-14, Adv. 15-20	1 Hr.		X	X		X		Arithmetic, Language	CAL
Dolch Base Sight Words	1	Individual	6-8	15 Min.			X					GP
Durrell Sullivan Achievement Test	2	Group	Prim. 6-8, Inter. 9-12	30 Min.		X	X					HBW
Gates Reading Survey	3	Group	8-15	1 Hr.	X	X	X					TC

Name of Test	No. of Forms	Type	Age Range	Approximate Administration Time, Reading Section	Speed	Comprehension	Vocabulary	Word Attack	Spelling	Auding	Other	Publisher's Code
										Designed to Assist in Evaluation of:		
Gates Reading Test	3	Group	Prim. 6-7 Adv. 7-8 Basic 9-12	40-60 Min.		X	X					TC
Iowa Test of Basic Skills	2	Group	8-14	70 Min.		X	X				Language Work-Study Arithmetic	HM
Metropolitan Achievement Tests	4	Group	6-8 9-12 12-18	50 Min.		X	X		X		Science Language Arithmetic Social Studies	HBW
Stanford Achievement Tests	4	Group	6-8 8-9 10-12 12-15	45 Min.		X	X				Arithmetic Study Science Social Studies	HBW
Wide Range Achievement Tests	1	Individual	6-18	40 Min.			X		X		Arithmetic	PSY
DIAGNOSTIC												
California Phonics Survey	2	Group	13-20	40 Min.				X				CAL

Name of Test	No. of Forms	Type	Age Range	Approximate Administration Time, Reading Section	Speed	Comprehension	Vocabulary	Word Attack	Spelling	Auding	Other	Publisher's Code
Diagnostic Reading Scales (Spache)	1	Individual	6-14	1 Hr.	X	X	X	X		X		CAL
Diagnostic Reading Tests	2-4	Group and Individual	5-13	Varies	X	X	X	X				CDRT
Diagnostic Reading Test Bond-Clymer-Hoyt	1	Group	8-14	90 Min.				X		X		L&C
Doran Diagnostic Reading Test	1	Group	8-12	3 Hrs.			X	X				ETB
Durrell Analysis of Reading Difficulties	1	Individual	6-12	40-60 Min.	X	X	X	X	X			HBW
Gates-McKillop Reading Diagnostic Test	2	Individual	6-12	1 Hr.	X		X	X	X	X		TC
Gilmore Oral Reading Test	2	Individual	6-14	15 Min.	X	X	X	X				NBW
Gray Oral Reading Test	4	Individual	6-18	15 Min.	X	X	X	X				BSM

Designed to Assist in Evaluation of:

Name of Test	No. of Forms	Type	Age Range	Approximate Administration Time, Reading Section	Designed to Assist in Evaluation of:							Publisher's Code
					Speed	Comprehension	Vocabulary	Word Attack	Spelling	Auding	Other	
Monroe-Sherman Group Diagnostic Reading Aptitude and Achievement Tests	1	Group	8-14	90 Min.		X	X	X	X		Arithmetic	NEV
Reading Versability Test	2	Group	11-15 16-Adult	25 Min.	X	X						EDL
Wepman Auditory Descrimination Test	2	Individual	5-10	10 Min.							Auditory Discrimination	JMW
INTELLIGENCE Arthur Point Scale-Knox Cube Test	1	Individual	5-13	10 Min.							Memory of Sequence	STO
Botel Reading Inventory-Listening	2	Group	6-18	15 Min.						X		FOL
California Test for Mental Maturity	1	Group	5-6 6-8 9-13 12-14 14-19 15-21	50 Min.							Language and Non-Language	CAL
Durrell-Sullivan Capacity	2	Group	Prim. & Inter.	25 Min.						X		HBW

Name of Test	No. of Forms	Type	Age Range	Approximate Administration Time, Reading Section	Designed to Assist in Evaluation of:							Publisher's Code
					Speed	Comprehension	Vocabulary	Word Attack	Spelling	Auding	Other	
Peabody Picture Vocabulary Test	2	Individual	2½-18	15 Min.								AGS
Stanford-Binet-Intelligence Scale	1*	Individual	2-Adult	1 Hr.						X	General Mental Maturity	HM
Wechsler Intelligence Scale for Children	1	Individual	5-15	1 Hr.							Verbal Performance, Mental Maturity	PSY

SCREENING TESTS

Vision:

Name of Test	No. of Forms	Type	Age Range	Approximate Administration Time, Reading Section	Speed	Comprehension	Vocabulary	Word Attack	Spelling	Auding	Other	Publisher's Code
Keystone Visual Survey Teli-binocular	1	Individual	5-Adult	15 Min.							Far and Near Point, Visual Skills	KEY
Reading Eye Camera	1	Individual	6-20	10 Min.							Photograph Eye motion	EDL
Spahce-Binocular Reading Tests	1	Individual	5-Adult	5 Min.							Binocular Reading Efficiency	KEY

Auditory:

Name of Test	No. of Forms	Type	Age Range	Approximate Administration Time, Reading Section	Speed	Comprehension	Vocabulary	Word Attack	Spelling	Auding	Other	Publisher's Code
Audiometer	1	Individual or Group	3-Adult	15 Min.							Auditory Acuity	MAI

*1963 Revision has 2 forms.

Name of Test	No. of Forms	Type	Age Range	Approximate Administration Time, Reading Section	Speed	Comprehension	Vocabulary	Word Attack	Spelling	Auding	Other	Publisher's Code
Personality: California Test of Personality	2	Group	5-8 9-13 13-15 14-21	50 Min.							Personal and Social Adjustment	CAL
Dominance: Harris Test of Lateral Dominance	1	Individual	5- Adult	5 Min.							Hand, Eye and Foot Dominance	PSY
STUDY SKILLS California Study Method Survey	1	Group	12-18	40 Min.							Study Habits	CALIF.
Survey of Study Habits and Attitudes- Brown Holtzman	1	Group	14-21	20 Min.							Study Habits	PSY

Designed to Assist in Evaluation of:

APPENDIX B

Remedial Materials

Appendix B provides a reference for reading aids based upon the materials which have been cited in this book. Specific information con-concerning these materials may be found in publishers catalogues and brochures. The publishers' key may be used by checking with Appendix C.

Many of the cited materials may be used in a variety of ways to help problem readers. The cited use is based upon our experience, but in no way is intended to suggest that a material be limited to these functions.

The suggested age level must be considered flexible and regarded as the difficult level. The educator will find many of these materials to be used with children of older age and interest levels.

MACHINE TYPE AIDS

Name of Material	Approximate Age Level	Interest Level	Orientation	Sight Vocabulary	Word Attack	Comprehension	Speed	Other	Publisher's Code
					Designed to Assist in Instruction of:				
Controlled Reader	6-Adult	6-Adult	X		X	X	X	Visual Exposure to Print is Regulated	EDL
Delacato Stereo-Reader Service	6-10	6-10	X	X			X	Hand-eye Coordination Exercises	KEY
Dolch Sight Words and Phrase Slides	6-8	6-8		X			X	Use with Tachistoscope	KEY
Flash-X	Use with child's personal vocabulary			X			X	Controlled Exposure	EDL
Iowa Reading Films	14-18	14-Adult				X	X		IOWA
Leavell Language Development Service	6-9	6-9	X	X				Stereoscope Exposure to print	KEY
Nichols Slides	7-15	7-18	X	X		X		Designed for use with Tachistoscope	KEY
Rateometer	Use with child's instructional material		X				X	Reading Rate Controller	AVR
Reading Accelerator	Use with child's instructional material		X				X	Reading Rate Controller	SRA

Name of Material	Approximate Age Level	Interest Level	Designed to Assist in Instruction of:					Other	Publisher's Code
			Orientation	Sight Vocabulary	Word Attack	Comprehension	Speed		
Tachistoscope	6-Adult	6-Adult	X	X			X	Words and Phrases by Controlled Mechanism	KEY
BOOKS AND WORKBOOKS									
Basic Reading Skills	9-11	12-14		X	X	X			SF
	12-14	15-18		X	X	X			
Be a Better Reader	12-18	12-18		X	X	X		Study Skills	PH
Better Reading Books	10-15	10-18		X		X	X		SRA
Cordts Phonics	6-10	6-12			X				HRW
Developing Your Vocabulary	9-12	9-12		X	X				SRA
Diagnostic Reading Workbook	6-12	6-12		X	X	X			CEM
Elementary Crossword Puzzles	10-12	10-12		X				Crossword Puzzle Designs	EPC
Frostig Visual Perception Materials	6-8	6-8	X						CPP
Herr Phonics	5-11	5-11			X				ERA
ITA	6-8	6-8		X	X	X		Initial Teaching Alphabet	ITA
Let's Read	6-7	6-7		X	X	X		Linguistic Basal	CLB

Name of Material	Approximate Age Level	Interest Level	Orientation	Sight Vocabulary	Word Attack	Comprehension	Speed	Other	Publisher's Code
The Macmillan Reading Spectrum	6-12	6-15	X	X	X	X			MAC
Merrill Linguistic Readers	5-7	5-7	X	X	X	X		Linguistic Basal	CEM
Phonetic Keys to Reading	5-12	5-12	X	X	X	X		Basal Phonics Approach	EC
Phonics Skilltexts	6-10	6-12			X				CEM
Phonics We Use	6-10	6-12			X				LC
Phonovisual	5-7	5-7	X		X			Basic Phonic Approach	PVP
Reading for Meaning	10-18	10-18				X		Study Skills	JBL
The Reading Skill Builders	6-14	6-Adult		X	X	X	X		RDS
Reading Skilltexts	6-14	6-14		X		X			CEM
Rochester Occupational Reading Series	13-18	13-Adult		X		X		Job Type Reading Material	SRA
Specific Skill Series									BL
Using the Context	6-11	6-11			X	X			
Getting the Facts	6-11	6-11				X			
Following Directions	6-11	6-11				X			
Locating the Answer	6-11	6-11				X			
Working with Sounds	6-11	6-11			X				

240

Name of Material	Approximate Age Level	Interest Level	Designed to Assist in Instruction of:					Other	Publisher's Code
			Orientation	Sight Vocabulary	Word Attack	Comprehension	Speed		
SRA Reading Series	5-12	5-12	X	X	X	X		Linguistic Basal	SRA
Standard Test Lessons in Reading	7-18	7-18				X	X		TC
Storybooks	6-7	6-7		X				Contextual Practice for Programmed Material	WMcH
Words in Color	6-8	6-8		X	X			Colored Letters in Beginning Reading	EnC
KITS AND PACKAGED MATERIALS									
Dolch Teaching Aids								Gamelike Procedures to Develop Vocabulary	GP
Consonant Lotto	6-7	6-9			X				
Vowel Lotto	7-8	7-10			X				
The Syllable Game	8-9	8-11			X				
Picture Readiness Game	5-6	5-6	X						
Match	5-6	5-8	X	X					
Basic Sight Cards	6-8	6-9		X					

Name of Material	Approximate Age Level	Interest Level	Designed to Assist in Instruction of:					Other	Publisher's Code
			Orientation	Sight Vocabulary	Word Attack	Comprehension	Speed		
Sight Phrase Cards	7-8	7-10		X					
Picture Word Cards	6-7	6-8		X					
What the Letters Say	5-6	5-7	X		X				
Group Word Teaching Game	7-9	7-11		X					
Gillingham	1-3	1-3	X	X	X			Spelling	ES
Building Pre-Reading Skills Kit-A-Language	6-7	6-7						Language Development Exercises	Ginn
Graph and Picture Study Skills Kit	9-12	9-15						Teaching the Use of Visual Aids	SRA
The Literature Sampler	12-18	12-18				X		Provides Samples of Books	LM
Linguistic Block Series	6-7	6-7		X	X				SF
Map and Globe Skills Kit	9-14	9-16						Use of maps and globes	SRA
Non-Oral Reading Series	6-8	6-8		X		X			PES
Organizing and Reporting Skills Kit	9-12	9-12						Study Skill Exercises	SRA

Name of Material	Approximate Age Level	Interest Level	Orien-tation	Sight Vocabulary	Word Attack	Comprehension	Speed	Other	Publisher's Code
						Designed to Assist in Instruction of:			
Peabody Language Development Kit	5-7	5-10						Speaking and Listening Vocabulary	AGS
Pilot Library	9 11 13-14	7-12 9-14 10-18						Provides Samples of Books	SRA
Reading for Under-standing	8-13 13-18 10-21	6-13 6-18 6-21				X X X			SRA
Reading Lab I-Word Games	6-9	6-9			X				SRA
Speech To Print Phonics	5-7	5-9			X				HBW
SRA Kits									
Reading Lab									
IA	6	6-8		X	X	X	X		SRA
IB	7	6-9		X	X	X	X		SRA

243

Name of Material	Approximate Age Level	Interest Level	Orientation	Sight Vocabulary	Designed to Assist in Instruction of: Word Attack	Comprehension	Speed	Other	Publisher's Code
SRA KITS									
Reading Lab									
IC	8	6-10		X	X	X	X		SRA
IIA	9	7-12		X	X	X	X		SRA
IIB	10	8-13		X	X	X	X		SRA
IIC	11	9-14		X	X	X	X		SRA
IIIA	12-13	3-16		X	X	X	X		SRA
IIIB	13-14	10-17		X	X	X	X		SRA
IVA	14-17	13-19		X	X	X	X		SRA
Tactics in Reading	12-18	12-18		X	X	X			SF
Webster Classroom Reading Clinic	7-13	7-18		X	X	X		High Interest Low Vocabulary Books	WMCH
PROGRAMMED MATERIALS									
David Discovers the Dictionary	9-11	9-15						Dictionary Skills	COR
Goals in Spelling	7-10	7-12			X				PSP
Lessons for Self Instruction	9-11	9-15						Dictionary Skills	CAL
Programmed Reading	5-9	5-14		X	X	X			WMcH

244

APPENDIX C

Key to Publisher's Code

AGS American Guidance
Service, Inc.
720 Washington Avenue,
S.E.
Minneapolis, Minnesota
55414

AVR Audio-Visual Research
1509 Eighth Street, S.E.
Waseca, Minnesota 56093

BL Barnell Loft Ltd.
111 S. Centre Avenue
Rockville Centre, New
York

B&M Bobbs Merrill Company,
Inc.
4300 West 62nd Street
Indianapolis, Indiana
46268

CAL California Test Bureau
5916 Hollywood Boulevard
Los Angeles, California
90028

CPP Consulting Psychologists
Press
Palo Alto, California

DRT The Committee on
Diagnostic Reading
Tests, Inc.
Mountain Home, North
Carolina 28758

CEM Charles E. Merrill Books,
Inc.
1300 Alum Creek Drive
Columbus, Ohio

CLB Clarence L. Barnhart
Reference Books
Box 359
Bronxville, New York

Cor Coronet Learning
Programs
Cornonet Building
Chicago, Illinois 60601

EC The Economy Company
529 N. Capital Avenue
Indianapolis, Indiana
46204

EDL Educational Develop-
mental Laboratories
Huntington, New York
11746

EnC Encyclopedia Brittanica
Press
425 N. Michigan Avenue
Chicago, Illinois 60611

EPC Educational Publishing
Company
Darien, Connecticut

ERA Educational Research
Association
2223 S. Olive
Los Angeles, California

ES Educational Service Inc.
P. O. Box 112
Benton Harbor, Michigan

ETB Educational Test Bureau
720 Washington Avenue,
S.E.
Minneapolis, Minnesota
55414

FOL   Follett Publishing
Company
1010 W. Washington
Boulevard
Chicago, Illinois 60607

GP   The Garrard Press
Champaign, Illinois 61822

Ginn   Ginn & Company
72 Fifth Avenue
New York, New York
10011

HBW   Harcourt, Brace & World,
Inc.
Tarrytown, New York
10591

HMC   Houghton Mifflin
Company
432 Park Avenue, South
New York, New York

HRW   Holt, Rinehart and
Winston, Inc.
383 Madison Ave.
New York, New York

IOWA   The State University of
Iowa
Bureau of Audio-Visual
Instruction
Iowa City, Iowa 52240

ITA   ITA Publications Inc.
20 E. 46th Street
New York, New York
10017

JBL   J. B. Lippincott Company
East Washington Square
Philadelphia, Pennsylvania
19106

JMW   Joseph M. Wepman, PhD
950 E. 59th Street
Chicago, Illinois

KEY   Keystone View Company
Meadville, Pennsylvania
16335

LC   Lyons E. Carnahan
Educational Publishers
Affiliate of Meredith
Publishing Co.
407 E. 25th Street
Chicago, Illinois 60616

LM   Learning Materials, Inc.
100 East Ohio Street
Chicago, Illinois

MAC   The Macmillan Company
Front and Brown Streets
Riverside, New Jersey
08075

MAI   MAICO Electronics Inc.
21 N. 3rd Street
Minneapolis, Minnesota

NEV   Nevins Publishing
Company
Pittsburgh, Pennsylvania

PAR   Programs for Achievement
in Reading, Inc.
Abbott Park Place
Providence, Rhode Island
02903

PES   Primary Educational
Service
1243 W. 79th Street
Chicago, Illinois

PH   Prentice-Hall, Inc.
Englewood Cliffs, New
Jersey 07632

PSP   Popular Science Publish-
ing Co., Inc.
McGraw Hill Text Film
Dept.
330 W. 32nd St.
New York, New York

PSY   Psychological Corporation
304 East 45th Street
New York, New York
10017

PVP	Phonovisual Products, Inc. Box 5625 Washington, D.C. 20007	STO	C. H. Stoetling Company 424 N. Homan Avenue Chicago, Illinois
RDS	Readers Digest Services, Inc. Pleasantville, New York	TC	Bureau of Publications Teachers College Columbia University New York, New York 10027
SF	Scott Foresman & Company 433 E. Erie Street Chicago, Illinois 60611		
		W McH	Webster Division McGraw Hill Book Company 1154 Roco Avenue St. Louis, Missouri 63126
SRA	Science Research Associates, Inc. 259 E. Erie Street Chicago, Illinois 60611		

Index